ROCK AND ROLL HIGH SCHOOL

Growing Up in Hollywood During the Decade of Decadence

MARISA TELLEZ

THIRD EDITION

Printed in the United States of America

Published by Pepperland Publishing

Cover Design by Casey Quintal

ISBN-10: 0-98864-810-5

ISBN-13: 978-0-9886481-0-4

CONTENTS

Foreword by Dave Zink   *v*

Preface   *vii*

Acknowledgements   *ix*

1 Valley Girl   *11*

2 Puppy Love, Brawling, and Discovering Hollywood   *17*

3 High School, Baked Squash, and Handcuffs   *37*

4 Is That a Boyfriend I Smell?   *49*

5 Welcome to the Jungle!   *73*

6 Boiling Bunnies   *87*

7 Girlfriend of a (pseudo) Rock Star   *105*

8 Emancipation, Cheating, and Rebounds   *129*

9 I'm So Goth, I Shit Bats   *161*

10 Crazy? Don't Mind if I Do!   *185*

11 Don't Let the Door Hit Ya Where the Good Lord Split Ya!   *225*

12 First Love…or Not   *239*

13 Social Resuscitation   *259*

14 Let Me Club Your Heart Like a Seal   *281*

FOREWORD BY DAVE ZINK

When writing about the past, however distant or near your current position in space or time, it is vitally important to get your facts straight. Examples could include *The Tale of King Arthur, The Warren Commission,* voting records in Chicago or even *The Hitchhikers Guide to the Galaxy.* (The latter being the only totally reliable source of facts thus far mentioned.) But I suppose that depends on whom you've asked for the facts.

For the purposes of the book you are about to read, just take my word for it. I've known Marisa Tellez since she was a teenager. She's like the dorky, kid sister my folks never got around to having. The differences between us are subtle but detectable. For starters, she has a slightly more encyclopedic knowledge of *Star Wars* than I do. I never got my first or any subsequent periods. She is often the brightest person in the room and almost always the prettiest. And unlike myself, she has never been prescribed antibiotics as the result of a romantic encounter.

As for facts, particularly about Hollywood in the late 80's and early 90's, she's cornered the market. The journals she's religiously scribbled in since the age of twelve are one of the guides she has relied on for the construction of her book debut. The other is a sharp wit and somewhat sober memory of all the bizarre shit you are about to read. (Bizarre only applies if you are from Utah, New Jersey or Yorba Linda.)

So come and dive into the shark infested waters of Hollywood! Let Marisa be your guide through the last turbulent years of excess and joy, fun and frolic, rock and roll! She'll be the one climbing up the side of the pirate ship with a knife between her teeth, and you'll be the one following behind, looking up her skirt.

D Zink

PREFACE

She barfed between my legs. He kicked me in the face. These are my first encounters in Hollywood with two people that I would come to know as the most genuine people on earth. Since then, I've made it a point to never judge anyone based on a first impression.

When I began keeping journals at the age of twelve, I did it only as a way to imitate my mom who had been writing her own journals for years. Most of my first entries were fairly generic. I would usually write about what I had done that day with no opinion on the events that took place whatsoever. But once I turned into a snarling, hormonal, foaming at the mouth teenage girl, the journals became my lifesaver. They morphed into an outlet I could use to express my happiest and darkest thoughts without any fear of judgment.

I had always bounced around the idea to write a book about my teenage years on the Sunset Strip. It wasn't until many years later when one of those bands did a reunion show, did I decide it was finally time to pull out my old journals and put this book together.

But I didn't want the book to be solely from my point of view. As the old saying goes, "there are two sides to every story." So I decided to interview some of the musicians and friends I hung out with back then and include their "testimonials" in this book.

At first I was really excited at the idea of writing a book about that time in my life. But once I began reading through my old journals, I quickly realized it wasn't all happy times. To be perfectly honest, a majority of it wasn't as happy as I had remembered. There were so many people and events that I had completely blocked out. It wasn't until I read specific entries over and over again, that I finally started to remember. But along with the bad memories were the good ones too, and you'll find a mixture of both included in this memoir.

I used to wonder whether it was a mistake to trade a normal teenage experience of growing up in the valley to go to rock and roll high school in Hollywood. But looking back on it now, I feel when a special moment in time is happening, so very few people are lucky enough to be a part of it. Even fewer can't realize when it's happening, so they don't take the time to cherish it. I'm fortunate enough to have realized both.

This book is dedicated to all the people that survived that crazy time with me. And more importantly to those that didn't.

ACKNOWLEDGMENTS

Special thanks to Casey Quintal for creating a monster book cover and also to Martin Kelly for using your artistic insight to guide me in the right direction.

Extra special thanks to the following for contributing their stories to this book:

Britt (Blackboard Jungle), Cassidy, Chris Penketh (Swingin Thing), Dave Zink (Blackboard Jungle), Dina Palmer-Gomes, Greg Warkel, J. Sinn aka "Skitz" (The Glamour Punks), Joe Howard, Joel Patterson (Blackboard Jungle), Kenny Price (Blackboard Jungle), Screaming Boy Mandie (The Glamour Punks), Spencer, Sunny Phillips (Swingin Thing).

Thank you to Evan for being my rock and providing me with an endless amount of love and support throughout the duration of this project. You calm my heart and make me a better person.

Unconditional love and thanks to my family, especially my mom and dad for never giving up on me when I was at my absolute worst. For every time you told me no, disciplined me, and grounded me, I thank you. It's the only thing that saved me.

1

VALLEY GIRL

The vibration of the bass drum rattles my liver and slowly shakes the foam earplugs out of my ears. I put my drink down, wipe the condensation from my hands onto my jeans and gently push my earplugs back in to muffle the sound of my friends' horrible band.

The drummer's mom grabs my arm and pulls me towards her as she dances offbeat to the song.

"This song is SOOOO good!" she yells into my ear.

I smile politely and look around the half empty club. The only people showing any sign of interest aside from the drummer's mom are the girlfriends of this band.

When the song ends, I give a mercy clap.

Is this what my life has come to? To be in my 30's and STILL going to see a friend's shitty band play at the Whisky a Go Go?

I'm quite familiar with the Whisky and the rest of the clubs along the Sunset Strip in Hollywood. I was well ingrained in that music scene during the late 80's and early 90's. It's where

I spent the span of my teenage years and the number one reason I racked up countless hours of being grounded at the hands of my parents. I can't say I blame them though. Compared to where they're from, I'm sure it was quite a culture shock to be raising a family in Los Angeles.

My dad was the youngest of 13 kids. My mom was the second youngest of 11. Both sides of my family grew up together in a small mining town in Arizona.

My parents and all their siblings went to school together, but my folks actually didn't start dating until they were in their late 20's. My dad joined the U.S. Army shortly after he graduated high school and was stationed in Germany during the Korean War. My mom on the other hand, came to Los Angeles after graduating to visit one of her older brothers who had just relocated with his wife and kids. Within a few weeks, my mom landed a job in downtown L.A. as a telephone operator and decided to stay in California.

When she broke the news to my grandma that she wouldn't be returning to Arizona, it didn't go over very well. Regardless, my mom left Arizona and made a life for herself in Southern California. It wasn't until years later that she got back in touch with my dad after running into one of his brothers in downtown L.A. By that time, he had finished his term in the Army and had a good paying job in construction. After dating only a few months they got married and settled down in Rosemead, a little suburb in the San Gabriel Valley about twenty minutes east of Los Angeles. A few months later, my mom became pregnant with my older sister Lucy. I came along about three years later, and my little sister Ginger followed seven years after that.

Our house had a big front yard and back yard to play in, and we spent our summers on the beach in Orange County. We would have barbecues in the afternoon and bonfires well into the night.

I had a few Barbie's growing up like every other little girl, but being around power tools were more my thing. My dad was a construction worker, so was always building things around the house, and I was more than happy to oblige. Since I was too young to handle power tools, he made me his assistant. He taught me simple things like how to change a drill bit in his power drill, how to tell the difference between a Phillips and flat head screwdriver, what nails were for as opposed to screws, and what washers and nuts were for. Anytime he started to build something, I would stand by and hand him whatever items he asked for just like a trusty assistant helping out a surgeon during an operation. I turned out to be a well-seasoned little construction worker by the time I started pre-school around the age of 4.

It was around the same time that I started getting into music, which was all under the influence of my parents of course. Artists like the Beatles, Elvis, Chuck Berry, and James Brown were always playing in our house, along with popular bands of the time like Blondie and Queen, which were my dad's favorites.

My parents had one of those old 1970's style stereos that was the size of a loveseat and made entirely of wood. You'd lift the top like it was the hood to a car and find a record player, a radio, and a little slot to put your records in. The fancier ones also came with an 8-track player. One of my dad's favorite records was a 45 of "Burning Love" by Elvis. He and I would dance so hard to that song that it would shake the whole stereo and cause the record to skip. I remember howling the words to "Bohemian Rhapsody" (or what I guessed were the words) and thought it was classical music like Beethoven or Mozart because it was so theatrical.

My mom on the other hand, was a huge Beatles fan. She had a collection of their original albums from the 60's and suckered me into liking them by showing me their animated movie, *The Yellow Submarine*. Despite my fear of blue meanies, I loved all the songs in that movie and became an instant Beatle fan. At that young age, singing "Yellow Submarine" was no different than singing the theme to *The Muppet Show*. It took me a while to realize that the Beatles were actually a REAL band and not in the same realm as Kermit the Frog. Unfortunately, I wouldn't realize how much I loved The Beatles until December of 1980.

My mom was sitting on the living room couch with my little sister, Ginger who was just a few months old at the time. We were watching TV when a live news report broke in. I had never really watched the news before. Considering I was only 7 at the time, I had no reason to. Cartoons were obviously more interesting to me than hearing about whatever Dan Rather was reporting on. I remember watching the first bits of news footage come in. Women were crying, children, even grown men. I had never seen anything like it. It wasn't until I saw footage of people holding pictures of John Lennon that it hit me.

"Mom…he was a Beatle huh? Our Beatles, like on the records we always play," I said as more of a statement than a question.

She shook her head and said, "Yeah, he was. *Aye dios*, I can't believe he's gone."

I don't recall seeing either of my parents cry, but I do remember things being a bit more solemn in the house during those first few days after John was killed. Even my teachers at school were acting differently. Day after day, people across the country and the world for that matter were holding vigils and singing John Lennon songs. It was as if a family member had died. It was awful.

While I continued to keep the music of the Beatles close to my heart, I also started to develop my own musical tastes due to a new cable channel called MTV.

MTV was the first cable channel to play music videos 24/7. It was THE channel for any young kid to have but my family couldn't afford cable. I got my music video fix by watching a local 1-hour show called *Video One*, which was hosted by a radio DJ named Richard Blade. I immediately took to bands like Duran Duran, The Cure, Depeche Mode, Culture Club, and soon to be pop icon, Madonna. There I was, not even in double digits yet and already being exposed to rampant sexuality and homosexuality by my favorite artists, which my parents tried to combat at every turn.

I was about 9 years old when an artist named Johnny Cougar released a single called "Hurt So Good". He was scheduled to appear on a Top 10 TV show called *Solid Gold*, which featured scantily clad dancers, grinding and spinning about as musical guests performed their latest hit. Johnny Cougar hit the stage, and I began singing the chorus to "Hurt So Good" as my mom walked into the living room with a plate of food for me.

"Come on mom, sing it!" I said shaking my butt.

My mom put down the plate of food, gave me a few choice words in Spanish like *cochina* and told me never to sing that song out loud again.

As for my crash course in homosexuality, that was the result of an offhand comment made by my older sister, Lucy, after I told her I liked Culture Club.

"Did you know that Boy George makes out with the drummer? They're boyfriend and boyfriend!" she blurted out.

My mom happened to be within an earshot when Lucy made that comment and noticed the confused look on my face. Slightly annoyed, she immediately took me aside and was forced to have a birds and bee's conversation with me way earlier than she had planned on. That was just the first of several mini heart attacks I would give my mom. A more significant one would be when I discovered Madonna.

I was obsessed with her as every little girl was during the mid 1980's. Sure my mom allowed me to get my ears pierced, wear pounds of jangling bracelets, and put lace ribbons in my hair. But she put her foot down when I wanted to cut off my long dark locks to bleach them blonde, and she had a fit when I asked her if I could wear the rosary I received for my First Communion as part of my daily ensemble.

And while we're on the subject of blond hair and overactive hormones let me tell you about my first crush, Brandon Weller, the boy who started it all.

2

PUPPY LOVE, BRAWLING, AND DISCOVERING HOLLYWOOD

I was in 5th grade when I met Brandon who was a year older and in grade 6. He had long blond bangs that cascaded over his big hazel eyes and was one of the most popular skateboarders at Janson Elementary. The first time I saw him was in a recreational dance class we had at school. I had no idea why he would be in a dance class because skaters were way too cool for stuff like that. It was much more suited to dorks like me, but nonetheless that's how we met.

My first encounter with Brandon was a brief one. After weeks of shuffling around with various dance partners, our dance teacher finally paired me to dance with him. My moment of happiness was cut short when he quickly lied to our teacher so he could get out of dancing with me. "Actually, Jeanne's my partner!" he said as he quickly grabbed her wrist.

Jeanne Wilkins was a 6th grader in Brandon's class and the most popular girl in school. I knew it was a lie when I saw

17

the look of surprise on Jeanne's face. I was immediately heartbroken.

I can't say I blame him though. This was during the peak of me being bullied in grade school. I was a scrawny little 5th grader with a massive overbite. The kids in school called me names like Buckie Beaver, forklift, trap jaw, can opener. The list was endless.

Despite the dance class incident, I wasn't ready to give up on Brandon just yet. Like any other girl who has a crush, I made the decision to find interest in the things Brandon liked to do. Since his life was all about skateboarding, I decided to take up skateboarding.

My house had a long driveway, which I practiced on daily and a huge lawn right beside it to break my many falls. I read up on the history of skateboarding and took to learning as much as I could about his hero, Tony Hawk.

I noticed Brandon walking by himself to class one day, so I immediately ran up to him with a head full of Tony Hawk related items to spark up a conversation. Unfortunately, one of my many bullies, a fellow 5th grader named Natalie caught up to us as well. She had made these huge walrus shaped tusks from white construction paper and put them in her mouth as I tried to talk to Brandon. Then she started dancing around us in circles like a monkey saying, "I'm Marisa, hardy har har!" Brandon ran away almost instantly. I was devastated.

Natalie was much bigger than me, so there wasn't much I could do about her heckling. I just hoped that someday soon she would see the error of her mean ways or that she would get hit by a car.

As if that weren't bad enough, a few days later, I met up with my buddy Robert during recess and overheard him saying something about a "snatch" as I walked up to him.

"What's a snatch?" I asked.

"You don't KNOW what a snatch is?" Robert asked."Nope. What is it? Some kind of animal?" I asked cluelessly.

His friend Rich began to laugh and said, "Well some people do call it a beaver..."

"It's hard to explain," Robert said. "Look, there's Mr. Cook," he said pointing in the near distance. "Why don't you ask him what a snatch is? He could probably explain it better than we can."

I shrugged my shoulders and walked over to our homeroom teacher, Mr. Cook.

"Hi Mr. Cook," I said.

"Hey Marisa, did you need something?" he asked.

Without hesitation, I asked, "Yeah, can you tell me what a snatch is?"

The color momentarily drained out of Mr. Cook's face, which was followed by a bright shade of red. By the dramatic look on his face, Robert and the guys must've known I asked him the snatch question because they burst out laughing moments later.

"Did Robert tell you to ask me that?"

"Uh huh. He said you could explain it better than he could," I said innocently.

Mr. Cook looked over to Robert and yelled, "Robert! To the principals office, now!"

Robert walked off and the bell rang for everyone to go back to class. I made my way back to my classroom and took my seat, which happened to be next to Rich. As Mr. Cook started our history lesson, Rich leaned over and whispered in my ear what a snatch REALLY was. I was mortified.

It only took a few days to get over the snatch humiliation, but I never got the courage to go up to Brandon again for the remainder of the school year. That was his last year at Janson because he'd be moving on to Muscatel Junior High in the fall. So I spent a majority of my summer pining and crying over what never was with Brandon.

In the fall of 1984, I started my final year at Janson. It was a year of firsts or should I say fists because the name calling and teasing of yours truly had reached epic proportions at the hands of my most ruthless nemesis, Roger Santos.

Roger and I were in the same grade. I had put up with his bullying for the last two years but it got much worse once we started the 6th grade. Not only did we end up in the same homeroom class, but our teacher also assigned us to sit next to each other, not knowing that he was making my life a living hell.

His teasing usually consisted of general name-calling in reference to my overbite. On rare occasions he'd actually throw something at me. But one day in homeroom class he decided to take it a step further.

While our elderly teacher was rambling on with her boring math lesson, Roger decided he would punch me in the arm every time she turned around to write on the chalkboard. Now I'm not talking about a simple tap on the arm. He would haul off and punch me like I was a guy. The kids around me saw what was going on and did nothing of course. The teacher didn't know what he was doing either. By the fourth punch, I could feel my face getting hot as tears welled up in my eyes.

I knew no one was going to do a damn thing to help me because everyone was scared of Roger. He was the biggest kid in our class. No one had ever gone up against him before, much less a girl. But I refused to let that asshole see me cry. So for the first time ever at the ripe old age of 11, I went completely ape shit.

Moments after the fifth punch I leapt on Roger like a frog, which knocked him completely off his chair and onto the ground. He fell flat on his back, and I started swinging. He was bigger than me, so he was able to block most of my punches. Even the ones I did land weren't doing much damage. I grabbed a fistful of his shaggy hair in each hand, held on tight and started slamming his head into the ground with every pound my tiny little frame could muster up.

Kids were screaming and our teacher was screaming. I knew he was throwing punches and landing them, but my hate for him numbed the pain of his blows. Every swing he took only made me slam his head to the ground that much harder. Not just for me but also for all the other kids he abused during his reign of terror. One of the boys in class tried to pull me off of Roger, but I wasn't letting go. I held on tight like a spider monkey and wasn't going to stop until one of us was dead. I don't remember exactly how long we were fighting for, but it took a few boys to finally pry me off of Roger and separate us. Then our teacher along with the boys that had pulled us apart escorted us into Mr. Towers office, the school principal.

Mr. Towers was a ginger. He had red fuzzy hair, freckles all over his face and big blue eyes. He asked both of us what happened. I didn't want to come off as a tattle tail, so I failed to mention that Roger was the demon seed of Janson Elementary.

The only thing I said was that Roger hit me, so I hit him back. Mr. Towers called our parents to tell them we would be suspended for the remainder of the week and sent us home.

My folks were cool about the whole thing though. I didn't get into any trouble. It was obviously self-defense and not like I had a history of being a bruiser anyway. My mom was upset over the blows I endured, but she was happy I came out of it without any serious injuries. Since I was the closest thing my dad had to a son, he was proud I held my own against a guy twice my size. My dad was an amateur boxer back in his day and offered a few helpful pointers in knocking Roger's ass out should he ever touch me again.

When I went back to school the following Monday, I wasn't worried about running into Roger. I was pretty fired up actually. Sure, there was a good possibility he would beat me to a pulp. He obviously didn't have any qualms about hitting a girl. But one thing I was determined of, I was never going to take shit from him again, even if that meant getting into another fight. To my surprise, Roger's teasing eased up considerably after our boxing match. He would still throw out a "Hey Buckie" every once in a while for good measure, but he never put his hands on me again.

As if having daddy's little girl turn brawler wasn't bad enough, enter Mötley Crüe into my innocent little world.

It was early 1985 when I heard about Mötley Crüe from some of the boys in my class. They would tell stories about the emerging music scene in Hollywood and how their older siblings were going to a place called the Sunset Strip, which sprouted out many heavy metal younglings like Mötley Crüe and Ratt to name a few.

After coming home from school one day, I tuned into *Video One*. They were playing Mötley Crüe's "Looks that Kill" video. It was the first time I ever laid eyes on Nikki Sixx. I slid off my couch in awe as I watched him move his body and bang his head with ferocity. My current musical tastes at the time were bands like Duran Duran, and the Go Go's. I had never seen anything like Nikki Sixx with his makeup-laden face and borage of spiky black hair. The only other guy in my music realm that wore that much makeup was Boy George, and I knew he was a fruit thanks to Lucy's outburst a few years earlier. But nothing

21

about Nikki struck me as gay; despite the dark shade of red lipstick he wore in the video. I decided then and there that I wanted to marry Nikki Sixx regardless of our 15-year age difference.

I immediately went out and bought copies of *Shout at the Devil* and *Too Fast For Love*. Considering the first album cover was a crotch and the second a pentagram, I decided for the sake of my poor, Catholic parents that I would keep my newfound love for Mötley Crüe under wraps for the time being. I would hide my *Circus* and *Metal Edge* magazines with a blood, whisky and groupie covered Nikki the way a husband would hide his *Playboy* magazines from his nagging wife. I'm sure my parents enjoyed happier days when I was crushing on clean cut boys my age like Ricky Schroeder, but the times were changing with the sound of glam rock and heavy metal overtaking Southern California.

In the fall of 1985, I started the 7th grade at Muscatel Junior High. It's where I met Sadie, Carla, and Tasha who would become my core group of girlfriends. Sadie was the cool metal chick, Carla was the clumsy one, Tasha was the cheerleader, and then there was me. I don't know what the hell I was, probably just loud.

I also became reunited with Brandon and I must say that karma really paid off this time around for the humiliating moments I suffered at Janson. Not only were we assigned to the same 7th period P.E. class, but we ended up on the same softball team as well!

Unfortunately, my reputation at Janson followed me to Muscatel because Brandon remembered me as the "walrus girl". It obviously wasn't one of my finer moments, but at least he remembered me and wasn't running away this time around. I had also just gotten braces and was counting down the days when my resemblance to any animal with big teeth or tusks would be long behind me. Things were definitely looking up!

Brandon talked constantly about skateboarding and Mötley Crüe. My knowledge of the Crüe was a given because I was in love with Nikki Sixx. I had also continued to keep up with the latest happenings in the skateboarding world during our yearlong separation. So this time around we had plenty of things to chat about.

Over the next few months, things rolled right along with Brandon. We would hang out during every softball and P.E. class, and he'd run up to me in the hallways at school. On a few occasions we even walked home from school together because his house was on my way home. It was more than I could've ever wished for, but I realized time was not on my side.

Muscatel was grade 7 and 8 only. Since Brandon was an 8th grader, I would only have that one semester to really make an impact on him before he left to high school.

While I worked on ways to win Brandon's heart, I was also becoming more obsessed with the Sunset Strip. My only connection to the music scene in Hollywood was through free local rock magazines like *Rock City News* and *BAM Magazine*. As the scene continued to grow in Hollywood, it wasn't long before *Video One* was giving equal if not more video airplay to a slew of bands like Ratt who I also became a fan of.

In the winter of 1985, Ratt was on their *Invasion of Your Privacy* tour with Bon Jovi as their opening act. I had just turned 12, and Lucy was 15. We begged and eventually talked our dad into taking us to their concert at the Forum in Inglewood. He had no desire to see either band play, so the night of the show he hung out in his truck with a cigarette and a book while Lucy and I rocked out in our nosebleed seats.

When Lucy and I walked back to his truck after the show, we caught him talking to a handful of cute glam boys in spandex pants. They had hair to the sky and were wearing more makeup than my mom had in her dresser drawer.

One thing I have to say about my dad is that he was such a laid back, non-judgmental person. He found everybody interesting and could strike up a conversation with just about anyone God bless him. He introduced us to the guys in the band and showed us a flyer they had given him.

"They're called Crimson Wave," he said cluelessly.

Lucy snickered. I didn't get the joke either. I wouldn't get it till two years later. LITERALLY.

According to the flyer they were playing a Hollywood club called the Troubadour that upcoming Saturday night at 9:00 p.m. Lucy and I bit at our dad's ankles like two annoying puppies in the hopes that he would take us to the show. One of the guys mentioned the Troubadour was an all ages club and handed my dad three tickets. *Perfect, problem solved.* It was a free all ages show and they were playing fairly early. There was no justifiable reason that my dad shouldn't allow his pre-teen and teenage daughters to go to a club in Hollywood right?

He pondered for a minute, and I knew we had him. One thing about my dad, if he didn't say no right away, I knew it was something he could be talked into. Actually, even if he did say no, I knew it was something he could STILL be talked into. But that's what daughters are for right? We are daddy's little girls sent from heaven to warm the cockles of his heart and pull those cockles fresh out of the oven when we need a favor.

The night of the Crimson Wave show was finally upon us. I could hardly contain myself! I wasn't crazy about having my dad follow us around at the show but he was on the higher end of the cool dad meter anyway, so I let it slide. I was just excited to be going to my first Hollywood show!

My dad battled his way through Hollywood freeway traffic as I tapped my foot with anticipation. I just wanted to be there already. *Why didn't all these people in their dumb cars understand that and get the hell out of my way?*

We finally got off the freeway and made our way down Santa Monica Blvd. When I saw the Troubadour come into view, I leapt towards the dashboard with excitement.

"There it is!" I yelled, pointing up at the club marquee.

As we slowly approached the front of the Troubadour, I noticed a guy on a leash being led into the club by a woman in a leather corset and hot pants. Hoping my dad hadn't already noticed, I quickly tried to divert his attention away from the proverbial bondage elephant in the room.

"Hey Chuck, look over there! There's a parking lot!" I said pointing in the opposite direction.

Chuck wasn't my dad's name. But for some reason I always called him "Chuck" from The Peanuts cartoons ever since I was old enough to speak.

My dad didn't look to where I was pointing. He stopped looking at the bondage couple and looked right at me. He was giving me that look of disapproval. I smiled optimistically. I was just as shocked to see the bondage couple as he was but I had to play it off like it was nothing. If I wasn't bothered by it certainly how could he be?

"Isn't this going to be fun?" I asked innocently.

Without saying a word, he turned the corner leading away from the parking lot.

"What are you doing?" Lucy asked.

"We're not going," he said.

"WHAT! What do you mean?" I squealed.

"Forget it. I'm not letting you girls in there," he said shaking his head and laughing.

As he drove further and further away from the Troubadour, I began to whine. I wasn't ready to give up. I was like a defense lawyer trying to plead my case. I told him he would be by our side the whole time. We had free tickets. We were already there. It was a waste of a drive and gas to not go in, blah blah. I kept bitching and trying to cop a deal with him, which lasted all the way through Hollywood and the freeway ride home.

"You act like it's the end of the world. It's just a show," he said calmly.

"No it's not, it's my first show! You wouldn't understand. You're old and don't like to go out and have fun anymore," I said with my arms crossed.

"Thanks a lot," he said.

My pleading continued as we turned the street to our house. By this time my dad was completely amused by my persistence.

"Do you really think I'm going to drive all the way back to Hollywood?" he asked.

"It's worth a shot," I said with a hopeful smile.

"NO," he said as we pulled up into the driveway.

I made a sour face as I got out and slammed the car door. This made my dad laugh hysterically, which me off even more. I stomped through the house, into my bedroom and climbed the ladder up to my bunk bed. I threw on my Walkman and listened to Mötley's *Shout at the Devil* album as I lay there bumming out that my first venture into Hollywood was a complete failure.

Even though we didn't made it into the Troubadour, I was fascinated by the small spectacle I saw outside the club. I wanted to be where the action was. I knew I just had to make my way back into the Hollywood music scene. My opportunity came a few months later thanks to the L.A. Street Scene in the fall of 1986.

The L.A. Street Scene was an annual two-day music festival in downtown L.A. where a few streets were shut down to host live bands and vendors galore.

Retribution over the Troubadour debacle hadn't been paid to Lucy or I yet. I was determined to milk the guilt out of that cow, hoping it would take the form of tickets for both of us to the festival. To my surprise, it worked. On our list of bands to see were Guns N' Roses, Jane's Addiction, Gene Loves Jezebel, Poison, The Ramones, and our newest obsession, Candy.

I had developed a momentary crush on Candy's guitar player, Ryan Roxie, after seeing their "Whatever Happened to Fun?" video on *Video One.* I didn't mention this when my dad agreed to take us on the 1st day of the festival. Sure the glam rock scene fascinated me, but going to the festival was more about seeing live bands than me drooling over Ryan. Besides my heart still belonged to Nikki Sixx and I had no intention of straying.

Whether or not my dad would take us on the 2nd day of the festival depended on how well me and Lucy got along on the 1st day. So at the risk of not ruining our music filled weekend we agreed not to kill each other for the time being. To act as a buffer, Lucy decided to bring along her friend, Christy who I wasn't a big fan of at the time. I had accidentally farted on her weeks earlier while we were playing in our backyard and she had been calling me "cheese" ever since. Not that I was any stranger to nicknames but still.

On day 1 of the festival, the first band on our list to see was Candy. Lucy and I wanted to meet and take pictures with the guys, but we were way too shy to go up to them. That's where my dad and his Grade A social skills came into play. We figured after the band finished their set we would pimp him out to go talk to the guys and wave us over once it was cool to meet them.

Candy played and I snapped a million pictures, which were mostly of Ryan. Shortly after their set ended, Lucy and I enforced our plan, which worked like a charm. Within ten minutes after stepping off stage, my dad was waving us over to meet the guys.

Ryan shook my hand hello. I said nothing and smiled like a lunatic. His black crimped hair was peeking out from underneath the white captains hat he was wearing. When we posed for a picture, Lucy and Christy immediately jumped on either side of Ryan, which left me having to squat out front. I was annoyed. After getting pictures and autographs from all the guys in Candy, they hugged each of us goodbye. As Ryan hugged me my face was engulfed with the comforting, familiar scent of Aqua Net Extra Super Hold.

I decided to let Lucy and Christy's sabotage of Ryan slide for the time being. I wasn't about to argue and jeopardize us coming back for the 2nd day of the festival. After meeting Candy, we strolled around for a bit and made our way to the stage where Guns N' Roses and Poison were supposed to play.

I asked a security guard standing nearby when Guns N' Roses was set to go on, and he told us we had just missed them. I was furious. He said there was a water leak near the stage during the Guns set, and they cut their set short due to a possible electrical hazard. When I asked about Poison he said they cancelled.

Lucy and I continued to be on our best behavior for the rest of the afternoon. And since the day went off without a hitch, my dad agreed to take us the next day to see Jane's Addiction and Gene Loves Jezebel.

On day 2 of the festival, we caught Gene Loves Jezebel's set and grabbed a bite to eat. Unfortunately, we ended up missing Jane's Addiction. We were missing all the bands we wanted to see!

We strolled around a little while longer eating delicious international foods and catching a song or two from random bands playing on the various stages. The only bands we cared to see had played, so we decided to head home early.

When we came home my mom was watching TV in the living room, so we joined her. She was watching a news report about a small riot that had erupted at the L.A. Street Scene shortly after we left the day before.

"Man, we miss all the fun!" I said with my arms crossed.

I was glad my parents didn't find out about the riot earlier. There's no way in hell my dad would've taken us back to the festival for the 2nd day if he had known that happened. It was also reported that in addition to the small riot from the day before, a few stabbings and at least one shooting had taken place within the last hour.

A short time later it was publicly announced that the L.A. Street Scene would be no more. After nine years of having the festival, the violence that ensued over those two days had ruined the fun for all of us. I also found out that Poison didn't cancel their set after all. They went on to play shortly after the water spillage/electrical issue was cleaned up.

About a week or so later, I started the 8th grade at Muscatel Junior High. It was a particularly odd time for me. For some reason, I had a wild hair up my ass and wasn't getting along with Sadie and the rest of the girls. I would get in random spats with them over the silliest things. It was always me against one of them. They never argued with each other, yet everything they did would get on my last nerve. So after another stupid fight, I stopped hanging out with them and took up with my friend, Vickie, and her friends Nancy and Drita who were fellow 8th graders.

Drita, Nancy, and Vickie were the most popular girls in school, which was certainly a far social leap from my Buckie Beaver days.

I met Vickie about a year earlier when I first started at Muscatel. Her hair was an odd shade of orange due to weeks of spraying a hair color lightener called Sun-In in her brown wavy locks. She was supposed to be a freshman in high school but flunked and was held back a year. Drita and Nancy had long curly black hair. They were best friends that constantly smacked bubblegum and wore way too much makeup. They were wannabe cholas, especially Drita who seemed to be the unofficial ringleader of the group. Nancy was always nice to me, but as for Drita, well, she was civil to me. She wasn't a complete bitch but she wasn't very friendly to me either. I always got a vibe off her like she felt I wasn't worthy to be hanging around in her circle.

I was a bit shell shocked during the first few days of hanging out with the popular girls because I wasn't used to getting so much attention from the other kids in school. Although I was missing Sadie and the rest of the girls, I was most definitely enjoying the perks of my new social standing.

During lunch one day, Vickie, Drita, Nancy, and myself had just picked up some food in the cafeteria and were looking for a place to sit. Drita noticed an empty table next to the biggest nerds in Grade 8, so we headed in that direction. We all put our trays down on the table except for Drita. She walked over to the table of nerds and leaned over the shoulder of a bookworm named Jennifer.

"I don't appreciate you making me look dumb in class today. If you pull that shit again, I'll beat your ass, got it?" Drita said in her ear.

Jennifer said nothing. She just sat there stiff as a board with her eyes bugged out through her horn-rimmed glasses.

The incident Drita was referring to happened earlier that day in English class. Drita messed up an answer when our teacher called on her, so Jennifer immediately raised her hand to give the correct answer. I didn't think she did it to make Drita look dumb. She was just one of those nerdy kids that knew the answers to everything.

I felt bad for Jennifer as she sat there frozen. She looked like she was going to drop dead of a heart attack. Drita was being such a bitch over something so stupid. But that's what she was, a pompous bitch with an unbelievable sense of entitlement. I needed to find a way to save Jennifer without getting my own ass kicked, so I nonchalantly told Drita that Jennifer wasn't worth the time. Luckily, Drita agreed and decided to back off. She took a seat at our table and laughed. Vickie and Nancy joined in while I stayed quiet as a mouse. Needless to say, the whole incident left a bad taste in my mouth.

When I came home from school that afternoon, I began to re-evaluate who my friends were. I really liked Vickie, but as a group coupled with Nancy and Drita, not so much. I didn't find interest in the things they liked, and the things they laughed about I didn't find funny. Having Drita walk around the school on her high horse was one thing. But threatening Jennifer for no good reason was the deal breaker for me. As someone who had been bullied first hand for years, I knew those were people I didn't want to be associated with.

A few days after the Jennifer incident, I called Carla. After some general pleasantries she asked how things were going with my new group of friends. I said I wasn't too happy hanging out with Vickie, Drita, and Nancy. That's when she told me she missed me. All the girls missed me, and I told her I missed them too. After a few minutes of catching up on our latest happenings, she invited me to sit with her and the girls during lunch at school the next day. I happily accepted.

When I had lunch with Carla, Sadie, and Tasha the next afternoon it felt like I had never left them. We picked up on each others little jokes and things seemed to be back in sync with no bickering what so ever. I finally felt like I could breathe again and just be me.

Although I retained my friendship with Vickie, I never went back to hanging out with her, Drita, and Nancy again.

A few weeks later, Drita came to school with a black eye and her tail between her legs. The rumor around school was she had been badmouthing a REAL chola named Leticia who was a sophomore at Rosemead High. Leticia "allegedly" beat the stuffing out of her at Rosemead Park while Vickie and Nancy stood by and did nothing to help Drita. I certainly don't advocate violence, but Leticia must have beaten the bitch right out of Drita because her attitude dropped drastically after that fight. She never quite walked with the same egotistical swagger for the rest of the school year.

Joining forces again with the girls couldn't have come at a better time because I was in desperate need of help with Brandon. We hadn't spoken much since he left to Rosemead High, so I wanted to call him and make sure he didn't forget about me during our separation.

The issue was that I had never called him on the phone before. I never had a reason to because we always saw each other at school everyday. But after a few motivating words from the girls, which was them telling me to stop being such a big chicken, I finally got the balls to call him.

During my conversation with Brandon, he mentioned he had just bought a VHS tape of Mötley Crüe's documentary, *Uncensored*. He hadn't seen it yet, so he invited me over to watch it. I calmly told him that sounded cool and we made plans for me to go over his house the following week after school. The moment we hung up, I immediately party lined Carla and Sadie. I was jumping up and down, squealing like a pig as I told them the news. Then the reality hit me that I was actually going to his house. That's when my joy turned to absolute terror.

I was only 12 and had never kissed a boy before. I hadn't even experienced a simple peck. Most girls my age had made out with at least one boy if not more. *What if he tries to kiss me? I don't know how to French kiss. Will I not use enough tongue? Or will I use too much tongue and end up swallowing his face?*

The next day at school, Carla mentioned she had stumbled across her stepfather's porn stash and suggested I watch it to get some pointers for my pseudo date with Brandon.

"Are you crazy? I don't want to have sex!" I said to Carla, mortified.

"I know you're not having sex, but you can watch the making out at least," she said.

"Is there making out in porn?" I asked cluelessly.

"I don't know. I've never seen one before either," she said.

We made plans to ditch school the following day with Sadie and Tasha to check out the porn tapes. It was my first ditch day ever.

When our classes broke for lunch the next day, we scattered across the schoolyard like a bunch of roaches. We felt it was less conspicuous sneaking out of school individually as opposed to a group. Everyone made it off campus without getting caught and we met up at Carla's house about a block away.

Carla's mom and stepdad both worked during the day, so that gave us free reign of the house. We raided the kitchen, making popcorn and other snacks as if we were about to watch a normal movie. The four of us gathered in the living room with our freshly made treats as Carla ran to a small closet in the hallway and pulled out a VHS tape. She came back to the living room and popped the tape into her VCR. Within mere moments, I was completely creeped out.

The movie was bad 70's porn with the typical role-play of a male teacher and a schoolgirl. It started with them making out, then progressed to them stripping each other's clothes off and exposing their wild pubic hair. There it was, plain as day on the snowy VHS tape that Carla had to keep adjusting the tracking on, my first penis and set of balls. Damn they were huge! The teacher began to spray shaving cream on the girls' crotch and pulled out a razor. We glanced around each other with confusion.

"Is that what sex is? You dress up in weird costumes and shave each other? I had no idea it was such a production," I said utterly perplexed.

I sensed the girls were just as grossed out as I was because no one was saying a word. I asked Carla to shut the tape off just as the teacher started to shave the girl down. The little bit of making out I did see didn't look like anything I could or wanted to learn from anyway. So we threw in a tape of *Sixteen Candles* and tried to enjoy the rest of our afternoon.

The following week, I showed up to Brandon's house on a random day after school. He greeted me at the door in a pair of jeans, some white and black-checkered vans, and a white Ocean Pacific t-shirt. I walked into his living room to find it really was JUST us two. I was excited, yet terrified.

I sat down on his sofa and noticed bowls of chips and nuts sitting on a coffee table in front of me. He asked if I wanted a soda and a sandwich. I declined on the latter because bread is the kiss of death when you have braces. You can't bite into it because it gets stuck everywhere. If you have to eat it, the best thing to do is tear it into small pieces and throw it in the back of your mouth.

Brandon came back to the living room with a sandwich in hand and soda's for both of us. He popped in a VHS tape of Mötley Crüe's *Uncensored* and took a seat in a reclining chair next to me, not on the sofa I was sitting on.

Oh. So we really are just going to watch the Mötley tape.

Not that I was expecting him to dress like a teacher and attempt to shave my private parts, but I thought he would at least try to sit next to me and give me a smooch.

I was so nervous that I started stuffing my face with nuts and chips as he told me about a band called The Cult who he was a huge fan of.

We ended up talking through most of the Mötley video. He told me about a new skateboard he had just bought and what life was like in high school as opposed to junior high. But as he babbled on, I wondered in the back of my mind when or if he was going to make a move on me.

When the video ended, we had a moment of awkward silence. We stared at each other, waiting for the other to say something. I was so nervous that I stupidly told him I had to go; even though that was the last thing I wanted to do. He walked over to me, thanked me for coming over and smiled. Our faces were mere inches away from each other. I thought for sure he was going to kiss me, so I began to close my eyes.

"Did you get taller over the summer?" he asked.

I quickly opened my eyes.

"Yeah, damn that puberty," I said mildly disappointed.

I was so angry at myself for saying I had to leave. I wanted another shot at hanging out with Brandon, but I was too embarrassed to ask. After a few more moments of awkward silence, he chimed in.

"Are you going to summer school at Rosemead after you graduate Muscatel?" he asked.

"I sure am. Are you?" I asked.

"Yeah, probably. I guess I'll see you then!"

Ugh. Brutal.

I've never been one to give up on something I want though. I may have failed at Janson, but at least I made some headway at Muscatel by creating a friendship between the two of us. So once I got to Rosemead High, I was determined to win the affections of Brandon.

Meanwhile, I was eagerly anticipating a major turning point in my life. I squealed with pre-teen delight as I counted down the days until my 13th birthday! I wondered if there would be any sudden changes after turning 13. Would I wake up one morning looking like Dolly Parton? Get my first pimple? Suffer a bad case of teen angst that I heard so much about? I didn't feel angry.

On the same note, Carla, Sadie, and Tasha had started surfing the crimson wave over the last few months. I was the only one in our little group who had yet to suffer the curse. So until I joined the land of cramps and water retention with the rest of my girlfriends, I would have to find something else to occupy my time. And thanks to Sadie, making my official debut on the Sunset Strip was just the distraction I needed.

Tony, one of Sadie's older brothers, happened to play bass in a band called Sapphire. She mentioned they had just booked their first show at the Whisky A Go Go, so of course I squealed at the opportunity to make my way back to Hollywood!

By the grace of god, my parents allowed me to go to the show. I'm sure the thought of a 13-year-old girl going to a rock club in Hollywood sounds scandalous, but it was more like a glorified family field trip. The only reason they let me go was because both of Sadie's parents and all her siblings would be there too.

I could barely contain myself the day of Tony's show. I ran home from school, grabbed Mötley's new album, *Theatre of Pain* to listen to and barricaded the bathroom. I didn't want anyone bothering me while I got ready.

I emerged an hour later, dressed and ready to go. My hair was stiff as a board, yet I still felt I needed more hair spray. I grabbed the white and pink can of Aqua Net Extra Super Hold, held my breath, and sprayed a flammable halo around my head.

If you used the pink and silver can of Aqua Net you were incapable of having a normal hairstyle. To go along with my ridiculous hair, I had an equally ridiculous outfit to match. I wore a black shredded tank top, flat suede boots with a chain around each ankle, and leopard printed stretch pants with a headband to match.

Once I finished getting ready, the only thing left to do was wait for my ride. I paced back and forth in my bedroom waiting for Sadie to pick me up. I was so excited about going to the show, that I would bum rush my bedroom window every time I heard a car come down my street.

About a half hour later, a clunky silver pickup truck blaring "Highway to Hell" raced up my driveway. I grabbed my purse and ran out the door.

Sadie's oldest brother, Tom, was driving. They had a few siblings in the front seat, so Sadie and I hopped into the back camper shell. We hadn't been sitting more than a few seconds when Tom tore out of my driveway like an ambulance driver, which caused Sadie and I to tumble across the bed of the truck like pieces of fruit.

We raced down the 10 freeway and hit traffic near downtown L.A. thank god, because it was the only thing that made Tom slow down. I peeked my dizzy head up, looked at the downtown skyline and saw a freeway sign that read "101

Hollywood". I had a little chill of excitement, quickly pulled a small can of Aqua Net out from my purse and started touching up my hair.

Twenty minutes later, Tom pulled into the back parking lot of the Whisky. Sadie and I happily ditched her siblings and stumbled down the slanted parking lot. I immediately noticed a big chested blonde. She was wearing a black bustier, tight leopard mini skirt and black heels. She emerged from a black corvette nearby and I looked at her in awe, hoping that my gangly frame would mold out to look like hers someday. I wondered how big my boobs would get and if I would ever grow out of my training bra. Sadie and I followed the voluptuous girl to the front door of the Whisky where she strolled right in. I walked up to the doorman and handed him my ticket.

"Put out both your hands," he said.

I put out my hands and smiled at him, wondering what he was going to give me.

"Palms down," he said sternly.

He grabbed a black marker out of his back pocket, pulled the cap off with his teeth and drew a big black "X" on the back of each of my hands. And just like that, within a few minutes of being in the Hollywood scene, I had been marked with the ultimate scarlet letter. Those "X's" were hostile and completely uncool. Looking back on it now, the outfit I had on was much worse but hey, I was only 13 and didn't know any better.

After doing the same thing to Sadie, we took our freshly branded hands and walked into the Whisky. I was in the holy land where Nikki Sixx once played just a few years earlier. I breathed in the stench of cigarette smoke and tried to picture him on stage in those red leather pants, lighting himself on fire.

A guy resembling a vampire interrupted my daydreaming by shoving a flyer in each of our hands. His hair was platinum blond but short and completely fried. He dressed head to toe in black with a dark trench coat to match. His face was plastered with pasty white makeup and he had black eyeliner smudged around his eyes. I was mesmerized by the plastic fangs that wobbled in his mouth as he told us how cool his band was and that we should come to his show the following weekend. As quickly as he had appeared, he disappeared and went to hound some other girls that had just walked in the door.

I suggested to Sadie that we take a stroll around the Whisky. As we walked upstairs, we were nearly sideswiped by a bony wannabe rock star that was fumbling down the steps. He had one arm around an unfortunate girl and the other was holding onto the rail. His patent leather pants seemed to be too big for his slender frame, which is probably why his girlfriend was holding them up with her other hand. Sadie and I shrugged our shoulders and continued making our way upstairs.

When we reached the top of the stairs, there were tables and chairs lining a railing that overlooked the club. I spotted a huge bouncer standing beside a door where a group of scantily clad girls burst out the door laughing and spilling their drinks on each other. I grabbed Sadie's arm and tore off in that direction.

"That must be backstage, let's go!" I said.

"We can't get back there. It's probably 21 and over," she said.

"So what? Your brother is playing tonight, which gives you clout."

"What about you?"

"I have clout by association."

As Sadie and I approached the bouncer, he stared me down the way my grandmother used to when I bum rushed her cookie jar before giving her a hug and kiss hello.

I quickly put my hands under my armpits to hide those obnoxious black "X's", and then smiled at the bouncer and said, "I'm going backstage."

"You can't go backstage," he said.

"Oh it's okay her brother is playing tonight," I said matter of factly.

"You kids are too young to go backstage, clear the way," he said, pushing us to the side as he opened the door to let Tony's singer walk up with two girls.

"Dude, we're eighteen, so I don't know what YOU'RE talking about," I said.

"You're not even old enough to be jailbait, now get out of here!" he barked.

Sadie and I walked away with our tails between our legs.

I stopped at the top of the stairs and looked over to find the bouncer still staring at us with that disapproving look. I stuck my tongue out at him and ran down the staircase.

3

HIGH SCHOOL, BAKED SQUASH, AND HANDCUFFS

After making my debut on the Sunset Strip with a resounding thud, I decided to take some time away from Hollywood to regroup and plan my next strategy. Okay, it was more like a forced hiatus because I couldn't find anyone to take me out there again, but I was working on that.

On the scholastic side of things, I had recently graduated from Muscatel and just started summer school at Rosemead High. I was looking forward to continuing the friendship I had built with Brandon, but he was preoccupied with his new anteater nosed girlfriend, Erica.

Erica dressed like a mod with little cardigan sweaters, tight cotton skirts, colored tights, and pointed flats. She always had a scowl on her face and constantly tucked her black bobbed hair behind her ears. Brandon and I would have a brief chat here and there when we passed each other in the halls at school, but

37

that was about it. Not wanting to be a home wrecker, I put my plans to pursue him on hold for the time being.

The summer semester went by in a flash. A few weeks later, in the fall of 1987, I officially started my freshman year at Rosemead High. I was the youngest in my class at only 13. This was due to my parents throwing me into kindergarten at the age of 4 instead of the mandatory 5. I guess they had the foresight to know I would become a big pain in the ass and decided to get me out of the house sooner rather than later.

Going to Rosemead High was the first time Lucy and I had gone to the same school together since Janson. But this time around she was a hotshot senior and didn't want much to do with the likes of a measly freshman like myself. That was fine with me though, I had bigger fish to fry.

I was still keeping tabs on the music scene in Hollywood and wanted so badly to be a part of what was happening on the Sunset Strip. But after the Troubadour debacle, not to mention the violence at the L.A. Street Scene, I figured my dad would never take me to Hollywood again. Even Sapphire had broken up over the summer, so there went my semi legitimate excuse to get out to Hollywood.

I was on my way to class one day when I happened to notice flyers posted throughout the hallways at school. It was promoting a free show the following afternoon on campus for a band called The Key. They were set to play in Panther Square, which was a large outdoor area on campus with a small faux stage.

The black and white photo on the flyer was pretty gritty, but I could see that all the guys in the band had long hair and were wearing makeup. After all my bellyaching of wanting to go to Hollywood to see bands play, the last thing I expected was to have one of them come to my dumb high school. I couldn't wait!

The following day, I was the first to bolt out the door from my English class on the other side of campus. By the time I wheezed my way into Panther Square, a crowd of kids had gathered for the show. About two or three songs into their set, I realized there wasn't anything particularly original or amazing about their music. Regardless, I was still excited to have a real living, breathing rock band play at my school. When they finished, a majority of the kids crowded around as the band members stepped offstage to sign autographs and take pictures, me included. The autograph session didn't go more than five minutes when the damn bell rang, which ended our lunch period and signaled for everyone to go to his or her next class. Some of the teachers who had been standing around acting as bouncers started breaking up the crowd and telling kids to go to class, but I wasn't budging.

As the old saying goes, if a tree falls in a forest and no one is there to hear it, does it make a sound? And if I don't hear a teacher telling me to get to class, (or at least pretend I don't hear them) that means I'm free to stay where I am, right?

Quite a few kids were sticking around, so the teachers started yelling, and I just kept right on ignoring. I was next in line to get an autograph from the singer when a teacher stepped in and said if I didn't leave right then and there she would send me to the attendance office. I looked over the teachers shoulder at the singer and looked back at the teacher. The singer was no Nikki Sixx and certainly not worth getting in trouble over, so I relented and skipped off to my next class.

With the possibility of me going to Hollywood still out of reach for the time being, I did what every other valley girl was doing at the time. Hanging out at the local mall with my girlfriends.

It was another typical Saturday afternoon of strolling around the Montebello mall with Sadie, Carla, and Tasha when we happened to come upon a music store called Mr. Entertainment. That's when I developed a crush on their youngest salesman, Brian Duncan.

Brian had long blond hair that just touched his shoulders and bright blue eyes. I wanted to spark up a music related conversation with him. I had recently started dabbling in guitar, but it was hardly anything to sneeze at. I was about to walk away with the girls when I noticed my neighbor, Carlos, walk out of a back room and go behind the register. I had no idea he worked there, so I seized the opportunity to meet Brian.

I was chatting with Carlos for a few minutes when Brian walked up and joined in the conversation. He said he was a junior at Montebello High and guitarist for a band called Razzle Dazzle. Against my better judgment, I tried to work the guitar angle. I told him I was learning to play, so he gave me his phone number and told me to call him if I had any questions about anything.

I didn't call Brian right away because I couldn't think of a thing to say to him. I felt dumb asking about guitar related matters because I was such a novice. Hell, I barely knew what a power chord was.

The following weekend, I went to the mall with the girls again and planned on stopping in to say hi to Brian. But the moment we walked into Mr. Entertainment and he looked at me with those baby blues, I clammed up and ran away like a squealing piglet.

A few days later, I was talking to Sadie about my dilemma with Brian. I couldn't understand why he scared the hell out of me. I certainly didn't have a problem going up and talking to Brandon when I first started crushing on him. Regardless, she said she'd help me, so an hour later my dad dropped me off at Sadie's and we put "Operation Brian Phone Call" into action.

Sadie and I drafted a series of questions in case I became nervous and stumbled during my phone call with Brian. We figured that ten questions would be more than adequate. But if I burned through all ten that meant the conversation was going VERY badly.

Another factor we took into consideration when writing the list of questions was demand. Like any normal girl talking to a guy she likes, she wants him to know that she's a hot commodity and wanted by other guys. We decided the alternate, 11th question would have me queuing Sadie to "accidentally" interrupt my phone conversation to ask me about Brandon in the hopes it would spark some interest for Brian to ask who he was. Sure Brandon was still with Erica and of course nothing was going on between us. Sadie knew that too but Brian didn't need to know that.

With my list of questions in place, it took Sadie a good half hour to calm my nerves and build up my courage to call Brian. And once I did, the phone call went as flawless as a car crash.

He breezed through all ten questions within a few minutes by giving me short answers. To make matters worse, when I queued Sadie to bring up Brandon, Brian said it sounded like I wanted to have a conversation with her and that he'd let me go, which he did rather quickly. *Damn it.*

A week or so later, I was walking home from school when I ran into Carlos. I mentioned that I liked Brian and he told me not to waste my time. He said Brian had a girlfriend that he was madly in love with who also went to Montebello High. I couldn't believe I wasted a whole month of my life on that guy.

With Brian being out of the picture for good, I went back to my standard daydreaming of Nikki Sixx until the next crush passed along my way.

Speaking of Nikki, it was shortly after my 14th birthday when I was listening to a local rock station in my bedroom and a DJ reported that Nikki Sixx might be dead due to a heroin overdose.

"Oh my god! Nikki might be dead!" I yelled to my mom after flinging open my bedroom door.

"Who's Nikki? A classmate from school?" she asked.

"No, he was supposed to be your future son in law," I said sadly as I walked back into my bedroom.

"Home Sweet Home" came on the radio and my heart sank. I figured it was a Mötley music marathon being played in memory of Nikki. I closed the door to my bedroom, lay down on my bed, and stared at a poster of Nikki on my wall. His hands and bass were covered with blood and he was holding a shank knife in one of his hands. *What a waste that I never had the opportunity to meet him.* The song ended and the DJ reported that Nikki had OD'd, but he was still alive and had been taken to a hospital. I jumped out of bed and flung open my bedroom door again.

"Mom! Nikki's not dead!" I said with excitement.

"Oh, that's good," she said unenthusiastically.

With Nikki's life being spared, I put my focus back on the Sunset Strip music scene and more importantly, finding a way to get back out to Hollywood.

Over the next few months, I began to hear about a new club in Hollywood called the Cathouse. It was THE place to be on Tuesday nights. Taime Downe, the singer of Faster Pussycat, and his roommate, Ricki Rachtman, a VJ on MTV, ran the club. What Studio 54 was to disco in the 70's, the Cathouse was to the glam rock scene in the late 80's. I was clawing at the chance to go, especially since Faster Pussycat played there quite often, and I was crushing big time on Brent Muscat, one of their guitar players. Unfortunately, I had a few things working against me.

For one, I had just turned 14 and the Cathouse was an 18 and over club. I couldn't even go the semi-legitimate route by using Lucy's ID because even she wasn't 18 yet. Now if I was a hot mama with big boobs and an ass you could rest a six-pack on, my age probably wouldn't have mattered. But um yeah, I didn't have any of that going for me. I was a scrawny tomboy with a flat chest who bore no resemblance to the vixens parading around in the rock videos of that time. It was like comparing a side of baked squash to a filet mignon.

But alas, it was around the same time that I finally got my period! Now that I was officially a full-fledged woman, I hoped the hormones would kick in quickly and I would wake one morning to find the curves and face of Cindy Crawford had taken over my body. *Come on hormones kick in already!*

I was too old for slumber parties and too young to have a driver's license. Until I could weasel my way back to Hollywood, I went the traditional high school route of going to neighborhood keg parties.

Keg parties were essentially kids from my high school having a party in someone's backyard. They were usually free, which was in my price range except for the occasional $2 or $3 booze donation they'd ask you to pitch in when the first keg was sucked dry. I tried marijuana for the first time and discovered the savory sweetness of Strawberry Hill.

The parties generally lasted a few hours until a disgruntled neighbor would call the police and bitch about the loud music or numerous amount of drunk, underage kids loitering on their street. Most were fairly uneventful with the exception being one of the last parties I went to at my friend, Dave's house.

I had been at the party for about an hour or so when the cops came to break it up. I sucked down my beer while getting in the cattle line with the rest of the kids as we slowly made our way out of the backyard and onto the street. I stopped in front of Dave's house to wait for Sadie, Carla, and their dates, Pete and Carl, who were these gross heshers they befriended just weeks earlier.

What is a hesher? Generally speaking, it is a guy with long fuzzy brown or dishwater blond hair that had bad skin and didn't wear makeup. If you had big hair because you teased and styled it with hairspray that was one thing, but if you had fuzzy, unstyled hair and walked around looking like a big cotton ball, then most likely you were a hesher.

Pete and Carl were seniors at Temple City High and had given us a ride to Dave's party that night. As far as personality goes, I didn't vibe with them. They were way too quiet for me. Their idea of fun was smoking pot 24-7 at Carl's house and lying around like a bunch of beached whales, which I found boring. I needed to be around livelier people. I was quite surprised that Carla and Sadie were even able to pry them out of Carl's place to go to the party.

When the four of them emerged from the backyard, they were talking about going back to Carl's house to "smoke a little ganja" and have a few beers. SNORE. I asked them to take me home.

While walking to Carl's car, we happened to pass one of the patrol cars.

"Fuck you pig," Pete mumbled loudly.

I rolled my eyes.

What a lame attempt at trying to be cool. This is exactly why I don't want to hang out with these heshers.

"What did you say?" the cop asked.

I ignored the cop and kept walking because obviously he was talking to Pete, not me. Pete ignored him as well and kept walking when suddenly the sound of footsteps rushed up behind me.

"Did you hear me? What did you just say!" the cop said as he grabbed my arm and spun me around to face him.

Sadie and Carla stopped beside me while Pete and Carl kept right on walking.

"Me? I didn't say anything," I said, completely confused.

"That's funny, I just thought I heard you say 'fuck you pig' a moment ago," the cop said.

"I didn't say that, he did!" I said pointing at Pete.

Pete and Carl stopped and turned around.

"Oh really?" the cop said smirking at me.

"Do I SOUND like an 18 year old guy?" I said with attitude.

I looked over to Pete and he said nothing. I couldn't believe he was going to let me take the fall.

"You fucking pussy! You know you're the one who said it!" I yelled.

He and Carl stood there quiet as church mice.

"Watch your mouth!" the cop yelled.

"I didn't do anything wrong!" I yelled.

I flung the cops hand off my arm to break free. I had taken two or three steps when he grabbed the collar of my denim jacket. I started flailing and swinging at the cop when he grabbed me by the neck and threw me against the back of the cop car.

"Put your hands behind your back!" he yelled.

"Are you fucking kidding me?" I yelped.

"NOW!" he yelled again.

I quickly put my hands behind my back and the cop threw a pair of cuffs on me.

"Do you know that assaulting an officer is a criminal offense?" he said.

"You touched me first!" I barked.

Without saying another word, the cop threw me in the backseat of the patrol car. Sadie and Carla started arguing with the cop, so he threw them in the backseat with me sans cuffs and shut the door. The cop and his partner climbed into the car, and the next thing I know we're being whisked away, leaving Pete and Carl behind. As we drove away, the cops told us they were going to take us home, talk to all our parents and explain what happened.

"See? This is why I don't hang out with stupid heshers. Now we're all going to get grounded," I said as I rattled my handcuffs.

My house was the first drop off and the patrol car pulled right in front of my house. I looked to the two windows in the front of my house, wondering if either of my parents happened to be peeking outside. Despite the pseudo boxing match I had with the cop, he had a momentary lapse of judgment in my favor, because as we both got out of the car, he took off my cuffs and didn't seem to be leading me up my driveway. He just stood by the patrol car holding my cuffs.

"You're going to tell your parents what happened tonight, right?" The cop asked.

HELL no.

"Of course I will," I said obediently.

"I don't want to see your face at anymore of these parties? Got it?"

I saluted him with my hand and said, "Loud and clear sir."

The cop stood there, staring at me and I panicked. *Shit, I didn't mean to be a smartass. Oh please don't change your mind. Just get the fuck out of here before my parents get up and look outside.*

"Take care kid," the cop said. Then he walked away and hopped into the patrol car.

I walked up the driveway and slowly opened the front door, waiting to get yelled at by my folks. Luckily, my dad was asleep in my parent's bedroom at the other end of the house and my mom was in the kitchen washing dishes. *Hallelujah!*

Unfortunately, Sadie and Carla didn't fare so well. The cops ended up talking to both of their parents. Sadie got a lecture, which wasn't too bad. But Carla got it the worst. Not only did her mom ground her for two weeks, but permanently banned her from hanging out with Sadie and I ever again. The latter didn't mean anything though, that kind of thing happened all the time. Every few months, one or more of us would always get banned from each other for doing stupid shit. After whatever debacle went down, we would give the parents a few days to calm down, and then go over to their house to make nice. We did the ritual shaking hands and kissing babies, throw in a mea culpa or two and all would be well again.

About halfway through my freshman year, two fellow freshman named Jude and Dagmar, transferred to my school. Dagmar was petite, but she always complained that her body was like a pear because she felt her butt was big and not in proportion with her tiny upper frame. She had wavy black hair and big brown eyes, but that didn't last long. Shortly after I met her, she started wearing green contacts and lightened her hair to a strawberry blonde. Jude, on the other hand, had a models body. She was tall and skinny with long blonde hair and eyes like a cat. Both Jude and Dagmar were rocker chicks that shared my same musical tastes, so I instantly found them cool and befriended them.

Dagmar lived with her mom and four younger siblings in El Monte about fifteen minutes east of Rosemead. All of her siblings were between the ages of 3 and 8, so the house was absolute chaos with kids and toys flying in every direction. Jude lived in an apartment with her mom and older brother, Paul, in Alhambra about five minutes down the street from me. Her bedroom was wallpapered with Metallica posters because she was in love with their guitar player, Kirk Hammett. She also had several pets named after her favorite musicians, like her two rats named Flotsam & Jetsam, and her beloved hamster that she named Kirk Hamster, respectively.

Jude and Dagmar introduced me to a girl from their old high school named Sasha who was also a freshman. She had long burgundy hair and oversized breasts. I had never met a girl my age with boobs anywhere near that size. Sasha was easily sporting a natural double D cup. Being around her showed a definitive missing link between hot mama and an ape, me obviously being the latter.

Jude's brother, Paul, had a set of friends that were all in their early 20's, two of which were Ron and Alex. Alex was about six foot with shoulder length dark brown hair, big brown puppy dog eyes and a smile that could melt lead. He was super sweet, very outgoing, and had a goofy sense of humor that went well with mine. He immediately became my new crush.

Only Jude knew of my feelings for Alex, but she insisted I tell Dagmar and Sasha to get some perspective on winning him over. Only after having her swear on the life of her beloved Kirk Hamster that the girls were trustworthy did I tell them about my feelings for Alex.

Their first order of business was clothes. The only thing more time consuming for a girl than getting ready is deciding on an outfit. They suggested I put together two or three ensembles to have on standby. Granted, I didn't have a killer body to fill out most of my outfits, so I was dependent on winning him over with my uh, great personality.

The next step was planning an event where I could see Alex. Jude quickly took care of that when she suggested to Paul that they have a party. Once he agreed, I pressed Jude for details on whether Alex was going and she in turn pressed on Paul. After a few days of non-stop nagging, he finally confirmed that Alex would be going! So the night of the party I pulled out one of my standby outfits and had Lucy drop me off at Jude's.

When I walked into Jude's, she was sitting at her kitchen table playing quarters with Dagmar and Sasha. I said hello to the girls and walked straight to the refrigerator to get a drink. I made myself a screwdriver and joined the girls at the table as I watched people trickle into the apartment.

Over the next hour, I scanned the faces coming in the front door. Once I saw Alex, I grabbed my purse and dashed into the bathroom to touch up. When I came out, he was sitting on the living room couch talking to Ron. The girls nudged me to talk to Alex, so I walked over and he greeted me with a big hug. I hadn't spoken more than a few words when Elanna the vulture swooped in and took Alex away like a piece of helpless prey.

Elanna was Alex's age and she wasn't even that pretty. She had a mediocre face with long straight brown hair, but she did have a killer body. She started talking to him in Spanish, and my fluency in Spanglish wasn't enough to keep up with their conversation. So I put my tail between my legs and walked back to the kitchen where the girls were still playing quarters. I hoped at some point Alex would break away from Elanna to come over to talk to me, but he never did. I didn't approach him for the rest of the night.

Dealing with rejection was something I had quite a bit of practice with unfortunately, so I took Alex's snub in stride as I did all the others.

With my back-to-back failures of Brian and Alex, it was back to fantasizing about Nikki Sixx for the time being until my next crush surfaced it's pretty little head.

47

4

IS THAT A BOYFRIEND I SMELL?

*T*oward the end of my freshman year, I had quite a few big changes coming my way. I had a designated curfew, which meant I could finally stay out till a somewhat decent hour. The sweet scent of Drivers Education class, aka getting my drivers license was just around the corner. Oh and miracle of all miracles, I got my first boyfriend, Ronan Morales.

Ronan was 17, with long black hair and brown eyes. His parents were divorced and he was the youngest of 3 siblings, all of which were scattered around Los Angeles. We met during my P.E. class when I was on the field playing baseball. I noticed him just outside the school fence standing near a bus stop with his friend Kyle. When my team came off the field and up to bat, Ronan waved me over.

Since it was during school hours, I wondered why he was lingering about and not in school. He said he was catching a bus that afternoon for no particular reason other than to just "hang out" somewhere in Arcadia. We only spoke for a few minutes, but during our brief conversation he seemed less than enthused to talk to me, which I found strange. *If he didn't want to talk to me, why the hell did he wave me over in the first place?* Regardless, he asked me for my number and I got his too.

During the first few weeks of phone calls with Ronan, he seemed to do most of the talking. He was in full rebound mode and had recently broken up with his girlfriend, Candice, who he had been dating for about six months. According to him, he ended up getting wasted at a party they went to and acted like a drunk idiot, so she dumped him. She wouldn't return any of his calls and he was absolutely devastated. He would go on for hours about his broken heart and how much he missed her. I don't know why the hell I became his shoulder to cry on but nonetheless, I tried to be supportive.

Ronan led a discipline free life that I wasn't accustomed to. He came and went as he pleased with no curfew and no steady home. He bounced between his aunt's place in Alhambra and a house in Montebello that his mom shared with his older sister. He earned money by unloading rolls of fabric at his uncles distribution company in downtown L.A. So on top of having complete freedom he also had spending money as well, which didn't compare to my pittance of an allowance.

Suddenly having a boy in my life worried my parents. Ronan and I would talk everyday after I came home from school and sometimes late at night too, which they immediately tried to put a stop to. My folks gave me a phone curfew of 10:00pm and Ronan scoffed at the idea that I would adhere to it. In an attempt to be cool, I devised a way to talk to him after curfew without my folks finding out.

I had a cordless phone in my bedroom but it wasn't my own private line. There was another phone in the kitchen at the other end of the house, right near my parent's bedroom.

The first thing I thought to do was unplug the phone in the kitchen before going to bed. But I noticed my mom would occasionally glance at the phone jack on the ground to make sure it was still plugged in, so I devised another plan.

I figured out a way to balance the plug in the jack to make it LOOK like it was still plugged in when it wasn't. Then I would set my cordless phone to its lowest volume setting and put it under my pillow to muffle the sound of the ring.

Once Ronan and I were done talking, I would conveniently walk to the kitchen to get a late night glass of water and plug the cord back into the wall jack.

As time passed, Ronan confessed that on the day we met it was his friend, Kyle, who originally spotted me and wanted my number, not him. That explained Ronan's less than enthusiastic attitude when we first exchanged numbers. Regardless, things were finally starting to progress between Ronan and I, and the subject of Candice wasn't part of our daily conversations anymore. He said he was really starting to have feelings for me and wanted to take me out on a date! I started thinking about what to wear when I remembered that I had never been on a date before. More importantly, I've never asked my parents if I could go out on a date with a boy, so I didn't know how they were going to react. After grilling me for a little bit, they actually allowed me to go out with Ronan and gave me an 11:30pm curfew, which Ronan bitched about of course.

We planned on going out to dinner. I was slightly mortified because I still hadn't experienced my first kiss yet. The closest I came was my botched attempt at Brandon's house almost a year earlier.

The night of our date, we ended up walking to Jim's Burgers just down the street from my house, which Ronan was upset about. His original plan was to pick me up in his mom's car, but she had to work that night. She ended up dropping him off near my house and told him to call his sister for a ride when he was done with our date. It didn't matter to me though. I was just excited to be on an actual date, and of course I was happy to be with Ronan who I was crushing on big time.

Ronan wanted to take me to a movie after dinner. But by the time we finished eating, I only had about an hour left till curfew. He told me to blow off my curfew, but I knew I had less than a handful of 'get out of jail free' cards with my parents ahead of me and getting grounded over a movie that I could see anytime wasn't worth wasting one on.

As we started the final walk down my street, he pulled out a pack of gum and asked if I wanted a piece. I knew exactly what that meant. That was the, "I'm going to kiss you, but we just ate so take this to freshen your breath" stick of gum. Me accepting that gum was making a pretty bold statement.

Am I ready to accept the gum?

"Yeah, thanks," I said as I took a piece.

And just like that, a stick of Wrigley's Winterfresh brought me one step closer to womanhood.

We stopped at the gate in front my house and our conversation came to a halt. I thanked him for the food to break the awkward silence. Instead of saying, "you're welcome", he slowly leaned in towards me. I froze and closed my eyes as if I were anticipating getting punched in the face. My muscles relaxed as his lips touched mine. But the moment I felt his tongue start to part my lips, I gasped and pulled back.

"Thanks again for the burger, I gotta go!" I said.

I gave him a playful punch in the arm and bolted up my driveway. I was mortified. I didn't turn around until I reached my front patio, but he was already gone. I peeked into my living room window to see my mom sitting on the couch, watching TV. I hesitated for a moment, wondering if she would be able to see the scarlet letter burned into my forehead when I walked in the door.

I said hi to my mom as I quickly walked in and headed towards my bedroom. I didn't want to be bothered or talk to anyone. I wanted to replay that first kiss over and over again in my head, sans the part where I freaked out and ran away like a squealing piglet.

Luckily, I didn't scare Ronan away. Over the next few weeks as I started my sophomore year in high school; I became his official girlfriend. I got to know his family whenever they sporadically came around, and we also hung out quite a bit with his friend, Kyle. While talking with Kyle one day, he casually mentioned he was friends' with a band called Taz.

I knew all about Taz through my free rock magazines because they were headliners on the Strip! I played it cool with him and Ronan though. I said I had heard of Taz and that I was "considering" whether to check them out. Ronan mentioned they had a show coming up at the Waters Club in San Pedro and that I could come with him if I wanted to. I very calmly accepted.

September 15th, 1988. That was the night of my first Taz show. When I walked into the Waters Club with Ronan and Kyle, the club was fairly packed and a band named Hysteria was on stage. I wanted to take pictures of Taz, so I found myself a good spot near the stage while the guys went to the bar to grab drinks.

I wasn't paying much attention to Hysteria. I began loading my cheap 35MM camera with a roll of film when a guy from the back of the crowd started heckling the band. He kept yelling that they sucked and to bring on Taz. The bassist gave the guy the finger, so the guy started throwing ice at the band until a bouncer came and escorted him out.

Hysteria finally finished their set and Taz took the stage. KK, the singer, strolled up in a pair of tight purple pants, black boots, a long sleeve lavender shirt, and a purple scarf wrapped around his head. Ronan had given me a demo tape of Taz a few weeks earlier, so I knew a few of their songs like, "Tattoo You", "Bad Religion" and "Cold Shoulder".

Song after song, a heavyset blonde standing next to me would howl to KK about how hot he was and kept grabbing at his crotch. She was a sloppy, drunk mess and could barely keep her balance while pawing at KK. During one song when he leaned over to sing to the crowd, she immediately grabbed him, flipped him over like a pancake and shoved her tongue down his throat. He was able to get away from her, but when he stood back up to continue singing, his chin was glistening from all her slobber.

The blonde had a fellow heavyset friend, a brunette with long wavy hair who seemed to be agitated with her friends' behavior. I overheard her call the blond girl, Rachel, as she yelled at her to stop being an idiot.

During the next song, another girl standing at the opposite end of the stage gave KK a red rose and wiggled her tongue at him when he took it. I couldn't believe how brazen these girls were about putting their sexuality out there. Meanwhile, Rachel, the porkly blonde who inhaled KK's face just moments earlier was still standing next to me stumbling around. Although she was annoying, I didn't want to move because I was in a prime location for getting good shots of the band. I was about to snap a picture of KK when Rachel jumped onto the stage and tried to charge him like a wild hog. She only took about two or three steps before she slipped and fell down though. KK had run to the other side of the stage and continued singing while she slowly tried to get up. Rachel's friend who was still standing in the front row, yelled at her to get offstage. Rachel told her friend to fuck off. Completely agitated, her friend leaned over onstage, grabbed Rachel's arm and gave it a hard yank, which sent Rachel flying into the crowd narrowly missing me.

"Those are the Taz fatties," Ronan said.

"That's kind of mean," I replied.

"Hey, I didn't name them the guys did. No matter where Taz plays, they go to EVERY show."

KK was clearly annoyed. When he finished the song, he told everyone (more specifically Rachel) to calm down and kick back. She finally took the hint and didn't make her way near the stage for the rest of the night.

After the show, I walked outside with Ronan to get some air. He led me over to Taz's van and introduced me to the guys in the band as they loaded up their gear. While I chatted with Kenny, the drummer, and Joel, one of the guitar players, Ronan quietly slipped away without saying a word. About an hour later, Ronan was still nowhere to be found. I was mildly annoyed that he snuck off. But when Joel and Kenny offered me a ride to the after party if Ronan didn't show up, I didn't seem to care as much. I mean technically if Ronan disappeared, I would need a ride home and being stranded in Hollywood was much closer to my house than San Pedro.

While I pondered the thought of how cool it would be to stroll into the after party with the Taz guys, Ronan reappeared. I asked him where he went and he said he was just off talking with a few friends. We said goodbye to the guys, they thanked me for coming to the show and Ronan took me home.

I became a huge fan of Taz after the Waters Club show and just like the Taz fatties, I went to every show from that point on. Well most anyway. I was still only 14, so if it wasn't an all ages' show I was shit out of luck. Another issue was transportation, not to mention my curfew. Headlining bands like Taz always went on late, usually around 11:00pm or so. By the time they'd finish their set, I would have just enough time to rush home and make my curfew…about twenty minutes late.

Ronan, on the other hand, was free as a bird with no rules. Going with him to Taz shows became a huge inconvenience for him because he would have to miss out on any after parties just to get me home on time. It's something he would bitch about frequently, so I would alternate between going with him and begging Lucy to give me rides.

Another Taz show was coming up at the Roxy, and Lucy was going to be out of town that particular weekend. My only shot at going was to ride with Ronan, but he was adamant about not missing another after party. Wanting to go to the show, I went against my better judgment and decided to take my chances at whatever grounding my parents would give me. So shortly after midnight when Taz finished their set, I was heading out to the Taz after party with Kyle and Ronan instead of racing my way home.

The after party was in an apartment on Highland, just north of Franklin by the Hollywood Bowl. When we walked in, there were about forty people hanging out in a surprisingly large apartment with high vaulted ceilings and a fireplace. I took a closer look at everyone in the room and realized I was the only girl there. Every other female was a fully sprouted woman with curves, boobs, and legs stemming from their necks. I was most definitely way out of my league.

Kyle, Ronan, and I found an uninhabited corner to hang out in. They pulled a few beers out of the stash we brought with us and spoke about the Taz show. I didn't say much though. I was just excited to be at the party and loved people watching. My eyes continued scanning the living room for new faces walking into the apartment and listening in on conversations that were within my range of hearing. Everyone seemed to have something "big" that was about to happen. This person was friends with that rock star or that celebrity and was definitely going places. There were showcases that had been played and demo tapes that were in the hands of big record executives. All that hot air being blown around the room by people with their inflated egos, yet they were still hanging out at the same party as my goofy teenage ass.

After a few beers my bladder was acting up, so I ventured off on my own to find the bathroom. I walked down a small hallway and must've looked lost because some guy asked me if I was looking for the bathroom. I said yes and he pointed to a closed door.

"I think I just saw KK go in there though, so it might be a while," he said before walking off.

Damn, I really have to pee too. I figured if KK had just walked in there though, he probably wouldn't be very long. But about five minutes later, I was still waiting. I was about to knock when I heard the sounds of male grunting from behind the door. *Is KK in there taking a shit? Who takes a dump in the middle of a party?* A few moments later, Kyle came to find me.

"Are you still waiting for the bathroom?" he asked.

"Yeah, but I heard grunting. I think KK is taking a shit," I whispered.

Our conversation was interrupted by the sounds of a female moaning from behind the bathroom door, followed by more male grunts. Kyle put his ear to the door, listened for a few moments and smiled.

"I think he's going to be a while," he said.

"He IS taking a dump isn't he?" I said completely oblivious.

"No, I think he's banging his girlfriend."

"Banging as in beating her up?" I said with my head cocked to the side like a confused dog.

Debauchery was in full effect on the other side of that bathroom door. Literally, right in front of my pre-pubescent face, and I still had no idea what he was alluding to.

"Banging as in fucking her in the bathroom," he said bluntly.

My eyes widened. Laughing at my reaction, Kyle led me down the hallway and back to Ronan. After another round of beers we decided to call it a night.

By the time I came home, I was only two hours late for my curfew, so I figured my punishment would be minimal. Back then my mom was always the disciplinarian and my dad went with whatever she said. Boy oh boy was she furious when she woke up the next morning. I ended up getting grounded for an entire week. But once my grounding was over, I resumed seeing Ronan and going to more Taz shows.

The more Ronan and I hung out, the more our lifestyles clashed. He literally had nothing to do everyday but wake up and breathe. I on the other hand, had school to tend to, homework to do and curfews to obey. I tried to talk him into going back to high school, but he wasn't having it. He hated school and said it was a waste of his time. Hell, he hated everything. It seemed like nothing made him happy, not even me.

Ronan told me I was a mindless puppet for doing everything my parents told me to do and that I needed to start thinking for myself. He also told me I didn't dress sexy enough and was a lousy kisser. I decided not to tell Jude and the Alhambra crowd what was happening. Instead, I confided in Sadie, Carla, and Tasha about the things he was telling me. Naturally, they said he was an asshole for saying those things to me and to dump him, which of course I didn't do because I didn't want to rock the boat. I took all his personal jabs as constructive criticism, and told myself those were things I needed to improve about myself.

I envied Ronan's life of being able to come and go as he pleased, and I was beginning to resent my parents for all their rules. I started fighting constantly with my mom about having a later curfew. My defense was that I was responsible, not doing drugs, and since I hadn't been in any major trouble she had no reason not to trust me. Therefore, I felt a 3:00am curfew for me to hang out in Hollywood wasn't an unreasonable request for a 14 year old to ask for.

Along with battling my parents and Ronan, I also began fighting with Sadie, Carla, and Tasha. They kept riding me to dump Ronan. I was sick of fighting with them over him, so halfway through my sophomore year; I stopped hanging out with them. Instead, I would alternate my time between hanging out with Jude or my new friends, identical twins Arwen and Ariah Gordon.

Arwen and Ariah were two pixie sized, new wave girls with multicolored styled bobs and funky clothes. I had only known them as acquaintances back at Muscatel, but we had recently become closer friends when the three of us landed in the same Home Economics class together at Rosemead High.

Arwen was older by a few minutes and the more laid back of the two. Ariah, on the other hand, was a hyper little spider monkey that had taken up the hobby of embarrassing my sister, Lucy. Whenever we saw her in the halls at school, Ariah would duck behind Arwen or me, then peek out and pretend to shoot Lucy with an imaginary laser blaster, making the sounds "P-tew!

P-tew!" in a squeaky voice as she shot her. Lucy would simply just shake her head at us and run away.

Arwen and Ariah knew all the skaters at Rosemead High including Brandon. Although technically I was with Ronan, a small part of me was still crushing on Brandon. Not that it would've mattered anyway since he was still with Erica.

I was lingering around campus after school with Arwen and Ariah one day when we got on the subject of Brandon and Erica. I had never officially met her before, but the twins had. They said she wasn't very friendly and that her and Brandon seemed very awkward around each other.

The three of us continued strolling through the semi empty campus. We entered a two-story building, which stood at the front of the school and our cackling echoed the halls as we made fun of Erica and Brandon. We acted out weird scenarios on how we thought they acted around each other. We made fun of her clothing and how Brandon's bangs had grown so long that he looked like a sheepdog and couldn't see what Erica REALLY looked like. We made farting sounds with our hands and laughed our asses off as we walked up the stairs. We had just reached the top of the stairwell and were wiping tears from our eyes when we noticed Brandon and Erica leaning against a wall staring right at us.

Arwen and I immediately froze. Ariah squatted down and decided to shoot them. "P-tew! P-tew!" she squeaked out and then ran down the stairs. Arwen and I turned on our heels and followed after her mumbling, "omigod...omigod...omigod" as we barreled down the stairwell. The three of us ran down the main hall, completely out of the building and didn't stop running until we were in Panther's Square on the other side of campus.

"You don't think they knew we were talking about them do you?" I asked.

"I don't know. Did we mention their names when we were walking up the stairs?" Ariah asked.

"Did you see the look on their faces? Of course they knew we were talking about them," Arwen stated.

Although we found the whole incident hysterical, I was worried Brandon might be mad at me. Surprisingly, he wasn't. I saw him in the halls at school a few days later, and he stopped to chat with me like nothing ever happened. Erica, on the other hand, would shoot me dirty looks every time I saw her the rest of the school year. Arwen and Ariah told me she would do the same to them too.

Shortly after my 15th birthday, I was chomping at the bit to get the ball rolling with my driver's license. At the time, my high school offered a free Saturday morning driving class called Behind the Wheel, which basically stuffed three students in a car with a teacher who would instruct you on how to drive.

The driving lessons I had with my dad over the last few months, not to mention the countless hours I spent playing Pole Position when I was little, came in handy when it came to my Behind the Wheel class. I was a pretty good driver that needed little to no correction and the same went for Ross, a hot skater friend of Brandon's who was also in my driving class. But our 3rd student, Clark, well, he was a hot mess. Our one-hour class consisted of ten minutes of me driving, ten minutes of Ross driving, and the other forty minutes of Clark trying not to take out random pedestrians.

Ross and I would sit in the backseat with our hands clinched and our eyes closed when Clark drove. After a few sessions, Ross and I asked our teacher if we could go home after each of our ten minute lessons were done rather than staying for the entire hour. We justified it by saying Clark was probably nervous with Ross and I riding in the car, and it would be best for him to give Clark 100% of his attention. Luckily, for Ross and I the teacher agreed.

On the shit side of things, my relationship with Ronan continued on a downward spiral. He was highly sensitive, extremely jealous, and continued to find more things wrong with me that he could bitch about. He also repeatedly pressed the sex issue. At that point, we had only got to first base, and I saw his penis once when it accidentally popped out of his boxers while he was changing. It had a lot of skin like a Shar Pei. Much more skin than I remembered seeing in the porno at Carla's house.

The subject for most of my fights with Ronan was my curfew because he wanted a girlfriend with the same freedom he had. Anywhere we went always had to be planned around my curfew so he could get me home on time, which got on his last nerve. There was one weekend when we went to a party a few blocks away from my house. I noticed he had been drinking quite a bit, so I told him he should probably cut back on the booze since he would have to drive me home soon. We ended up getting into a huge fight, and he left me stranded at the party with my curfew rapidly approaching. I didn't want to call my parents for a ride because I didn't want them to be mad at him for leaving me. So I ended up walking the entire way home by myself and of course I was grounded for being late.

By this time my friendship with Sadie, Carla, and Tasha was almost non-existent. As for the twins, I rarely talked to them about Ronan nor did I bring him around them, so they didn't know what a dick he was. The only group of friends that hadn't began to hate him yet were Jude and the rest of the Alhambra crowd. I would only bring him around if her or Ron had a party, but even that quickly stopped once I heard rumors that he was flirting with random girls when I would leave. I wanted to believe the best in Ronan despite the fact he was showing less and less of that towards me.

On another bad note, my Uncle Gilbert, one of my dad's older brothers, had recently passed away. His funeral was going to be in Arizona. Lucy, my dad, and I were going to make the drive out there for the funeral services while my mom stayed at home with Ginger who was sick at the time. We would be away for an entire weekend, and I welcomed the forced vacation from Ronan. I hoped that being with my family would help me clear my head a bit and that my time away would help him get his shit together too, aka stop being such a big asshole to me. It was wishful thinking on my part because nothing changed when I came back to L.A. I cringed to think what or who Ronan was doing while I was gone. Even though he made me crazy, I thought I was "in love", so I stayed in the relationship.

The only highlight of my sophomore year was reaching the 15½-year mark. That was the minimum age to apply for a drivers permit, which I received right after I was eligible. The remainder of the school year was essentially a blur of Taz shows and fighting with Ronan. I couldn't wait to turn 16 so I wouldn't have to depend on anyone to give me a ride anywhere again.

In the fall of 1989, I started my junior year at Rosemead High and was pleasantly surprised when Brandon and I landed in the same guitar class. Aside from a few small chats in the hallways at school, we hadn't spoken much since our softball days at Muscatel. Having a guitar class together quickly changed that, and it wasn't long before we rekindled our friendship. I didn't realize how much I missed him and was so happy to have him back in my life on a regular basis. He and Erica had long been broken up, and he'd recently started dating another senior, a chubby Goth girl named Grace.

I vented my frustrations to Brandon about the problems I was having with Ronan. To my surprise, he seemed to be having similar issues with Grace. She was extremely jealous and wouldn't let him go anywhere without her. One of his best friends was a girl named Jenny that he'd known since 1st grade, but Grace didn't like that he had a good friend who was a girl. She badgered him into ending the friendship with Jenny, which he eventually ended up doing.

The first few weeks of the semester, our guitar teacher, Mr. Simmons, taught us some basic chords. But from then on every class became "practice time", which essentially was kids disappearing into one of five small rehearsal rooms to sleep, goof off, or for the few of us that were actually interested, play guitar. As long as we learned to play a song each Friday for our weekly tests he didn't give a shit what we did.

Aside from learning how to play guitar, that class became relationship therapy for Brandon and I. Sometimes we would camp out in one of the rehearsal rooms with the other kids to learn a song for our weekly tests. But usually we would get our own room, jam a little bit and give each other advice on our dysfunctional relationships, both of which we knew we had to get out of.

Meanwhile, my one-year anniversary with Ronan had recently passed and it was certainly nothing to be excited about. I was still enduring his hostility and critique when I finally realized it was beginning to take its toll on me. All we seemed to do was fight and I wasn't a fun person to be around anymore. I dressed the way he wanted me to dress. I wore the makeup he wanted me to wear, and yet it still wasn't good enough for him. All of my friends hated him. Even the Alhambra crowd turned on him after they caught him cozying up to Elanna the vulture after I left a party one night. The daily fights with Ronan were stressing me out. I needed to plan a ditch day to blow off some steam, so Arwen and Ariah suggested we plan a day to go to the beach.

Getting my absences excused on ditch days wasn't a problem. I had spent a solid year putting a fail proof system into play. When I was in grade school and junior high, my mom would usually write the sick notes for me to bring to the attendance office. During that time I learned how to forge her signature but certainly not an entire letter in her writing. But once I started high school, on occasions when I was legitimately sick, I made it a point to write out the notes in MY writing then have my mom sign off on them at the bottom. Of course it looked shady to the office administrators, so I told them to call my mom to verify the notes. After a few instances of receiving that type of letter and speaking with my mom, they stopped calling to confirm my absences. Naturally, that left me free to write a note anytime I felt like ditching school. I was a resourceful little shit back then.

When I came home from the beach that afternoon, I mean, "school", there were no phone messages from Ronan. We had a fight the night before, so I was expecting some kind of mea culpa when I walked in the door. Coming home without any messages from Ronan made me furious. I stomped into the living room and slammed my bedroom door. A moment later, there was a knock on my door.

"Are you okay in there?" My mom asked.

"Yeah, I'm fine," I said as I threw my backpack on my bed.

"Why did you slam the door?"

"Cuz it slipped out of my hand."

"Why is your door closed?"

"Because I want to listen to music."

"Are you mad?"

I started to get heated and said, "No, I just want to be alone and listen to music."

"You sure?"

"Yes mom. Everything's fine," I said with my teeth clinched.

"Okay. Dinner will be ready in a few minutes," she said finally relenting.

I put on Mötley Crüe's new album, *Dr. Feelgood,* and curled up on my bed. Surely fantasizing about Nikki would calm my frazzled nerves. I pictured him rocking out on stage with those beautiful green eyes piercing through me. Sigh.

A half hour later, my mom knocked at my bedroom door and interrupted my fantasy.

"Dinners ready whenever you're hungry," she said softly through the crack of my bedroom door.

"WOULD YOU JUST LEAVE ME ALLOOONNE!" I screamed with my fists clinched.

By the volume of my scream, I'm sure the neighbors thought my parents had just adopted a wild banshee. My mom said nothing. A few moments later, I heard her footsteps fade away from my bedroom door.

In my mind this wasn't teen angst. I had a justifiable reason for being angry. My mom was hassling me to eat food I didn't give a shit about, and I was irate that Ronan had alienated me from all my friends. I couldn't understand why he was always such an asshole to me when I didn't deserve it. I couldn't do anything right in his eyes. I never had problems with anyone before I met Ronan, much less with my parents or friends. Nobody understood what I was going through, and Ronan was turning me into a fucking mental patient.

As I lay there stewing, I realized the fantasies about Nikki would have to wait. I had to focus on what the hell to do about my and Ronan's relationship. He did end up calling me a few hours later and said we needed to talk. So he picked me up and we went to the house in Montebello.

I didn't even get a chance to sit on the couch before he started bitching at me over the same old bullshit I had heard for months. I was a weak puppet for always obeying my parents. My girlfriends were jealous bitches because I had a boyfriend and they didn't. My guy friends just wanted to fuck me and that's why they hated him, blah blah, and of course the sex issue always reared its ugly head, no pun intended.

Maybe it was women's intuition, but there was always something about Ronan that never sat right with me in terms of us having sex. Even though I thought I loved him, something in the back of my mind (beyond the scariness of losing my virginity) kept telling me I shouldn't have sex with him. Since I could never shake that uneasy feeling, I simply kept telling Ronan I wasn't ready to sleep with him, which he obviously wasn't happy about.

Our fighting escalated. He told me I was nothing but a cock-teasing bitch for our entire relationship. He also found out I used to have a crush on Alex and said I was probably sleeping with Alex since I wasn't giving him (Ronan) any sex. *Hell I wish.*

One by one, he went through all my male friends and had these crazy ideas in his head on how I was cheating on him with each of them. I was so sick and tired of everything revolving around sex.

"If you want someone to have sex with, how about you go fuck yourself!" I yelled.

"Oh yeah? How about you're not leaving this bedroom till you fuck me!" he said looking me dead in the eye.

That shut me right the hell up. There's no way he would do that to me. He stood and glared at me for a few moments. The next thing I know, he jumps on top of me and pins my arms to the bed. His lips were pressed against mine. I tried kicking my legs up to get him off me, but he pinned those down too with his legs. My arms were pressed against my chest, so I couldn't take a swing at him. He continued pressing his face against mine, telling me he was going to treat me like the whore I was being with every other guy but him.

Although my hands were pinned against my chest, they were facing him, so I dug my claws into his neck. Unfortunately, that didn't seem to do much damage. The only weapon that wasn't restricted was my overbite. I quickly jerked my head, wrapped my mouth around his nose and clamped down with my big choppers. He started screaming and told me to let go of his nose. I released my bite, and he quickly jumped off of me.

It was almost as if a light switched on in his head. He immediately started apologizing and said he didn't mean to get carried away. He wanted everything to be okay with us and for things to go back to the way they were when we first met. I told him he was a worthless piece of shit for trying to force himself on me.

Although he apologized profusely, he said he wasn't going to let me leave until I promised that we were okay. I told him he was out of his fucking mind and to get the hell out of my way, but he physically wouldn't let me leave the house. He kept telling me I had to promise everything was cool between us and that we were still a couple.

As he and I verbally went back and forth, it finally hit me. You can't reason with a crazy person. You have to play their game.

Me telling Ronan he was an asshole and to take me home was not going to get me out of that house. I knew my only option was to relent and play along. So I took a deep breath and calmly said we both were out of control for the last hour but that everything was fine. He told me he loved me and although it made the bile in my stomach rise up in my throat, I told him I loved him too.

When he dropped me off at home, he apologized again for what happened and suggested we take a small "break" from dating each other. I wholeheartedly agreed.

Despite the fact that Ronan was a psychotic dickhead, I was still hurt by our pseudo breakup and took it as a sign of failure. That's how fucked in the head I was.

And by the way, what constitutes a "break" anyway?

According to Ronan, the "break" meant we wouldn't see each other for a few weeks but would still talk sporadically. Ronan dictated the rules for our "break" and because I was still a bit of a spineless jellyfish, I let him call the shots.

I spent my hiatus from Ronan trying to mend my friendships with Sadie, Carla, and Tasha where the most damage had been done. I had heard that Pete, the hesher responsible for my first semi arrest, had recently committed suicide by hanging himself. The girls were close to him. I knew they were hurting, but we hadn't spoken in months. I wasn't sure if it was appropriate for me to chime in with condolences after being M.I.A. for so long. I tried to make small talk with them as a means to open the doors of communication, but at that point things had been distant between all of us for quite some time. Although we would still chat when we saw each other in the hallways at school, we weren't our little clique of four anymore. Everyone had branched off into different groups. Carla had joined school clubs like the yearbook and newspaper, Tasha's new circle was the varsity cheerleaders, and Sadie was preoccupied with her new boyfriend. Collectively, they had zero interest in going to Hollywood and seeing bands play, which was all I wanted to do. With nothing really in common anymore, I reluctantly watched my friendships with the girls fade away.

Since I had become Ronan repellent, it kept him from going to most of my friends parties, especially the ones in Alhambra. I partook in mild flirting with Alex to ease my bruised heart and also took a forced hiatus from going to all Taz shows. Not only because Lucy was tired of being my Hollywood cabby, but I also didn't want to run into Ronan. I knew I needed the time away from him to clear my head.

A few weeks into my hiatus with Ronan, a new face popped up in the Alhambra crowd. His name was Justin Pierce. He was 21, soft spoken with long dark hair and hazel eyes. He had his own apartment and his own car. I was instantly intrigued.

According to Ronan, our time apart also included the freedom to date other people. At first, I was crushed that he would even consider being with another girl. But once I noticed Justin showing interest in me, my "break" from Ronan didn't seem like such a bad idea. I couldn't believe a cool older guy like Justin would give someone like me the time of day. I had never been presented with actual options before. None of the guys I liked had ever liked me back with the exception of Ronan.

Justin and I began talking on the phone every day. We would meet up at parties and find quiet spots to go make out. He didn't care that I was only 15 with a curfew. He never criticized the way I looked or dressed. It was nice to finally just be myself without having to walk on eggshells all the time.

Ronan and I didn't talk much during the beginning of our "break". But a few weeks after I started hanging out with Justin, Ronan's calls became more frequent. I figured he had heard through the grapevine that we were hanging out because he was suddenly very interested in how I was and where I was going on the weekends. I knew exactly what Ronan was doing and took great satisfaction in his jealousy. When he finally confronted me about whether or not anything was going on with Justin, I told him the truth and said we had hung out a few times.

"Oh so now you're fucking this asshole Justin, huh?" he barked.

"No I'm not, and even if I was we're on a break remember?"

"This is supposed to be time for both of us to think about our relationship. Not for you to go out whoring around with some asshole!"

"Aww boo hoo. Someone's jealous of Justin," I said egging him on.

"I'm not jealous!"

"And what have you been up to? You've probably fucked half of the San Gabriel Valley by now."

"Maybe I have."

"Maybe I could give a shit!" I yelled and hung up the phone.

The thought of Ronan being with another girl was devastating, but I couldn't let him know that. I still didn't want it to be over with him, god only knows why. Justin certainly treated me better than Ronan ever did.

About a week later, Justin's friend, Tate, decided to throw a party at his house. Tate was a former classmate of Lucy's, so she planned on going to the party with her boyfriend, Tim. Although I couldn't wait to get to the party to see Justin, I wasn't happy about being under the watchful eye of my big sister.

About an hour or so into the party, we were out of alcohol and Justin asked if I wanted to go on a beer run with him. Seeing an opportunity for us to be alone, naturally, I agreed. He said he had to make a quick phone call before we left and ran inside. Unfortunately, Lucy and Tim overheard our conversation.

"You can't go with that guy," Lucy said.

"It's fine. We're just going to the corner to get beer," I said.

"He's 21 and you shouldn't be hanging out with him. He's way too old for you."

"I'm not 'hanging' out with anyone. I'm just driving down the street to get beer. I'll be back in a few minutes, GAWD," I said rolling my eyes.

Justin walked back outside and asked if I was ready to go. Lucy and Tim gave me a parental look of disapproval, but I didn't give a shit. They weren't my parents.

"Yeah, lets go," I said and left with Justin.

Justin and I were putting cases of beer in his car when he said he had to stop by a friend's house to pick up "something" before we went back to the party.

"Where's the house?" I asked.

"In Montebello. It'll just take a second," he said.

Montebello was about ten minutes down the street. I didn't think anything of it and agreed to go with him for the ride.

When we pulled up in front of his friend's house, he said it would only take him a minute to grab what he needed and to wait in the car. Again, I didn't think it was anything out of the ordinary, so I sat in the car flipping through the radio stations while he went inside.

Justin walked out of the house a few minutes later as promised. He hopped into the drivers seat and pulled out a thumb sized resealable baggy that contained white powder. He pulled his car keys out of the ignition and dipped the tip of one of the keys into the white bag of power. He put a small pile of powder on the tip, placed it under his right nostril and took a big sniff. My jaw dropped to the ground.

"Did you want a bump?" he asked as he dipped the key back into the baggie.

I sat in silence. I'm sure the expression on my face was self-explanatory.

"Oh man, I'm sorry. I didn't mean to freak you out," he said.

"Oh it's totally fine," I said, trying to sound cool.

He did another key bump with his left nostril.

"I just figured you had done it before," he said wiping his nose.

"It's cool." I said with a forced smile. "Um, can we go back to the party though? I'm really craving a drink." I continued.

Justin changed the subject and began to ramble about nothing in particular, which I later found out to be the 'coke rambles'. As he cackled on, I couldn't get that visual of him doing coke out of my head. I had never been around any hardcore drug before, so I was completely freaked out. I can't explain why, but as we drove back to the party that night, all the feelings I had for Justin disappeared faster than the bumps that went up his nose. I was immediately disgusted by the cocaine and disgusted with him. I wanted to go back to the party and forget I ever met him.

When we came back to the party, Justin and I were like oil and water, which was fully enforced by me, of course. Any part of the house he was hanging out in, I would be on the opposite end. Lucy picked up on this and asked why I had done a complete 180 within the last hour. I knew her and Tim would flip if I told them what happened, so I lied. I told her that on the ride to get beer he said a few dopey things that got on my nerves and that she was right. He was too old and we didn't have much in common after all. I'm sure she didn't believe me because it really was such a lame excuse, but she didn't press the issue. I'm sure she was just happy I didn't want to hang around him anymore. I didn't even say goodbye to Justin when I left the party. I just snuck out and caught a ride home with Lucy and Tim.

After avoiding Justin's calls for about a week or so, he finally got the hint and stopped calling. Ronan, on the other hand, wanted to meet for dinner and talk. Against my better judgment, I stupidly agreed to see him. He mentioned we would have to give his mom a ride home from work before we could grab dinner. I said that was fine.

I really liked Ronan's mom. She was always so sweet to me. She would shower me with affection and buy me gifts with what little money she had as if I were her own daughter.

I was always on edge when Ronan borrowed his mom's car because it usually started an argument between them. Not that she minded him using the car. The issue was its expired tags and numerous unpaid tickets, not to mention a broken taillight. That car was a police target. If they ever got pulled over, the car would immediately be impounded, so they tried to drive it as little as possible.

When Ronan came to pick me up that night, the backseat of the car was filled almost to the ceiling with junk. So when we went to get his mom, we all had to sit in the front seat with me being sandwiched in the middle. He told her he wanted to use the car to take me out to dinner. She tried to reiterate as she always did that the driving should be kept to a minimum and offered to make dinner for us, but he was insistent on taking the car.

The bickering continued back and forth for about ten minutes. She didn't want him to drive the car, he said he would take side streets where there were less cops. For some reason, the arguing took a drastic turn. He began to scream at her that he was going to take the car whether she liked it or not. She told him she wasn't going to let him. The next thing I know, he abruptly pulls the car over and lunges for her with me getting caught in the middle, literally.

The way she curled up in a ball as he landed blows across her back, led me to believe this had happened before. I screamed at him to stop and tried to push him away from her, but he wasn't stopping. I immediately had a rush of adrenalin like the time I had fought with Roger in the 6th grade. Without thinking, I started to throw right hooks across Ronan's face. It took about four or five blows to finally make him stop.

The three of us sat there disheveled and out of breath. A few moments later, his mom started to cry uncontrollably. Ronan broke the silence by saying he was taking me home because he wanted to talk to his mom alone.

As we pulled up to my house, I had never been so happy to be home. But I was afraid for his mother. I hated walking out of that car and leaving her alone with him. I hugged her goodbye and said nothing to Ronan as I got out of the car.

I walked up my driveway and peeked through one of the windows in the front of my house. My parents were watching TV in the living room. I decided to stay outside for a few minutes to collect myself. My mind was racing, trying to comprehend what had just transpired. I could never tell them what happened. I couldn't tell anyone. There was no reason to anyway. I knew the moment I stepped out of the car it was over with Ronan.

A few days later, Jude and Sasha suggested we buy last minute tickets to the L.A. Guns show at Irvine Meadows Amphitheatre. I jumped at the idea and begged my parents for the money to go. After the few hectic weeks I just had with Ronan, a fun concert with the girls to blow off some steam was exactly what I needed.

As part of a birthday gift from his parents, Jude's younger cousin, Jerry, had received concert tickets and limo transportation to and from the L.A. Guns show. Being the cool older cousin that Jude was, she invited Sasha and me to mooch in on the limo perks.

I was running late the night of the show, and Lucy dumped me off at Jude's as the limo was arriving. I was the last to climb in along with Jude, Sasha, Jerry, and his friend, Cory. After sitting down I noticed a few unmarked glass bottles sitting on a little floor shelf, which I assumed was booze. The bottles were full. I was surprised the driver had left them there. I was about to reach for one when the driver opened up the divider between him and the rest of the limo.

"I wasn't told you kids were underage so hands off the bottles," he said.

"Can we stop at a market at least? We wanna grab some snacks," I said.

"Of course," he said and closed the divider.

"Great. What's the point of having a limo if we can't drink?" Sasha asked.

"Oh don't you worry, we're drinking this booze," I said.

I grabbed the bottles of alcohol, pulled the top off each one and took a few sniffs like a bloodhound.

"Looks like we have tequila, whisky, and this one is clear, so it's probably vodka or gin," I said matter of factly.

"How do you know what everything is?" Jerry asked.

"Because my family has a lot of barbecues and they drink everything," I said.

"So here's the plan," I continued. "We'll refill the tequila with apple juice, the whisky with a dark cola, and the clear one with water."

"Whisky doesn't fizzle genius," Jerry said.

"Who gives a shit? It's so dark in here he's not going to notice anyway. Now everyone throw in a few bucks for the chasers," I said.

"You don't think he's gonna check when we go watch the concert?" Jerry asked.

"The flasks will be full when we get to the show, and if he does check who cares? He's the one that's gonna get into trouble for leaving the bottles in here, not us," I said.

Over the next hour as we made our way to Irvine, bottomless cocktails ensued in the limo. Despite our nosebleed seats, we were all drunk off our asses and had a great time at the show. On the way home our limo had a flat, so we used the breakdown as a photo shoot opportunity to commemorate the night.

Going to the L.A. Guns show was the first time in months I had fun. I was finally starting to feel like myself again, and my feelings for Ronan were fading at a light speed rate.

Although my fling with Justin was long over, the fact that I had dared to date another guy set Ronan on fire.

He wanted to meet up again and talk things out, but I lied and said I had finals to study for. The truth was, I didn't want to have "talks" or anything else with Ronan. I didn't want to deal with him in any capacity because I was still disgusted at the way he treated his mom. So I kept dodging his calls and making excuses, hoping that he would get the hint and let our relationship fade into oblivion.

Just my luck, Taz had a show coming up at the Roxy that Ronan wanted to take me to. I hadn't seen him since the incident with his mom. I wanted to see Taz since I missed their last few shows, so I played the curfew card to get out of going with him. I told him I would catch a ride and see him there so it wouldn't interfere with him going to the after party, a point which he certainly couldn't argue with.

When I arrived at the Roxy, I managed to avoid Ronan for most of the night. He preferred to stand in the back of the club and act cool, whereas I would go up front to take pictures. I nestled myself near the stage right between the Taz fatties. When Taz finished their set, I darted out the side door of the Roxy without saying goodbye to him, ran down Sunset Blvd. and had Lucy pick me up by the Whisky.

5

WELCOME TO THE JUNGLE!

*W*ith my 16th birthday just a few exciting squeals away, I decided it was time for a fresh start. I wanted to leave everything that was negative in my life behind and Ronan was the first thing on my list that absolutely HAD to go.

After going to the Taz show at the Roxy, I realized I didn't like them as much as I did before. I decided to stop going to their shows, which would also lessen my chances of seeing Ronan. I also busted my ass studying for my driving test, and it paid off because I got my drivers license just a few days after my 16th birthday.

I felt I was on the right track in terms of getting my life together and wanted to share my sudden enlightenment with Brandon who was still knee deep in drama with Grace. We had bonded over the school year venting our relationship troubles to each other and expressing how miserable we both were. Now that the clouds were starting to part and I could see things clearly, I wanted to bring Brandon into the light with me.

Although I hadn't made it official by telling Ronan to his face that we were broken up, I knew in my heart we were over. I had a long talk with Brandon and told him he should break up with Grace too. Neither of us had been happy in those relationships for months. Life was too short to be with people that made us miserable. We needed to be free!

A few days after my heart to heart with Brandon, he began to act strangely. He would barely talk to me in guitar class and started getting his own practice room rather than sharing one with me as we had done almost every day through the school year. While strolling through the halls at school one day, I noticed Brandon walking with Grace. She glared at me as they headed in my direction. Brandon looked visibly uncomfortable. He didn't even say hi or make eye contact with me as they walked by.

Later that day in guitar class, Brandon bolted to a rehearsal room by himself as he had been doing for the last week or so. I followed him in and asked what was wrong. He said nothing and that everything was fine. After pressing him for a few minutes, I demanded to know what his problem was. It was then that he finally opened up and told me what was going on.

He said it was nothing I did. It was Grace.

She hated that I was a close friend he could talk to, so she threatened him, or me I should say. According to Brandon, she told him she would beat the shit out of me if he didn't stop being friends with me. With Grace being twice my size, he made the choice for my own safety as he had done with his old friend, Jenny.

"This is EXACTLY why I'm dumping Ronan. It's all about having control. You can't let her do this!" I pleaded.

"I don't want you to get hurt. It's for the best anyway. I'm going to try and work it out with Grace," he said sounding defeated.

"Are you out of your damn mind? You're a bigger wacko than she is if you think it's going to work out. Look at you, you're miserable! We've been talking about breaking up with both   of   them   for   months."

"It's not that bad really," he said as if trying to convince himself.

"I can't believe you're doing this. Is this what you really want?"

"You wanted to know what was going on, so now you know."

"That's not an answer."

He looked up at me with these sad, puppy dog eyes and said nothing. I could tell by the look in his eyes he didn't want this. I knew he didn't want this.

"Yes, it's what I want," he said.

I stood there waiting for him to take it all back but he didn't. He began playing his guitar like I wasn't in the room. Our entire friendship flashed before my watery eyes.

"I can't believe you're throwing away our friendship because you're too big of a pussy to stand up to her. You're a fucking coward," I said.

I grabbed my guitar and slammed the door behind me.

Weeks passed and nothing changed between Brandon and I. It wasn't long before the last few weeks of the school year were upon us, and Brandon, along with the rest of his fellow seniors, prepared for graduation.

I felt bad about the fight I had with Brandon. I wanted to make things copasetic between us before he graduated. In a lame attempt to open up the doors of communication between us, I signed up at the Student Body office to send him a Gram for graduation.

No not THAT type of Gram.

The Grams at my high school were basically a simple card with a Blow Pop sucker stuffed inside for the cost of $1. Students would send them to their classmates throughout the school year for different occasions like birthdays, Valentines Day, and graduation. I figured for a buck it was worth it if I could get another shot at getting through to Brandon.

After sending the Graduation Gram, I saw Brandon in guitar class during finals week. He walked in and sat a few seats away from me. He didn't say a word to anyone. Once his name was called to do his test, he stood up and played one minute of "Stairway to Heaven". When he finished, he asked Mr. Simmons if he could go to the bathroom, which he in turn said yes. Brandon left and never came back to class.

Later that day, I was walking with Arwen and Ariah through campus when I saw Grace coming down the hallway in my direction. She glared at me as she came my way, but that was nothing new. I continued with my conversation because I was used to her giving me dirty looks. Grace had just passed us when she suddenly grabbed my arm and stopped me dead in my tracks.

"Why are you sending things to Brandon?" she snarled.

"I'm not sending THINGS to Brandon," I said tearing my arm back.

"Yes you are. You sent him a Graduation Gram."

"So what? I also sent grams to ten other seniors I'm friends with."

"You're only going to get yourself into trouble. HE DOESN'T LIKE YOU. He ripped up the Gram as soon as he got it. He only thinks of you as this dumb little girl that follows him around like a love sick puppy dog," she said venomously.

And just like that, my longstanding crush on Brandon turned into a crash. I didn't know what to say to her, so I said nothing and continued glaring at her as she was doing to me.

"I bet he tells you that he doesn't like me and how he wants to break up with me doesn't he?" she continued.

"I haven't talked to Brandon lately, so I don't know what he does or doesn't like," I said calmly.

"Oh really? That's not what I heard."

It was then that I realized how much Brandon truly cared about me. If I were some annoying little shit to him as she claimed, she wouldn't even waste her time with me. We were very close and that's why she had a wild hair up her ass, so much so that she had to walk up and say something to me about it.

As Grace and I continued to stare each other down, Ariah started purring like a kitten. Her purrs turned into a howling cat, and she started making clawing gestures at Grace. It wasn't long before Arwen joined in. I couldn't help but laugh. Grace shot them a dirty look and walked off.

Speaking of psycho's, I had my own to contend with since I was still doing the avoiding dance with Ronan. He continued to nag me about having that "talk". He suggested we grab dinner over the weekend, but I wasn't ready to deal with any of that heavy shit yet. It was the first weekend my dad was lending me his truck since getting my drivers license. The last thing I wanted to do was commemorate my first unsupervised drive by going to see Ronan.

Just like clockwork, Ronan called me that Saturday night as I was getting ready and asked if we could meet up. I told him I was home sick for the weekend. I also let out a few fake sneezes, then hung up with him and left to pick up Dagmar and Sasha. We planned on going to a friend's birthday party in Arcadia about fifteen minutes up the street from me.

When I turned the corner toward the party, I noticed three cop cars at the end of the street. People were trailing out of what we figured was the party. I was pissed. I had a car, a brand new drivers license, and it was a Saturday night. There was no way in hell I was going home.

Some friends walked up to the truck and mentioned they were going to our friend, Frankie's house to have some drinks. Nothing about that sounded like fun to me. I had been to Frankie's house a million times before. I wanted to do something a little more exciting since I had a car at my disposal.

"I don't really feel like going over there. I want to do something different," I said.

Dagmar wanted to go to Frankie's. She hopped out of my dad's truck and took off with our friends as they continued walking down the street.

"Why don't we go to the Strip?" Sasha asked.

"Yeah right," I said.

"Why not?"

"Um, I don't know. I have no idea why I said that."

"You're a licensed driver, aren't you?"

Sasha was right. There was no reason we couldn't go. I had never driven that far away from home before though, not by myself anyway. But technically, I wouldn't be alone because Sasha would be with me. Of course it's not normal rationale, but in our 16-year-old minds it made perfect sense. So we hopped on the 101 freeway and made our way out to Hollywood.

As we turned the corner of Sunset Blvd and approached the Whisky A Go-Go, it looked like a building evacuation had taken place. A blanket of people covered the entire sidewalk, so much so that people were spilling into the streets. It was like a freak show. Spiked hair, colored hair, no hair, leather and spandex clothing, or very little clothing, and this circus continued as we drove up Sunset just past a club called Gazzarri's.

SKITZ (The Glamour Punks): There will never be another time in history that resembles Hollywood in that era. I can't speak for everyone who was there (because not everyone had it so good), but my experience was AWESOME. I don't have to sit around and wonder what it would be like to be a rock star because I lived it. Anything I needed was given to me. I never had cash in my pocket, and it didn't matter because everything was free. I had a bag with all of my belongings, along with my guitar and amp. Wherever that stuff was is where I was living at the time. I had my little clique and nothing else really mattered. We looked out for each other. It was non-stop adventure to the point that it really started to cloud my thinking and made it easy for me to get side tracked. There's just no way to fully explain how crazy it was. I've tried to explain it to people and they just think I'm making shit up. If you weren't there you wouldn't be able to comprehend the madness. Sometimes I question it myself. Did that REALLY happen?

SUNNY PHILLIPS (Swingin Thing): The scene was great back then because people were coming from all over the country and all over the world to this one place for one purpose, to create music and try to make it big.

JOEL PATTERSON (Blackboard Jungle): The most fun times we had back then were when we hung out with Kim Fowley early on. We'd always go to dinner with him at Ben Franks or Rock and Roll Denny's and that was always an adventure because he was such a personality.

Neither of us had money for parking. After driving around for a few minutes, we found free parking down the hill on Cynthia Avenue, a residential Beverly Hills street just off Doheny Blvd.

A few minutes later, as we huffed and puffed our way up Doheny, we finally reached Sunset Blvd. We walked past Gazzarri's and our empty hands were instant magnets as various musicians bombarded us with their show flyers from every direction. It was a semi familiar scene from going to all the Taz shows, but I never had the chance to really hang out on the Strip before. I was usually bolting through the crowd in a mad rush to make my curfew.

I listened in on a few random conversations as we walked down Sunset Blvd. The street was like a sick and twisted networking session. Band members shook hands and kissed babies, schmoozing underage and overage girls into going to see their band play in the hopes of moving up the show ladder to the coveted headlining slot. Gone were the days of walking into a club and just being able to play. The clubs wanted bands that had a guaranteed draw, not a borage of crickets and tumbleweeds. Unless you were able to pack a club, which few strip bands were able to do, the club promoters would require bands to sell pre-sale tickets, thus coining the term "pay to play".

CHRIS PENKETH (Swingin Thing): Our worst show ever was in Orange County. Everyone left because it was so horrible. I was so drunk that I came running out on stage at the beginning of the show, fell off the stage into the pit and busted up my guitar. And this was just the intro to the set!

I gave my busted up guitar to my tech. He gave me another guitar, but it was tuned to the wrong tuning because it was for another song that was tuned different. So I start trying to play, it was all out of tune, then Henry's bass amp went out and it was just horrible. I remember some chick walked up to us after the show and said, "Oh my god! You guys are amazing!" and we were like, "You're fucking stupid."

SUNNY PHILLIPS (Swingin Thing): The worst Swingin Thing show was our 2nd show at The Whisky for the No Bozo Jam. During the 2nd song, everyone got lost at the same time and we fucked up that song so bad. It was embarrassing as hell because we had to stop the song and start over again. My little sister had come in from Michigan for the first time to see me play and she had to witness that train wreck.

The best show was in Venezuela. We played in front of about 7000 people. The place was going crazy and they hadn't even heard us before. There were pyrotechnics on the stage and it was a total pro show, it was awesome.

MANDIE (The Glamour Punks): My worst show memory is from the Red Light District. We sounded so horrendously bad. After the first song I jumped off stage, walked right out the front door and went home. I'd have to say the best Glamour Punks show was the first big show we did with Dizzy, and we had Punk Rock Dave in a cage. I believe it was at the Roxy.

DAVE ZINK (Blackboard Jungle): We were playing The Palace in Hollywood and went on after some band that wore overalls and had bales of hay on the stage. The bales of hay were moist and had water in them. As they dragged them off the stage after their set, it left this huge wet trail behind that no one cleaned up. So when we came out for our first song, "Paint You a Picture", I went running onto the stage in Beatle boots with my Telecaster, and I started hydroplaning on that stupid water trail. I went right into one of the monitors and landed head first into a sea of people. Luckily, my head never hit the ground.

JOEL PATTERSON (Blackboard Jungle): One of the best shows I remember playing was around the time of the L.A. Riots. I think we were playing at the Roxy. It was packed, and it was the first time I noticed people singing along to the songs. The crowd had an amazing vibe and such great energy. On the flip side, we had a show in Virginia where we had five people in the audience including the sound guy.

SKITZ (The Glamour Punks): All of our shows were fun. I don't have a favorite. The worst show was definitely the last one we played at the Troubadour. It sucked loving a band so much but knowing it just couldn't work with the way things were going internally.

As Sasha and I approached the Rainbow Bar & Grill, a guy wearing a black suede cowboy hat and dirty leather trench coat stopped us. His hair was pulled back into a ponytail of long skinny braids and he was carrying an armful of multicolored long stem roses.

"Hello ladies. I'd like to invite you to our show next Saturday night at the Roxy," he said as he handed each of us a rose with a tag attached.

We smiled as we each took a rose and he walked off. I read the tag to find it was a mini flyer for his band, Trash Cowboys. *What a great way to plug a show.*

When we passed the Roxy, I noticed a man walking in the street playfully fingering a blow up doll with one hand and carrying a stack of flyers in the other. He shoved a few flyers into the hands of some girls that were about to pass him. The girls smiled and took the fliers, then threw them on the ground as soon as they passed him.

"I don't even want to know what band he's trying to promote," I said to Sasha.

He targeted us immediately or should I say Sasha's boobs that were practically spilling out of her top. He tucked the blow up doll under his arm, pulled out a few flyers and handed them to us. The flyer read, "Toss That Doll".

"Hey girls, what are you doing next Friday night?" he asked.

"Going to a slumber party. We gotta go!" I said dragging Sasha away.

We furthered our way down the Strip and noticed a group of bikers parked by a pizza place near Hilldale Avenue. They weren't bothering anyone. They just seemed to be hanging out on their bikes amongst themselves, but they seemed a bit out of place considering what was going on around them.

We continued walking past the bikers when I heard someone yell, "Wow what a great ass!" I felt a hard pinch on my butt and turned around to find a guys face near my rump. He had spiked out black hair just past his ears and small beady eyes. He stuffed a flyer in my hand for a band called Fraidy Cats and tore off down Sunset Blvd. I would later find out my attackers name was Taj.

"Did he really just bite my ass?" I asked.

Sasha cracked up and said, "I'll say he did."

A few moments later, still standing in shock over my bite and run, a guy with long platinum blond hair walked up to Sasha. He was wearing a white shirt with fuchsia colored biker pants and a hat to match. It was just never ending. Her boobs were like a magnet.

He introduced himself as Mick and said he was the singer of a band called Ana Black. He handed us flyers and invited us to come see his show at the Whisky, blah blah. It was the same sales pitch from every guy to see his band play.

"Hey that's a pretty rose," he said as he looked at my rose.

I inhaled the bud and said, "Thanks, I think so too."

"May I?"

"May you what?" I asked cautiously.

He leaned over slowly as if he were about to smell my rose, then quickly wrapped his mouth completely over the bud and bit it off clean.

"Thank you," he said with petals falling out of his mouth, and casually walked off.

My head was spinning from all these crazy characters and we still hadn't completed one lap down Sunset Blvd yet. I noticed a car dealership just past the pizza place with a little 2-foot wall that people were sitting on. Needing a breather, we decided to walk over and sit down.

We chatted a little bit, but I was more preoccupied with people watching. A musician would walk up to some girls, give them a flyer, talk about his show and walk off. The girls would either keep the flyer or throw it right to the ground as soon as the guy would walk away. It was the same cycle over and over again.

After people watching for a few minutes, I noticed another guy with long platinum blond hair and a black leather jacket staring at me. I looked away and focused back on my conversation with Sasha. When I glanced back to him a few moments later, he was still looking at me.

He was kind of cute, but I found his staring a bit annoying. It was borderline creepy. It wasn't just a glance; it was like he was challenging me to a staring contest. Sure enough, he started making his way in my direction. I was still carrying the stem from my freshly pillaged rose and squeezed it tightly in case my ass or any other part of my body needed defending.

"Is your band playing this weekend too?" I said before giving him a chance to speak.

"Is that your name?" he asked.

"I guess that was bitchy of me," I said relenting. "Sorry. I'm Marisa."

"Sheldon. It's nice to meet you," he said kissing the back of my hand. "And we're playing next Saturday at Gazzarri's since you wanted to know."

Sheldon was 19 and the drummer of a band called Dancer. We had been chatting for a few minutes when a fair skinned guy with long black hair and a slight belly walked up beside Sheldon. He was sporting a black leather jacket as well and said he was Sheldon's guitar player, Nima.

"Nice to meet you ladies, but we need to head to Gazzarri's," Nima said.

We said our goodbyes and Sheldon told me to come to his show the following weekend. He wrote his number on the back of a Dancer flyer, handed it to me and walked off with Nima. As they walked away, I noticed the name "Dancer" was silkscreened on the back of each of their jackets in sky blue and bright pink. *What a horrible name for a band.*

Sasha and I made a few more laps up and down the Strip, chatting with random people. About three hours later, we left with our hands full of flyers and the latest issue of *Rock City News* in our hands.

On the way home, we talked of all the crazy people we encountered that night and how much fun we had. I seemed to be having a lot of fun nights without Ronan. It was a constant reminder that I had to stop dragging my ass on our breakup. I needed to face him once and for all to tell him it was over.

The following weekend, Sasha and I went to the Strip again. Only this time it was my idea to go and we dragged Dagmar along with us. On Friday night, we went to hang out and stroll around the boulevard. But on Saturday, we planned on going to Sheldon's show at Gazzarri's.

I managed to dodge Ronan's calls Saturday afternoon, but I made the mistake of answering my phone later that evening, as I was getting ready to go out. He was still on my case to get together, but I was already running late to get the girls. I also wasn't in the position (or mood) to have a long conversation with Ronan about our relationship. I told him I was having dinner and would call him back in a few minutes. Then I grabbed my purse and walked out the door.

When I arrived at Gazzarri's with the girls, the door guy refused to let Sasha in because he didn't believe she was 23, which she was according to her fake ID. It was the first time she ever had trouble using that ID. She had the face and body of a *Penthouse* centerfold for Christ sake. Even I had a hard time believing she was only 16. But the door guy wasn't giving in to Sasha, so Dagmar and I didn't bother trying to get in either. After all, we still had the endless street party on the Sunset Strip to keep us preoccupied for the night, so we did just that.

About an hour later, we were chatting with a few people in front of the Roxy when I noticed Axl Rose walk through the parking lot of the Rainbow. He was wearing a white shirt underneath a navy blue jacket with a simple pair of jeans. During this time, Guns N' Roses were in their prime. Rumor had it they were working on a double album, which later became the *Use Your Illusion* albums.

I continued to watch Axl while he made his way through the crowded parking lot. He was sipping on a can of Cherry Coke as he walked in my direction. I wondered if it really was him because he was alone and nobody seemed to recognize him as he walked right by them. By the time he reached the sidewalk, Dagmar and I turned on our heels and decided to follow him.

We started to lose him as he darted across Sunset Blvd, so I yelled out his name in the hopes of slowing him down. He came to a stop in front of Ten Masa Sushi.

"Hi Axl, I'm Marisa. Can we take a picture with you?" I said slightly out of breath.

"Sure," he said unenthusiastically.

I grabbed a random person that happened to be standing nearby and asked if they could take the picture. I hoped for a hug, maybe even an arm over the shoulder from Axl, but I got nothing. He didn't move an inch. He just stood there sipping on his soda while Dagmar and I posed around him as if he were a mannequin. There wasn't a bit of warmth in his demeanor. I wanted to ask what was happening with Guns N' Roses, but based on the cold reception he was giving me, I felt it was best if I just get the picture and let him be on his way.

"Thanks so much!" I said smiling, hoping that my happy face would warm him up a little.

"Sure," he said in a monotone voice and walked away.

When I came home a few hours later, I found a note from my mom saying that Ronan had called twice after I left.

I had so much fun that night, and I didn't want it to be ruined by a guaranteed fight with Ronan. I decided I would wait till the morning to call him back and that would be to finally break up with him.

When I called Ronan the following afternoon, it took about a minute or two before he went into his normal berating behavior. He said I was an inconsiderate bitch for not calling him back the night before and for blowing him off over the last few weeks. He also heard I was hanging out on the Strip and said I was probably out fucking every musician in Hollywood. He told me I was a whore, I was stupid, yeah yeah yeah.

As I listened to Ronan hammer away at my self-esteem, I realized I had not one drop of affection left for him. Everything my friends had been telling me since the beginning of our relationship was suddenly crystal clear to me. Ronan was a douchebag and nothing more than an insecure, controlling asshole that would never add anything positive to my life. I didn't want to hear his voice, see his face or have contact with anything that remotely reminded me of him. His destructive words didn't hurt me anymore. They annoyed me. *Why am I even taking this shit from him when I can be having fun on the Strip? Hell, the guys there are way cuter anyway.*

"If I'm such a horrible person, why are you with me then?" I asked.

"Maybe I shouldn't be," he said as if to test me.

Normally at that point in the argument where he would threaten to leave me, is where I usually cowered and started apologizing.

"Then don't be with me you worthless pile of shit!" I yelled.

I hung up on Ronan, fell back on my bed and let out a big grin. It was the first time I had genuinely smiled in months. It felt like someone had lifted a huge weight off my shoulders. I turned on the radio and danced around the room as I happily gathered old letters, cards, and pictures of Ronan and threw them into the trash.

A few days later, still enjoying my newfound freedom, Arwen, Ariah, and I weaseled our way into the graduation ceremony for the class of 1990. When the festivities concluded, we flooded onto the field along with other friends and family, hugging and congratulating the seniors we knew. I noticed Brandon across the way, and we stared at each other for a few seconds. He gave me a little smile. I smiled back. That one little smirk of his flashed me back to Janson, Muscatel, and our years together at Rosemead High. Seeing him stand there in his cap and gown made me realize we weren't kids anymore.

Where did the time go? Will I ever see him again? I've been in school my whole life and have never known anything else. What the hell am I going to do next year when I graduate high school?

As we stood there staring at each other, I could tell by the look in his eyes that he missed me. I certainly missed him too. He was my first childhood crush. More importantly, he had become one of my closest friends, or so I thought. With my new sense of empowerment after dumping Ronan, I wanted to surround myself with strong, positive people. Brandon obviously was not one of them. I didn't regret calling him a pussy that day in guitar class. I wanted friends who would not only stick up for me but stick up for themselves as well. I knew I couldn't force myself to be in his life anymore, so I wished him well in my heart and knew I had to move forward.

Their graduation song, "Never Say Goodbye" by Bon Jovi began to blare out over the PA system. My gaze with Brandon was broken when Grace walked up to him to give him a hug. Even to this day, every time I hear that song I still think of him on his graduation day looking so handsome in his cap and gown.

6

BOILING BUNNIES

A few weeks after the class of 1990 graduated, I started summer school. I couldn't believe it was to be my last summer in high school, forever. If I passed all my summer school classes, my senior year would consist of an easy breezy schedule of only five classes, three of which were optional electives. With such a light academic schedule, I didn't have to worry about my studies getting in the way of my socializing.

To make matters even better, Dagmar moved out of her mom's house and went to live in her grandmother's condo on La Cienega, just south of Sunset. Her grandmother set her up in her own private bedroom with two twins beds. It was the perfect playground for our weekends on the Strip. Not only because it shortened our commute to a mere five minutes, but spending the nights with her negated my curfew. I didn't have to worry about rushing home anymore. I would've loved to live there every weekend but residing with two loud, teenage girls wasn't exactly what her grandmother had in mind. So I only stayed as often as I was asked, which was roughly every other weekend.

Shortly after starting summer school, Jude, Dagmar, and I decided to take a ditch day. We ended up going to a dive motel down the street from school where a bunch of kids had been partying the night before. It was about 11:00am when we walked into the unlocked motel room. The curtains were closed. The lights were out. There were about seven or eight people in the room, all of which were passed out. A few were in bed others were on the floor. Jude stepped on a pile of blankets that let out a big "Ouch!" and realized our friend, Frankie, was underneath. As Jude and Dagmar tried to wake everyone up, I decided to mooch the room phone and call Sheldon.

Sheldon had been asking me out for weeks, but I was avoiding him until I could officially give Ronan the boot. Now that I was newly single, I gave him a ring and asked if he wanted to hang out. He said he did and would pick me up in about an hour.

A fellow senior named Tommy was the first to get up and began waking everyone else up to drink more. He was a total Jekyl and Hyde when it came to his drinking. When sober, he was a sweetheart. But once he got drunk, he turned into a loud, obnoxious asshole. Tommy was a full out hesher with dirty blond hair and a wide smashed face. He always reminded me of those angry mushroom people that chase Mario and Luigi in the old school Super Mario Bros game.

Tommy began to pound beers and would throw the empty bottles at the wall. I told him to stop before someone called the cops. He said he wouldn't until everyone woke up, which happened rather quickly. I wasn't about to visit the back of a patrol car again because of his drunk ass, so I figured the best thing to do would be to wait for Sheldon in the parking lot. I was about to walk out when Sheldon appeared and knocked on the frame of the open motel door. Tommy looked over at Sheldon. Not recognizing him as someone he knew, he told him to fuck off.

"Go fuck yourself Tommy, he's with me," I said.

I grabbed my things and walked out the door with Sheldon.

We hopped into his beat up '72 Chevelle and went to Dancers rehearsal studio in Van Nuys. The studio was by the Anheuser Busch Brewery, and the scent of hops and barley filled his car as we pulled off the 405 freeway.

The rehearsal space had 70's style wood paneled walls, and the only furniture in the room was a black leather couch. We sat down, chatted for a little bit and started making out. When our kissing became hot and heavy, he started to unzip my jeans and that's when I had to ruin the party by pulling back and telling him I was a virgin. He didn't seem to be too shocked by the news and was actually pretty cool about it. After a little more making out, he dropped me off at home around the time I normally would have been strolling in from school.

As the summer kicked in, I saw more of Sheldon and much more of the Sunset Strip. On Sunday mornings, I would have my breakfast while putting together my social calendar for the week. I would go through the magazines and flyers I had gathered from the weekend and penciled in any upcoming shows on my calendar that I wanted to see.

I incorporated a number of different factors on whether or not I would see a bands show. The first was word of mouth. Were they actually a good band or did they suck? Looking back on it now, I realize that 90% of the bands were shitty back then. But hey, I was 16. I didn't know any better.

Yes, I'll admit that looks did matter. It was all I had to go on if I hadn't heard their music. Although it wasn't a sole factor, it was a minor point that could sway me into going. If a band wasn't good looking and sucked, I didn't necessarily rule them out. But only if they happened to be playing with a band I wanted to see and here's why.

In terms of getting into a show for free, it was all about survival of the fittest. Generally, a pretty face and a big set of tits was the only ticket a girl needed to get into a show. But yours truly was not one of those girls. I was more like the goofy little sister that was friends with all the bands. They would usually get me in for free unless there was some new hooch on the scene that they were trying to hook up with. If it were the latter case, then I was shit out of luck and would have to pay my way in unless I knew the door guy. But that's where the sucky band came into play.

There was a pecking order of bands at every show. Generally, the earlier you played, the less of a following you had. The only exception was the 11:00pm 'ish time slot, which was reserved for the headlining band who they usually sold their tickets for about $10 a pop. The worst time to play was after the headlining band, which I called the "crickets and tumbleweeds" slot. By that time, everyone that came to see the headlining band had cleared out. So you played to a pile of barf on the floor and the five friends you berated into coming to your show. That band usually sold their tickets for $5 and that's how I would get in. Sure it's only a $5 difference from the headlining bands ticket, but take into consideration I was a teenage girl without a job. That extra $5 paid for gas to the show and an optional midnight snack.

Things continued to progress with Sheldon over the summer. Everything seemed to be going right on track, except for the fact that Ronan was still calling me. I stopped returning his calls, and we hadn't spoken since the afternoon I hung up on him. I certainly had no desire to talk to him anyway because my feelings for him were long gone. I was completely gaga over Sheldon. But as the weeks passed, Ronan wouldn't give up. He even started sneaking into the parking lot at my school to leave letters and other gifts on whatever car I drove that day. His cards would say all this lovey dovey bullshit about how he wanted to work things out. I ignored all of his gestures. I figured he would get tired of trying and leave me alone, but that only seemed to make things worse.

During my lunch break at school one day, I was walking to my dad's truck to grab something when I caught Ronan leaving another of his many notes on the windshield.

"What the hell are you doing?" I asked.

"I was just leaving you a gift," he said.

He pulled the note off the truck and handed it to me with a rose attached. I didn't accept either.

"I don't WANT your gifts," I said with my arms crossed.

"Oh yeah? Now that you're a Sunset Strip whore, you think you're hot shit?"

"Yes Ronan. I am a Sunset Strip whore, and I think am hot shit," I said rolling my eyes.

"You know those guys only want one thing."

"Oh, the same thing you've been hounding me about for the last year and a half?"

"Sex is what people do when they love each other!"

"WHEN they're ready!" I barked.

Why in the hell am I even arguing with this moron?

"Oh and you're going to be 'ready' with some band guy?" he said snidely.

"Damn right, I plan on banging half of Hollywood before my 17th birthday," I said raising my eyebrow.

Even I was shocked those words came out of my mouth. It was a bold statement considering I was still a full-fledged virgin, but I only said it in the hopes that it would hurt him.

"You're not worthy to wear a cross you fucking whore!" he yelled as he tore off my necklace and threw it across the parking lot.

I ran in the direction of the cross's flight pattern. I could feel the back of my neck burning from where the necklace had torn across my skin. He followed me as I looked between cars for my cross.

"You fucking asshole! I can't believe you broke my necklace!" I yelled.

"Your Hollywood outings are just a phase you little bitch, and I might not be here when you're over it. Just think about that."

"Good! Then start right now by getting the fuck out of here!"

He gave me a cocky smile and walked off.

Stupid asshole.

In the weeks that followed, I continued to split my time between hanging out with the Alhambra crowd and going to Hollywood. Ronan continued to pursue me, so I avoided answering the phone all together, which was completely abnormal behavior for a 16-year-old girl. I had my parents screen my calls and told them to say I wasn't home anytime Ronan called. Obviously they were suspicious. I downplayed the situation by telling them it was a minor squabble that I needed space from. I wanted to handle the Ronan problem on my own and wasn't about to tell them what was really going on. I kept hoping at some point he would just give up and stop calling me. But on a random Saturday afternoon, I was home alone watching TV when the phone rang. I answered it without thinking and just my fucking luck it was Ronan.

He immediately started bitching as to why I hadn't returned any of his calls and called me every name in the book. I just couldn't take it anymore, so I unleashed a venomous tongue-lashing on him like I had never done before.

I told him he was a stupid, worthless loser for the way he treated me throughout the course of our relationship and that I didn't love him anymore. I said he was an ugly motherfucker inside and out and that's why his family didn't give a shit about him. I also said a prayer, thanking god that I had the good sense to not lose my virginity to a piece of shit like him. I hung up on him in the middle of his rebuttal. A half hour later he was pounding on my front door. I was irate that he had the nerve to show up at my house and flung open my front door.

"What the hell do you want!" I yelled.

He lifted his bloody, right forearm, which had my name carved into it and yelled, "See what you made me do!"

"Are you FUCKING crazy? What the hell is wrong with you!"

"I just want to talk to you!" he pleaded.

"Fine! We'll talk tomorrow! Now get out of here before my parents get home!"

I slammed the door in his face, ran to my bedroom and shut the door behind me even though nobody else was in the house.

Thank god my parents weren't home. The blood running down Ronan's arm made it blatantly clear that things had been taken to a whole other level. This wasn't some bad *Beverly Hills 90210* episode anymore. It was most definitely some fucked up shit that I was going to have to contend with. I just didn't know how.

When I woke the next morning, I thought about what Ronan did to his arm. It was fairly clear that he was a certified crackpot. There was no way in HELL I planned on seeing him that day or any other day. I only told him that to make him go away. And besides, I already had plans that afternoon to borrow Lucy's car and go to the beach with Alex and Ron. A day of relaxation on the beach was exactly what I needed. It didn't hurt that I had Alex as eye candy either.

At the end of our leisurely beach day, I drove us back to Ron's so we could clean up before heading out to dinner. I called my mom to see if I had any messages. She told me Ronan had called three times. I could hear the concern in her voice and I was beyond furious. Not at my mom for caring, but at Ronan. I didn't want my family involved. Him repeatedly calling the house like a damn psycho was making it harder for me keep that whole mess under wraps. I had no other choice but to call his stupid ass and tell him to stop harassing my mom.

Alex and Ron were chatting in the background when I called Ronan at his aunt's house. He asked where I was. I told him to not worry about it. I played it off like I forgot we were supposed to meet up and to stop making a big deal over nothing.

"Hey Marisa, you ready to go?" Ron yelled out to me.

"You're at Ron's aren't you?" Ronan asked.

"No, I'm at my cousins house in Covina," I said lying through my teeth.

Ronan immediately hung up.

SHIT.

The only thing separating Ronan's aunt's house and Ron's apartment was a ten-minute walk across a freeway overpass. Alex and Ron asked if everything was okay. I lied and said it was. I hadn't told anyone about the things Ronan was doing, so I played it cool and tried to rush the guys out of the apartment as calmly and quickly as possible.

We walked to Lucy's car and I was relieved to find no signs of Ronan anywhere. We hopped into her car and I rolled my window down because it was a bit stuffy from the warm summer day. I turned on the engine, the lights, and that's when I saw Ronan running towards the front of the car. I quickly locked my door and tried to crank up the window as quickly as I could. I only got it about ¾ of the way closed before Ronan was able to reach his arm in the driver's side window. He grabbed a fistful of my hair and started slamming my head against the window. Ron and Alex immediately hopped out and pushed Ronan away from the car, releasing the lock on my poor aching head.

"She was supposed to be out with me today! She lied to me!" Ronan yelled.

"What the fuck is wrong with you! Get outta here!" Alex yelled as he gave Ronan a hard shove.

I sat trembling in the drivers seat while they argued with Ronan. He left a few minutes later. Ron asked if I was okay and told me to get out of the car. Alex moved my hair around to make sure my head wasn't cut. I said I was fine. I told them I wasn't hungry anymore but they didn't want me driving home in that frazzled state. Not taking no for an answer, we hopped into Alex's car and they treated me to dinner at a Mexican restaurant just off Fremont Avenue in Alhambra.

Since Alex and Ron had a front row seat for Ronan's psychosis, it was pointless in trying to downplay the situation. So as they stuffed me with delicious Mexican food, I told them everything that had been happening over the last few weeks. They consoled me and said if he ever bothered me again to let them know. I thought it was sweet of them, but to be honest, I was incredibly embarrassed over the entire situation and didn't want to get anyone else involved. I felt the entire mess with Ronan was something I had to clean up on my own.

When we came back to Ron's, the boys walked me to Lucy's car and made sure I drove off safely without another ambush from Ronan. When I drove home that night, I didn't turn on the radio or listen to any music. There was nothing I felt like listening to because I was still reeling from what happened earlier. Instead, I listened to the sound of the summer wind hit the car windows.

A few minutes into my drive, I heard faint jangling like the sound of bracelets. I took a quick glance into my backseat and saw nothing. I looked at the radio and it was off. The jangling stopped.

A few minutes later, the jangling started back up. Again, I looked into my backseat, still nothing. I looked in the side mirrors to see if maybe something was caught on the sides of the car but there was nothing. The jangling stopped.

The jangling started again. This time when I looked into my rearview mirror, I saw Ronan slowly crawl out from the trunk of the car and into the backseat like a slithering snake. I quickly pulled over, grabbed the keys and ran out of the car across a residential street.

"Oh my god! Get the fuck away from me you psycho!" I yelled as he climbed out of the car.

"Stop yelling! I'm not gonna hurt you," he said.

"How the hell did you get in there?" I said yelling, rather than asking.

"You left the doors unlocked."

Yeah, right.

"Why can't you just leave me the alone?" I said starting to hyperventilate.

"Why do you keep avoiding me? Why won't you just talk to me?"

"Because you're an asshole who never loved me and you've treated me like shit since the day I met you!"

"But I do love you!"

"Bullshit! Now that you can't control me anymore you can't stand it!"

"Fine. Tell me you don't love me anymore, and I'll leave you alone."

"I don't love you anymore," I said without hesitation. "Now get the fuck away from the car! Completely away, across the street!"

It was as if we were in one of those old western movies, staring each other down and waiting for the other to draw. He slowly started to walk back across the residential street. As he took steps back, I took steps forward. When he reached the curb, he sat down, put his head in his hands and started to sob.

I contemplated for a moment and wondered if I was being a cold-hearted bitch. I honestly felt no sympathy for Ronan as he sat there crying. But I quickly came to my senses.

Fuck him. He's just getting a pinch of what he's put me through over the last year and a half.

I quickly jumped back into Lucy's car, locked the doors, and sped off, leaving him still blubbering in the street.

Almost a week had passed since the incident at Ron's, and there were no signs of Ronan what so ever. No phone calls and no notes on my car at school. But after all the bullshit he pulled, I didn't believe for one second that he had given up. I was under a tremendous amount of anxiety during that time because I never knew when or where he was going to pop up.

When the weekend arrived, Sasha and Dagmar picked me up so we could go to the Strip as usual. We started our socializing along the boulevard and immediately ran into Mick from Ana Black just outside the Roxy. We had been chatting with him for a few minutes when I noticed Ronan walk out of the Rainbow. I was in shock because Ronan never hung out on the Strip, not even when we went to Taz shows.

Based on his behavior at Ron's, it was obvious he had no problem causing a scene in front of people. I was worried what he might do. It was unfortunate that some of my Alhambra friends had to witness one of his crazy episodes, but none of my Hollywood friends knew anything about my problems with Ronan. I was also still dating Sheldon, so I certainly wasn't about to tell him what was going on and scare him away. I quickly told Mick we had to go. I grabbed the girls, told them what was happening and we scurried away.

Just my luck, Ronan caught up to us and started in with his bullshit. To make matters worse, I spotted Sheldon just off in the distance. He waved to me as he made his way in our direction.

Running away wasn't an option. That would've set Ronan on fire, and I didn't need him chasing me down Sunset Boulevard like a lunatic.

Sheldon walked up to us, completely oblivious to the situation and gave me a big hug.

"Hey honey bunny," he said.

"Who the hell is this?" Ronan said looking at me.

"Hey dude, just kickback," Sheldon said mildly defensive.

"What's it to you? Are you with her?" Ronan asked.

"Look stalker, nobody wants you here. Why don't you just go away," Sasha said.

"Yeah, seriously. What the hell is your problem?" Dagmar added.

The four of us stood there staring at Ronan. He said nothing and suddenly ran away. I downplayed the situation to Sheldon and told him Ronan was just an idiot I briefly dated. He looked a bit concerned for obvious reasons, but I told him everything was cool and quickly changed the subject. We continued on our way down the Strip and ran into Sheldon's roadie, Alan. We hung out with them sporadically throughout the night, and thankfully Sheldon didn't bring up what happened with Ronan for the rest of the evening.

When Sasha took me home that night, I was running late for curfew as always. Since she was driving her moms old clunker, I had her drop me off a few houses away so the car wouldn't wake anyone in my house while I tried to sneak in. As Sasha drove off, I noticed Ronan's mom's car parked about three or four houses past my house. He saw me, got out of his car, and quickly started to walk towards me. I picked up my pace as well. My heart was racing as I fumbled to open the gate to my driveway. Once I got the damn thing open, I had only taken a few steps in when Ronan grabbed me. I wanted to scream but controlled myself since I didn't want to wake up my parents.

"Get the fuck out of here before I call the cops!" I whispered angrily.

"The cops? What the hell is wrong with you! I just want to talk to you!" he said as he grabbed my arms and shook me like a rag doll.

"Get the fuck off me!" I said throwing his hands off me.

I started run up my driveway, but he was right on my heels and grabbed me again. I don't know what he was aiming for, but in the midst of him trying to hold onto me he ended up hitting me in my ribcage. I got angry and punched him in the face.

He clinched my wrists tightly and said, "Why are you acting like this!"

I broke his hold and gave him a hard shove with my entire body, which knocked him back a few feet. I just couldn't take it anymore. I was ready to brawl. If I had to beat the shit out of Ronan to get him out of my life then I was more than prepared to do so. Even if that meant doing it right on the front lawn of my own house.

"You wanna fight you piece of shit? Then lets go already!" I said giving him another hard shove.

"I don't want to fight. I just want to talk to you!"

I shoved him again and said, "I don't want to talk to you! Why can't you get that through your thick head!"

"I fucking love you Marisa! Why won't you give me another chance?"

"I've told you a million times I want nothing to do with you! I fucking hate you!"

Ronan looked at me like I was a nut.

"Did you hear me? I fucking hate you! I hope you die! Get out of my life!" I said giving him multiple shoves with all the strength I could muster.

He looked like a deer caught in headlights. He said nothing and suddenly ran out of my driveway. He didn't stop running till he reached his moms car. I stood in my driveway a bit out of breath as Ronan drove off. I put my hand on my ribcage, which hurt a little bit. I looked around and was surprised that my yelling didn't wake anyone up.

I was out of breath and didn't feel like going inside my house. There was a nice breeze outside, so I quietly walked down the driveway along the side of my house and went to my backyard. I looked at a swing my dad had made years ago for my sisters and me when we were little. It was gently swaying from the wind as it hung from our big oak tree. I climbed onto the swing and sat there. I hadn't been on that thing in years and thought about how simple my life was the last time I sat on that swing. I also thought about something my mom told me not too long ago. She said, "You have the rest of your life to be an adult and only a few years to be a carefree kid. So enjoy these years while you can and don't be in such a rush to grow up."

I wouldn't say I had an epiphany but more a moment of clarity into my future. I knew I was at a crossroads and had to decide what kind of woman I wanted to grow up to be. I could continue down the path I was on, let my self esteem dig even further into the dirt and fill my life with abusive boyfriends, or I could learn from the mistake I made by letting Ronan into my life and never let another guy treat me like that again. Luckily, I went with the latter option.

I sat outside on the swing for a few minutes and then snuck into my house. I was sweaty from the struggle I had with Ronan, but I couldn't take a shower because that would've woken up my parents. Instead, I turned my fan on, peeled off my sweaty clothes and put on some clean pajamas. I turned off the light in my room and lay in bed. It took me well over an hour to finally wind down before I was able to fall asleep.

A few days passed and Ronan was M.I.A. again. Needless to say, I was worried about going to the Strip the following weekend. While I got ready to go out, I couldn't shake the uneasy feeling that something wasn't right. I turned off the lights in my bedroom, closed the door and peeked out my bedroom window. There were no cars parked in front of my house. The porch light was lighting my entire driveway. I closed the curtain, turned the lights back on and continued getting ready.

About a half hour later, I was about to leave and pickup Sasha when I decided to check outside one last time. I shut off the lights in my room again and peeked out of my bedroom window. This time, I saw Ronan's mom's car parked across the street. My stomach began to churn and a heavy wave of anxiety came over me as I quickly closed the curtain.

Calling the police wasn't an option because I was still under the dumb impression that I could handle him on my own. Ronan knew damn well I went to the Strip every weekend. He also knew I usually went with Sasha and Dagmar. He knew where Sasha lived too, so I called her and devised a plan to ditch him.

"Hey, I need you to be waiting outside in front of your building when I come get you okay?" I said.

"Why? Is Ronan up to his old tricks?" she asked.

"Yes, so wait ten minutes then go outside. I'm about to walk out the door right now."

"Oh screw him. He's just doing shit to piss you off."

Sasha didn't know about Ronan hitting his mom, the incident at Ron's, or our boxing match in my driveway from a week earlier. I had done a pretty good job of hiding his more extreme behavior from her and everyone else for that matter. So as far as she knew, Ronan was just being an annoying pain in the ass.

"Listen, just be outside your apartment in ten minutes okay?" I said sternly.

"Okay okay, fine," she said relenting.

I hung up with Sasha, then grabbed my things and held onto them tightly. I bolted out my front door to Lucy's car, and quickly locked the doors behind me. To my surprise, Ronan didn't attempt to get out of the car. He just sat in his mom's car watching me. It wasn't until I pulled out of the driveway and made my way down the street that he started to follow me. Luckily, I knew a shortcut to Sasha's and quickly lost him. I just prayed that she would do as I told her and be outside waiting so I could scoop her up and go to Hollywood.

When I turned the corner to Sasha's and approached her apartment building, she was nowhere to be found. I punched the dashboard in frustration and pulled around to park in the back of the building. I just hoped that Ronan would keep driving if he didn't see Lucy's car out front.

Seeing no signs of Ronan, I got out and ran up the flight of stairs to the 2nd floor. I ran down a hallway and was almost to her front door when I saw Ronan jogging up the staircase from the opposite end. Being faster than me, he made it to Sasha's front door before I could and wouldn't let me go in.

"Please, just talk to me for a minute!" he pleaded.

"It's over! I have nothing to say to you! Gawd, just leave me alone already!"

"You heartless bitch! I should kill your fucking family so you can feel half the pain I'm going through!"

Every time I thought Ronan's craziness had pushed it to the furthest level, he'd push it a little more. I decided to call his bluff.

"Oh yeah? Well my friends know about all your little antics, so if anything happens to me or my family you're going to jail you psycho piece of shit!" I yelled.

Flustered, he frantically climbed over the railing.

"Don't make me do it! I'll jump!" he yelled.

"Go ahead! I hope you do!" I yelled back.

I stormed into Sasha's apartment, slammed her front door behind me and charged into her bedroom. She looked up at me cluelessly as she touched up her makeup.

"I'm late aren't I?" she said.

"What the fuck is wrong with you? I ask you to do ONE little thing."

"I'm sorry, I'm sorry. I know I'm lagging. I'll make it up to you. Midnight snack, my treat okay?" she said with a big smile.

I hardly thought greasy take out was a fair exchange for my possible homicide outside her front door, but I didn't want to ruin the night by being a sourpuss. I reluctantly accepted her offer and tried to put myself in a better mood.

Sasha finished getting ready and we hopped into Lucy's car with no sign of Ronan. When we got to the Strip, I met up with Sheldon and found myself constantly looking over my shoulder during our brief conversation. He asked me what was wrong. Of course I lied and said everything was fine. Sure everyone brings some type of baggage to a relationship, but I wasn't about to tell him that mine was an ex that moonlighted in stalking and boiling bunnies *Fatal Attraction* style.

Sasha and I roamed the Strip on our own for the next few hours, and then met up with Sheldon and Alan at the end of the night. As we walked to Lucy's car, they mentioned they were going to stick around a bit longer, so I offered them a ride back down to the Strip.

I pulled into the AM/PM store across from the Whisky and leaned over to get a hug and kiss from Sheldon who was sitting in the passengers seat. After exchanging a few smooches, I pulled back to find Ronan thrusting his arms into the passengers side window. He clasped both hands around my throat, but Sheldon quickly broke the choke. Alan flipped the passenger seat forward to get out, shoving Sheldon right into the dashboard. Alan barreled out the door from the backseat and chased after Ronan with Sheldon following right behind him. Alan caught up to Ronan at the back of Lucy's car and planted a right hook that threw him across the trunk of the car. I quickly rolled up the windows and locked the doors as Sasha cheered and clapped with delight.

"Beat his ass!" she yelled as she smacked her hands repeatedly against the rear window.

Not being able to do anything about the situation, I just sat in the drivers seat and watched in my rearview mirror as Ronan got his ass kicked. When Alan and Sheldon finally let up on Ronan, he immediately ran over to the driver's side door and started pounding on my window.

"How could you do this to me you cheating whore!" he yelled with his freshly beaten face.

"I'm NOT your fucking girlfriend you psycho asshole!" I screamed at the window.

After a little more pushing and shoving, the boys told Ronan if he didn't leave me alone they would beat the shit out of him again. Ronan looked at me as if he were waiting for me to say something in his defense. I ignored him and stared straight ahead with my arms crossed, focusing on a bum rummaging through a dumpster beside the AM/PM. A few moments later, Ronan walked away. I rolled down my window.

"Are you okay?" Sheldon asked.

"Yeah, I'm fine. I am so sorry about all of this. Believe me, he's not my boyfriend anymore. He's a fucking nut and won't leave me alone."

On one hand, I was horrified that Sheldon had to get involved. But after hanging out in Hollywood for the last few months, I realized that crazy shit like that was commonplace on the Sunset Strip. So it wasn't like Ronan's outburst was going to stick out and become gossip fodder.

While I was grateful that Alan and Sheldon had given Ronan a good pummeling, I wasn't sure they had beat the crazy out of him. I could only hope. I was worried about seeing his mom's car parked outside my house when I came home that night. I couldn't take another boxing match or possibly worse. I wished that I had someone, a bodyguard to make sure I got into my house safely. That's when I thought of my dad.

During the warm summer evenings, he would often hang out on our porch late at night, sipping a cup of coffee and reading whatever new book on war stories he had just picked up. I called my dad before I left Hollywood that night in the hopes he would still be up.

"Hey Chuck, are you still awake?" I asked.

"Yeah, I'm just doing some reading. What's up?" he said.

"I'm going to be home in a few minutes, and I was wondering if you could wait up for me."

"Sure. I just poured myself a fresh cup of coffee."

"But you're outside on the porch right?"

"I'm outside right now."

"Okay, wait outside for me till I get home okay?"

"Why? What's wrong?"

My dad was the last person I could tell all my Ronan drama to. With him being an Army veteran, I could only imagine how he would have handled the situation.

"Umm, nothing. I just saw this really scary movie, and I'm totally scared of the dark right now. Stay outside though, okay?" I said.

"Okay, I'll be outside waiting for you," he said.

We hung up and my eyes welled up with tears. With that one little sentence he put my heart and fears to rest. When I had the love and protection of my dad it was like an indestructible wall that no man, no machine, nor any psycho for that matter could penetrate.

After dropping off Sasha, I made my way home. When I turned the corner to my street there was no sign of Ronan or his mom's car to be found. I pulled in the driveway and breathed a sigh of relief once I saw my dad. As promised, he was sitting under the porch light. He had his feet up on a small brick ledge and was sipping a cup of coffee with a book in his hand. When my dad smiled at me as I got out of Lucy's car that night, it suddenly put everything into perspective.

The entire time I dated Ronan, I always resented my parents for their rules and enforced curfews. Sure Ronan may have had more freedoms than I did, but he also didn't have anyone to provide a steady home for him. No one made him delicious home cooked meals or gave him fresh bed sheets to sleep in because he didn't have his own bed. His family wouldn't notice if he were gone for days on end because no one cared what happened to him. He thought he was king of the world for being a teenager with no rules, but in reality he had nothing. I, on the other hand, seeing my dad on the porch that night felt I had everything.

"Hey Chuck, what's up?" I said as I got out of the car.

"Nothin much. What's the word, bird?" he asked.

"The word is 'crap'. What a crappy night. I just want to go to sleep."

"The movie was bad huh?"

"It was horrible. The most HORRIBLE movie I've ever seen. I hope I never ever see it again."

"What was the movie?"

"You don't want to know. I'm going to bed. Thanks for waiting up Chuck."

"Up Chuck?"

We both shared a laugh, then he gathered up his things and we went inside.

Maybe Ronan came to my house, saw my dad and drove off. It's also possible the beating at the hands of Alan and Sheldon actually worked. I would probably never know either way. Instead of stressing about what could happen with Ronan, I tried to put it all behind me and focus on my new social circle in Hollywood.

7

GIRLFRIEND OF A (PSUEDO) ROCK STAR

As the summer turned into fall, I started my senior year in high school and continued to be a regular on the Sunset Strip. I was meeting more bands and seeing things my budding, pubescent eyes were too young to see. I had no desire to go to neighborhood keg parties and school dances anymore. I found them boring in comparison to hanging out in the Hollywood scene with an older crowd.

With me bowing out of just about all high school related activities, I found myself becoming alienated from a majority of my fellow seniors, with the exception of Arwen and Ariah. Jude rarely went to Hollywood because she preferred to be local and hang out in Alhambra, which I found boring. Even Dagmar wasn't going to the Strip with Sasha and I every weekend like she used to. The rest of my classmates thought I was a stuck up Hollywood snob because I wasn't hanging out in Rosemead anymore. I did feel bad that I was coming off that way, but I've always been the kind of person that welcomed change and was eager to see what the next big thing was. I felt I had done everything there was to do in Rosemead. I wanted to do something different. So I continued going to shows in Hollywood where I met a flock of high school girls like myself that I could relate to. One of those girls was a doe eyed brunette named Faye Warner.

Faye and I met at a Dancer show. I couldn't take my eyes off her the first time I saw her. She was absolutely stunning with long honey brown hair and big brown eyes. She had the body of a *Playboy* model and could've easily passed as Cindy Crawford's younger sister. She actually approached me first by asking if I was Sheldon's girlfriend. I was surprised by her inquiry because I had only been dating Sheldon for a few weeks. I wasn't aware anyone else knew we were hanging out. Although we were spending a majority of our time together, even I wasn't sure if I was his official girlfriend yet.

Going back to Faye, she was an only child who lived with her parents in Burbank. Her mom was a homemaker and her dad was a district attorney. He would often give her rides to Hollywood and drop her off by herself, which I found shocking since she was only 14.

One of the things I liked most about going to Faye's house strangely enough was playing with her pet rabbit, Chloe. The poor thing sat in her cage most of the time except when I came to play with her. Faye knew how much I loved rabbits and told me I could have Chloe because she knew I would give her a better home. Unfortunately, my mom didn't want to deal with the responsibility of having another pet in the house even though she was a huge animal lover.

Speaking of my mom, it was around the same time that she told me her and my dad were separating. I don't know why she used the word "separate" when I knew it was a flat out divorce. They had been arguing quite a bit over the last few years, and I had braced myself for the possibility that it might happen. But when those words came out of my mom's mouth I can't say it didn't bother me. Not because I wanted my parents together. I knew they were better off being apart. But I knew that meant my dad would move out and I would miss seeing him everyday.

As the divorce proceedings went through, I noticed each member of my family slowly drift apart from our once close little unit. My dad was already starting up a new relationship with some woman named Pamela, my mom was in an emotional limbo because she didn't want to get divorced, and Lucy was rarely home because she was always over Tim's house. I didn't realize the extent of how much my family was growing apart until my drama class in high school performed their first semester play, *The Crucible*.

I was set to play the character of Ann Putnam and told everyone in my family when our first and only performance was. They didn't say anything about going to see me perform, but they didn't have to. I knew they would be there because they were big on those kinds of things. It didn't matter if I was in a Broadway play or a puppet show on a street corner. I knew my mom would wrangle the family together to support me.

The play wasn't going to be an official school wide production performed in our schools auditorium. Instead, it would be in the classroom where we had our drama class, which was twice the size of a normal classroom. It was going to be an intimate performance, only for family and a few friends of the students that were in my drama class.

The day of the performance was absolute chaos. I wasn't able to go home after school because I had to stay for last minute rehearsals. I rushed to eat a brief snack and had just enough time to put on my costume before my drama teacher literally threw me on stage for my first scene. When I finished my dialogue and walked off stage, I peeked from behind a corner wall to see where my family was sitting. I scanned the packed room full of parents and friends with bouquets of flowers in their hands and realized not one member of my family showed up to see my performance.

Despite being blown off by my family, I decided to focus on my new budding relationship with Sheldon. One of the downsides of dating him was the constant flow of groupies that had less than no regard for our relationship. Oh and of course every musician has to have at least one stalker. Sheldon's happened to be a plump, curly haired brunette named Misha.

Misha was a Sunset Strip regular. The first time I heard about her was through Faye. According to Faye, Misha walked up to her at the Whisky a few months earlier and threatened to beat her ass if she ever came to Hollywood again. This didn't surprise me though. Faye was always having problems with girls in Hollywood. They absolutely hated her, and I couldn't understand why. She was always super sweet to me. I never saw her be mean to anyone. I just chalked it up to them being jealous of her beauty.

Going back to the subject of Misha, Sheldon did admit that he had sex with her. He said it only happened once. According to him, it happened about a year earlier and only because he was really drunk (isn't that always the case). He avoided her after they hooked up, so naturally she became angry and resorted to crank calling and other antics like putting sugar in his gas tank. But her cries for attention didn't faze me in the least. Compared to the nightmare Ronan had just put me through over the last few months, her hijinks were childs play.

Regardless of Misha's shenanigans, I continued to see Sheldon. He had just moved to a small house in Sylmar with his mom and younger sister, Laney, about forty-five minutes north of Hollywood. His mom seemed to like me the few times I did see her. She was a nurse that constantly worked double shifts at a nearby hospital. As for his dad, well he never spoke about him. Then there was Laney who he didn't get along with to put it mildly.

Laney and I were the same age. She hated most of Sheldon's girlfriends with the strange exception of yours truly. We got along quite well and when Sheldon would go to band rehearsal, I would stay at the house and hang out with her till he came home.

Laney was quite a character. She was abrasive, in your face and didn't hold anything back. She always told you exactly what was on her mind. I can understand how that would rub people the wrong way, but it didn't bother me. I've always preferred people to be up front with me rather than smile and lie to my face. She had a constant string of violent relationships, but underneath the cigarettes and foul mouth, Laney really was a nice person, well to me at least.

Even though our sixteen-year-old lives were 180 degrees different from each other, we somehow found a common ground on which we could relate. She was living a tumultuous life that I was mildly curious about…well, until I had a little taste one Saturday afternoon of what a day in the life of Laney was all about.

Sheldon had just left the house to go rehearsal, so I spent the afternoon hanging out with Laney as I always did. She had been dating a guy named Miller who had a psycho ex-girlfriend. She was telling me all about him when the house phone rang. Laney answered. She began cursing at the person on the other line and slammed down the phone. A few minutes later, the phone rang again. She angrily picked up the phone.

"Go ahead bitch! Come to my house! I'll beat your fucking head in!" she yelled and slammed the phone down again.

Laney stomped into the kitchen and came back to the living room with two large knifes in her hands. Meanwhile, I'm sitting on the couch, munching on carrots and trying to watch a harmless episode of *I Love Lucy*.

"Here, in case they try to come in the house," she said as she shoved a steak knife into my hand.

I think a bit of carrot actually fell out of my mouth as I stared at her.

She opened the front door, leaned against the doorframe and stared out the screen door, glancing back and forth at the street. About fifteen minutes later, a truck pulled up to the front of the house.

I peeked out the window to see three girls hop out of the back of a truck and walk up to the front gate. Each had small, potted plants in their hands. Despite the screaming match Laney had on the phone, I stupidly wondered if they were friends of hers since they came bearing gifts. The next thing I know, one of the girls hurls a plant at the front door like a pitcher in the 9th inning.

CRASH! The plant and its ceramic pot exploded across the small porch. I flew away from the window like a scared cat and ran to a recliner on the other side of the living room. Laney kicked open her screen door.

"This is MY house you fucking cunts! Just try and come on my personal property!" she yelled.

I sat straight up on the edge of the reclining chair like a prairie dog, wide eyed with knife in hand, trying to focus on *I*

Love Lucy, rather than the real life version of *Boyz in the Hood* that was taking place outside.

CRASH! Another plant came flying and hit the frame of the door.

"Why don't you come outside your gate you chicken shit!" a girl yelled from outside.

"You're the chicken shits! Come into my yard so me and my girl can cut you into little bits you fucking whores! You didn't think I would have backup did ya!" she yelled.

Then it hit me that I was the backup.

The banter went back and forth for about ten minutes with Laney screaming and pots flying. I was actually glad they were causing such a spectacle. It prompted a neighbor to call the police who showed up just minutes later and were able to diffuse the situation.

I never told Sheldon about what happened that afternoon because he and Laney already had a pretty volatile relationship. He would have flipped if he knew she had involved me in any of her hijinks.

My social and personal life seemed to be going at a comfortable, steady pace. That's when my dad dropped the bomb that he was getting married to Pamela, and I would be inheriting three younger stepbrothers.

I wanted nothing to do with my dad's wedding to Pamela. Neither did Lucy, but my dad wanted us to attend the wedding. Shortly after my dad broke the news, there was a family get together at a nearby park. When Lucy and I arrived, it was packed with people from my dad's side of the family. We worked our way through, saying hello and hugging cousins, aunts and uncles when we finally came upon a table where my dad was sitting with Pamela. We hugged him hello and she immediately chimed in.

"Do you girls mind going for a little walk with me?" she asked sweetly.

Lucy looked at me. I shrugged my shoulders.

"Yeah, I guess," I said.

The three of us took a walk around the park and Pamela went into a long speech about how she wasn't trying to replace my mom and how much it meant to my dad to have us at their wedding. She wanted us to be honest about any issues we had in regards to them getting married. I knew that was the last thing I should do because the things I had to say to her were going to be far from pleasant. As far as I was concerned, she was nothing but a home wrecker.

Lucy and I exchanged occasional glances as Pamela went on with her monologue. I knew by the look in Lucy's eyes that she was ready to pull the trigger on this if I was. Of course that was my first instinct, but as I listened to Pamela drone on, I thought about my dad. The dynamic in my house was drastically different from not having him there everyday. I would only see him once a week or every other week when he would come to pick up Ginger. I knew that causing a blowout with Pamela at a family function wouldn't accomplish anything. It would only put more distance between us. So for the sake of wanting to keep some semblance of a relationship with my dad, I decided to bite my lip and make things copacetic with Pamela.

Their wedding took place a few weeks later. I felt like a traitor as I got ready for the ceremony in front of my mom. She seemed to be keeping a brave face though. The wedding itself was fairly uneventful. It was a short ceremony at a chapel in San Gabriel, filled with some family and a few of my dad and Pamela's friends. The reception though was a little more colorful thanks to my Aunt Mona, one of my dad's older sisters.

The reception was held in a small banquet room at a hall in Alhambra. When Lucy and I arrived at the banquet hall, so had most of the wedding guests. My dad and Pamela were sitting at the main table with her three sons sitting to the left of her. Sitting to the right of my dad were a man and a woman who I didn't know. I figured they were there to chat with him for a little bit and then move. Certainly they would have to move because those two seats were reserved for Lucy and me. I mentioned this to Lucy, and we noticed they weren't even talking to my dad. He had his back turned and was talking to Pamela and a few other people standing behind them. I don't even think he knew those two people were sitting there. Lucy and I decided to take action and find out what was going on.

"Hi there," I said with a smile as I walked up to the two people. "We're his daughters and I believe these are our seats," I continued.

"Oh…uhh…well we are Pamela's cousins and we were hoping to sit here," the man said in a stern, yet friendly tone.

Just then, my Aunt Mona walked up.

"What's wrong *meja?*" she asked me. "Everyone is taking their seats. Why aren't you girls sitting down?"

"We were trying to, but I guess these people want our seats," I said innocently.

I certainly had a temper, but it was no match for the wrath of my dad's sisters. Some were calmer than others, but there were no wallflowers in that bunch. They were upfront, no bullshit, strong Mexican women that weren't afraid to tell you what was on their mind. I knew the situation with Pamela's cousins would be resolved in a matter of seconds by my Aunt Mona. Lucy and I stood back, smiled at each other and waited for the fireworks to fly.

"Who the hell are you?" My aunt asked bluntly to the gentleman.

"We are Pamela's cousins, we were hoping to…" he began to say.

"I don't give a shit what you were hoping for. These are his daughters, MY nieces. So get THE HELL out of their seats before I throw you out," she said looking at the man dead in the eye.

The two people grabbed their things and hurried away.

"*PENdejo.* Who the hell does he think he is? You girls need anything else?" she asked me sweetly.

"Nope, we're all good now. Thank you!" I said smiling as I took my seat.

My dad was still talking to the people behind him. I don't think he noticed what took place with my Aunt Mona. Or maybe he was so used to that kind of thing with his sisters that it didn't even faze him anymore. Pamela, on the other hand, saw everything that happened and seemed disturbed by it. I didn't give a shit; let her take on my Aunt Mona. Served her right for having rude family members.

Luckily, the rest of the reception went off without a hitch. There were no more outbursts from Aunt Mona, and Pamela never confronted her about what happened. Smart woman.

With the wedding out the way and my dad embarking on his new life with Pamela, I felt I should do the same and put my focuses back on my personal life as well.

Although I had met Sheldon on the Strip, now that I was his girlfriend, he wasn't thrilled with me hanging out in Hollywood. Apparently there was band girlfriend etiquette that I wasn't aware of according to him. For starters, he felt it was disloyal for me to see other bands shows. Especially other headlining bands that were in direct competition with his. One band in particular that he had major issues with was The Glamour Punks.

The Glamour Punks had a punk sound with the look of a glam band (thus the name). They were the only of their kind playing in Hollywood during that time. They were well known for their violent shows, which always resulted in a guaranteed mosh pit no matter what club they played. Sheldon told me that the Punk's bass player, Dizzy, had recently busted the rear view mirrors on car belonging to a friend of his. That was the main reason why Sheldon didn't like them. I had never been to a Glamour Punks show before and neither had Sasha. So when we heard they had a gig coming up at the Whisky, we made plans to go. But kept it on the down low of course.

When I went to the Strip, I never spent a majority of my time with Sheldon anyway. He was always busy "promoting", which basically translated to passing out flyers and talking to pretty girls. With him being preoccupied, I figured he wouldn't notice if I disappeared into the Whisky for a half hour or so to see the Glamour Punks play.

MANDIE (The Glamour Punks): I moved to Los Angeles with the sole intention of starting a band called The Glamour Punks. I never sang in a band before, I'd only played drums. I had this whole plan of what I wanted it to sound like, and I had some songs written. I knew what I wanted to do; I just didn't have anyone to be in a band with me. I met Fly T. Hooker the first night I was in L.A. and from there we met Mickey a few weeks later. Staci moved out from the east coast a few months later and that was it. We were formed.

SKITZ (The Glamour Punks): I was living in New York City and playing bass in a band called The Love Tribe when I first heard

113

of The Glamour Punks. I instantly knew that I would fit into the band perfectly. I decided to pack my bags and take a bus to Los Angeles. I was in L.A. for about three weeks when I heard they were having some internal problems and might be looking for a guitar player.

I walked straight up to Dizzy and said, "I'm gonna play guitar for the Punks." He said, "WHATEVER! You're a bass player!" and I said, "Fuck Off! I'm pretty sure I can handle two more strings, it's not BRAIN SURGERY." One thing led to another, and although I don't remember the exact details, he ended up shoving a large safety pin through my arm, told me I had balls and said, "If you can play the songs then you're in."

I didn't own a guitar or an amp at the time, so I borrowed one from a friend of mine and auditioned by playing along to a cassette tape in Dizzy's bedroom. He and Mandie stood there snickering at me while I rocked out all by myself. (laughs) That night we celebrated by drinking a half-gallon of Jim Beam.

Somehow it ended with all of us on the roof of an apartment building, beating the shit out of each other while helicopters hovered over and yelled at us to get off of the roof. We ran from the cops, and I threw up while falling down a flight of stairs.

The next morning, I woke in the back of a car with a note pinned to my chest. It had directions for me to get back to where I was staying at the time. I walked home battered and bruised. Dizzy called about five minutes after I walked in the door and said, "How's it feel to be a Punk?" I remember thinking, "It doesn't feel all that great."

The weekend of The Glamour Punks show, I picked up Sasha and we made our way out to Hollywood. As we walked down the always-crowded sidewalks on Sunset Blvd., I noticed Sheldon standing near the Whisky with quite a few people around him. He seemed to be busy chatting away, so we tried to sneak by. Just as I thought I passed him without recognition, he called out my name.

"Marisa! Where are you going?" he asked.

"Um, just across the street to AM/PM," I said casually walking back to him.

"Oh. Well I'm heading up to the Rainbow, then I'll probably head home."

"Cool, I'll be leaving soon too."

"Okay honey bunny, call me tomorrow."

Sheldon gave me a kiss and then walked off with Nima.

Sasha and I walked to the corner and stood there like we were waiting for the light to change. But once Sheldon was a good distance away, we scurried back like rats and ran into the Whisky.

The Glamour Punks were onstage when we walked in. A mosh pit of punk kids with an overabundance of safety pins and brightly colored hair was already in full effect.

"Lets go in the pit!" Sasha said with enthusiasm.

"You're out of your fucking mind, we'll get killed in there!" I said.

Without saying another word, Sasha grabbed my arm and dragged me through the pit where we ended up dead center near the stage. I was shoved and bumped around a bit throughout the show, but it wasn't that bad. For the most part, the crowd was like a small wave of water swaying back and forth across the club and no one found themselves in the same spot for more than a few minutes.

The last song of the set was a cover of Beastie Boys "No Sleep Till Brooklyn", at which point a very tall, skinny kid with purple hair jumped behind the drums to play. The band was thrashing and Punk Rock Dave, the unofficial band mascot, was stomping around the stage in his straightjacket and bugged out eyes. Just as they finished the song, Dizzy grabbed a microphone.

"Do you wanna hear a bass solo!" he yelled.

The crowd cheered and yelled.

Dizzy laid down his bass, pulled out a bat from the drum riser and started to smash it on stage. A huge chunk of his red bass came flying in my direction, and I caught it before it nearly took my head off. The next thing I know, the singer, Screaming Boy Mandie, takes a few steps back towards the drum riser and stares out to the crowd from behind his fire engine red hair. Before I could bat my fake eyelashes, he was already airborne towards my side of the crowd with his steel toe combat boot landing perfectly on the left side of my face.

I dropped to the ground, flat on my back and felt the remnants of spilled drinks begin to soak into the back of my shirt. Hands suddenly clamped all over my arms as a handful of people sprang me back up on my feet like a yoyo.

"Oh my god, dude! Are you okay?" Sasha asked.

"Yeah, I think so," I said bewildered.

"Come on, let's go to the bathroom."

Sasha grabbed my hand and slowly began pulling me through the crowd towards the bathroom.

"Oh man," Sasha said after looking at my face in the light of the bathroom.

The only type of mirror in the ladies bathroom was a distorted piece of reflective plastic, which only gave you a general idea of how you looked. I had to depend on Sasha's dramatic facial expressions to tell me exactly what was wrong with my face.

"It's gonna be a shiner. You're swelling a little already," she said.

"Awe, damn it! How am I supposed to explain this to Sheldon?"

"Tell him you got into a fight after he left. It's not TOTALLY unbelievable."

Sasha spent the next few minutes cleaning me up as best she could. Then made our way through the club, out the front door and right smack into Sheldon.

Damn it.

"What were you doing in there?" Sheldon asked sternly.

"Using the bathroom," I said casually.

"What happened to your face?"

"Umm...I got in a fight?" I said smiling.

After pressing me for info about my puffy cheek, I did confess that Mandie accidentally kicked me in the face while stagediving. As Sheldon and I argued, I could feel the vultures circling around me. The girls who were waiting for any kind of weakness so they could swarm in on the potential carcass of our relationship. I knew I needed to present a united front between Sheldon and I. Even though I had no intention of keeping the promise, I told him I would never go to another Glamour Punks show just to shut him up.

DAVE ZINK (Blackboard Jungle): I was about 17, and I think I was at the original Red Light District at Sunset and Hudson

before it moved to Hollywood Blvd. I was on a date with some girl that I fancied when some dude and his brother started in with me. It quickly turned into a brawl, and the next thing I know, they're kicking the crap out of me. One guy even broke my nose. And guess who came to my rescue? Mandie.

I barely knew him, but Mandie got these guys off me and even walked me home. A couple of days later, he made contact with me to make sure I was okay. I've always had a fondness for him and respected him over the years for doing that. I don't know that I ever properly thanked him because god knows what those guys would've done if Mandie hadn't jumped in. He'll always have a special place in my heart for doing that.

Sheldon didn't speak to me for a few days after The Glamour Punks show. We had never gone that long without talking before. I was surprised at how angry he was over the whole ordeal. But my 17th birthday was just around the corner and that helped melt the ice between us. The plan was to have a small dinner at Benihana on La Cienega with Dagmar and his singer, Vince.

I have no idea where Sheldon and his band mates found Vince. He was originally from Hungary and barely spoke any English. The most English he knew was in the songs he sang for Dancer, and even then he barely understood what he was singing.

As the four of us ate dinner, Sheldon brought up The Glamour Punks show and got on my case about going to other bands shows. He basically forbade me from ever going to the Strip again, which I found hysterical. The remnants of Ronan trying to rule our relationship with an iron fist were still very fresh in my mind. After surviving that nightmare, I swore I would never let a guy control me again.

"I was going to the Strip before I met you ya know?" I said.

"It looks bad when you go to other bands shows," Sheldon replied.

"It does not," I said rolling my eyes.

"Yes it does. You look like a hussy."

"What is hussy?" Vince asked in his thick Hungarian accent.

"Be quiet and eat the scallops," I told Vince.

117

"I don't look like a hussy," I said directing my attention back to Sheldon. "It's not like I'm standing by the stage, flirting with these guys and flashing my boobs. They're just friends and I've known them a lot longer than I've known you."

"You don't understand that I have a reputation to uphold."

I burst out laughing.

"What reputation? You act like we're Tommy Lee and Heather. No one gives a shit about what we do except for the girls that are trying to hump you," I said.

"I also don't want you getting hurt anymore."

"That's a crock of shit. You could care less that I was kicked in the face. You still haven't asked if I'm okay."

"Look, you shouldn't go down there because it's not safe. I only go because I have to promote. I hate being down there."

"Yeah, I bet," I said raising my eyebrow.

I was sick of arguing with Sheldon. In another attempt to shut him up, I lied and told him I would stop going to the Strip. And besides, there were more than enough people packing those sidewalks for me to go and not run into him anyway.

The following weekend, I made plans to go to the Strip and recruited Sasha to be my wingman. Her only job was to keep an eye out for any potential landmines aka Sheldon or friends of Sheldon that would rat me out.

Friday night went off without a hitch. It wasn't until Saturday night when Sasha and I were doing a final lap up Sunset that Moses himself parted the debaucherous seas and there was Sheldon, Vince, and Nima right in front of Gazzarri's.

Damn it.

Sheldon glared at me as I walked up to him. But before he could start barking at me, help came in the most unexpected form, his personal stalker Misha. I had noticed her earlier in the night passing out flyers for a band called Liquor Sweet.

I continued to make my way towards Sheldon, but Misha reached the boys first and sparked up a conversation with Nima. Annoyed by Misha's presence, Sheldon turned his back and began talking to Vince. Wanting to get Sheldon's attention, Misha jokingly tried to pull on a stack of flyers he had rolled up and put under his arm.

"Get away from me you bucktoothed bitch!" Sheldon said venomously.

"Fuck you, you stupid asshole!" she said as she lunged for Sheldon.

Nima immediately grabbed her and pulled her off to the side as she continued screaming obscenities. Not to say I was happy that crackpot was trying to attack my boyfriend, but it certainly took the heat off me for the time being.

"I don't want any part of YOUR drama. I'm going home," I said with disgust to Sheldon as I walked off.

Once Sasha and I were out of facial view of Sheldon and his band mates, I cracked a smile and giggled with her all the way back to the car.

Needless to say, Sheldon eventually gave in as far as banning me from the Strip. But that didn't stop him from giving me shit every time he saw me there. Especially when I went to see other bands play.

Speaking of girls on the Strip, let me tell you a little bit about the various groups of ladies that hung out in the scene, which I mentioned briefly in an earlier chapter.

At the top of the food chain were the hot girls, and the world was their oyster. They got into shows for free, had their drinks paid for and pretty much anything else they wanted. But a vast majority of these girls were groupies that were passed from band to band like a joint at a keg party.

At the bottom of the food chain were the ugly girls who were usually fans of the band. They would foot the bill for whatever particular band member they were crushing on, JUST so they could be around them. Mixed in with the ugly girls was also a stalker or two.

Then there were the group of girls I belonged to, which were caught somewhere in the middle. We certainly weren't hot but we weren't hideous either. We had befriended a majority of the bands on the Strip without having to sleep with them and actually had their respect. We all got along for the most part, but in every group there always has to be one. That one girl that rubs you the wrong way and completely annoys the shit out of you. For me, that girl was a skinny, lanky little thing named Casey.

Casey was a year younger than me with stringy red hair just down to her shoulders. She had a gap between her two front teeth and a pointy witches nose. She knew all the same bands I did including Dancer. I knew damn well she had a crush on Sheldon too. At first, I found her mildly annoying. But after several instances of her pulling the giggly, flirty act with Sheldon and showing no regard for me as his girlfriend, well, I was just about ready to choke the bitch.

Despite all the dirty looks I shot her, it was blatantly obvious she didn't care how much I hated her. She seemed to feed off it. I quickly realized that Casey was the bratty kid dragging the stick across the fence, and I was the dumb dog chasing it back and forth barking. Sure I could've pulled the caveman act and flat out told her to back off of Sheldon, but that's never been my style. And besides, I wasn't about to give her the satisfaction of knowing she had completely got under my skin. I decided to take a more clever approach in dealing with her.

I was hanging out with Sheldon and his band mates one evening near Bank of America on the Strip, when I spotted Casey and her sister, Terry, near Gazzarri's. They were talking to my friend, or should I say OUR friend, Pepper who was in a band called Strawberry. Casey was holding Peppers hand and laughing at the things he was saying like he was the best thing since sliced bread.

Terry and Casey hugged Pepper goodbye and made their way toward us. Casey was wearing platform combat boots. I secretly hoped that as she crossed the "hill of death" she would fall and snap her neck.

The "hill of death" was a small residential street called Wetherly Drive that divided Gazzarri's and Bank of America. It was one the steepest hills on the small stretch of the Sunset Strip. I witnessed many girls try to maintain their sexy composure in spiked heels while attempting to cross that little street. A majority of them never made it across without eating shit at least once. Luckily, I never fell victim to Wetherly Drive, no pun intended.

As Casey happily skipped over Wetherly Drive unscathed (unfortunately), I knew I was in for another session of her hanging all over Sheldon just to piss me off. She immediately gave Sheldon a big hug and enthusiastically asked when his next show was. *Little kiss ass.*

Terry stood by not saying much to anyone. I decided to spark up a conversation with her, which I had never done before. She was wearing a dress that I thought was really cute, so I asked her about it. Although she was surprised by my inquiry, she went on to tell me about where she bought her dress and a lot of her clothes. Towards the end of our friendly exchange, I noticed Casey ease up her pawing on Sheldon.

"Well I have to meet a few people by the Whisky, so I'll see you guys in a little bit," I said.

After giving Sheldon a big kiss, I smiled at Casey instead of shooting her my normal daggers and then happily walked off. I kept up my cheery demeanor for the next several weeks and noticed Casey gradually start to warm up to me. She stopped slobbering all over Sheldon and even began saying hi to me when she saw me. On a few occasions, she even hugged me hello before saying hi to Sheldon, which shocked the hell out of both of us.

I did start to be genuinely nice to her after a while, but I still held a small bit of resentment from all the times she cozied up to Sheldon. Or maybe I should've directed that anger towards him because he never did anything to stop the flirting. God knows it was never his fault.

"I have to be nice to my fans," he would always say.

Being "nice" was understandable. But to use that as justification for the flirting, kisses, and letting girls hang all over him? Um no. I never bought into that horseshit for a minute. It was all just a test of patience on my part as to how much I would actually put up with.

Strangely enough, once things seemed to be kosher between Casey and myself, I noticed my relationship with Sheldon start on a rapid decline. He became very irritable and we weren't talking everyday as we normally did.

After a few weeks of Sheldon continuing to be elusive, my anxiety began to kick into overdrive. I was sitting in class one day and my mind was going in a million different directions, wondering what the hell could be wrong with him. Instead of waiting till I came home to call him, I decided to do so during my lunch break at school. It was there that I reluctantly ended up discussing my personal life on a public pay phone in front of every hungry kid running in and out of the school cafeteria.

121

Sheldon said he was having "problems" that he wasn't ready to discuss with me yet and needed "space" to figure these things out. He also said he wouldn't be able to call me as much anyway because he couldn't afford his phone bill.

"So we're breaking up then? That's what you're saying?" I said with a lump in my throat.

"I didn't say that. I care about you, but I just can't have a girlfriend right now."

"That means we're breaking up," I reiterated.

"Just hang tight. All I need is a little bit of space."

I began to cry.

"It's really immature to cry. I hate when girls cry," he said.

"Well it's just me being human and we cry sometimes. If you need space, then call me when you're ready to talk."

"Okay Rambo."

"What the fuck? You call me a baby for crying and Rambo for trying to be strong about it? You're an asshole!" I yelled and immediately hung up on him.

In the weeks that followed, things were pretty choppy with Sheldon. We spoke here and there, but not as much as we used to. He still invited me to shows, and I would stupidly go. We would hook up sporadically and that made things even more confusing. It was all just a big mind fuck as to whether we were together or not, which according to him, we weren't. We were on a little bit of a "break".

Great. Just what I need, ANOTHER fucking "break".

One weekend I was sick as a dog, so Sasha went to the Strip with Dagmar while I stayed home and hacked up a lung. The next morning, Sasha called me with some interesting news.

"Dude, when Dagmar and I were walking to her car behind the Whisky, we saw Sheldon and Casey scamming in the parking lot," Sasha said bluntly.

"Scamming" back then was a slang word for making out. I was immediately sick to my stomach. I knew something had been going on between them. It made perfect sense as to why he would always let her hang all over him.

Even though we technically weren't together at the time and on a damn "break", it still pissed me off. I confronted him about it and he did admit to making out with Casey that night, along with a few other nights during our separation. He said they first hooked up shortly after he met me but they never had sex. Yeah, right.

A few days later, Sheldon and I met up in person to hash everything out. He also told me about the personal family problems he was struggling with. We had a really good talk and said we still loved each other, so we decided we would try to give our relationship another shot.

With the end of the school year fast approaching, there was still one more teenage milestone I did want to participate in. Senior prom.

Unfortunately, finances in the family were very tight because my dad was on disability leave due to a recent back injury. His income was considerably less than what he earned while he was working, so I knew I couldn't ask him for money. I had the cost of a prom dress, a yearbook, and a class ring coming up with no money to pay for any of it.

I mentioned my dire straits to a classmate named Hannah who worked part time as a telemarketer for Culligan Water. She was able to work a little magic, and within a few days I was making minimum wage with her at Culligan. For three days a week after school, I would cold call people and bother them during their dinnertime, asking if I could have a representative come over to set up a sample water filter on their faucet.

As with any sales job there was a quota, which I came nowhere close to making. Needless to say, about a month later I was fired. The money I saved up from Culligan wasn't enough to pay for everything I wanted. I decided I would have to graduate high school without a class ring.

The financial strain put a damper on my prom. I wanted to buy a beautiful dress with beautiful jewels and shoes to match, and be taken in a limo. Instead, I chose a neutral color for my dress so it would match jewelry my mom already had, I would borrow Lucy's car to pick up Sheldon, and the tailor that made my dress felt so bad I was literally counting pennies to pay for everything, that he threw in a pair of shoes for half price.

Hannah needed a date for the prom. Since she had gone with me to a few Dancer shows recently, she ended up asking their roadie, Alan, to be her date. Sasha wanted to go too, but the prom was for Rosemead High students only. Luckily, Hannah knew a fellow senior who wasn't going, so we had them buy a ticket and give it to Sasha. When I asked who her date was going to be, she said she was bringing Alex. I'll be honest, I was a little jealous when I heard she was bringing him. It certainly sparked some residual feelings I had, but I was still very much focused on trying to make things work with Sheldon.

As I drove to pick up Sheldon on the night of my prom, I wondered what he might be wearing. He didn't mention anything about buying or renting a tux. I figured he might be decked out in rocker clothes, which would be a little weird, but I didn't have a problem with it. I felt I was just a tiny bit cooler than the rest of my classmates because I was dating a musician, as opposed to a typical high school boy.

When I arrived at Sheldon's, he opened the front door fully decked out in a tuxedo. He even took a shower and did his hair. I was surprised that he went to that trouble. He only got that gussied up when he had a show, sans the tux of course.

My prom was held at the Hyatt Regency in Long Beach. When we arrived, Hannah and Sasha were already at our table with Alex and Alan. I hate to admit it, but once I caught a glance of Alex in his tux, I was a little jealous that he was Sasha's date and not mine. I did love Sheldon don't get me wrong, but Alex was much more suited for an event like this. He was friendly, funny and loved to dance, whereas Sheldon literally bolted outside with Alan within moments of us walking into the ballroom.

I spent most of the night talking with Alex. We laughed about old times and caught up on all the recent happenings of everyone in the Alhambra crew. We danced with the girls, and although I was having fun, I was slightly disappointed that Sheldon wasn't engaging with my friends and the event in general.

Sheldon and Alan finally made their way back into the ballroom as dinner was being served. Unfortunately, Sheldon and I stayed just long enough to eat and take some professional portraits. Before heading out, Alex asked me if I wanted to slow dance at least once before I left. He didn't seem to care whether or not that would piss off Sheldon. Quite frankly, Sheldon didn't seem to care either. I didn't take Alex up on the offer, although I should have. Instead, I thanked him for being so sweet. I tried to play it off like it was my idea to leave even though it was blatantly obvious Sheldon was the one chomping at the bit to get out of there.

Aside from maintaining a relationship with Sheldon, I was also balancing the chaos of wrapping up my last few weeks of high school. Finals were just around the corner when I realized I didn't have a walking partner for the graduation ceremony. The school faculty wanted the walking partners to be boy/girl. I was shit out of luck because all the guys I knew in my class already had walking partners. When I mentioned this to Arwen and Ariah, I was happy to find Arwen was in the same solo boat I was, so we agreed to walk in the ceremony together.

My last week of high school was hectic with graduation rehearsals and finals. Senior Wills were also distributed, which were basically a book full of dedications from seniors to other seniors, wishing them well in the future and recalling high school memories.

I read through the Senior Wills and noticed that Sadie had put in a Will. She made a dedication to her boyfriend then wished well to Carla and Tasha. To my complete surprise, she included me too.

I happened to see Sadie at her locker later that day and asked her why she included me in her Senior Will. She said she had a change of heart and wanted to put the Ronan drama behind us. We immediately warmed up to each other and caught up on everything that had been going on in our lives. There was so much to talk about! I didn't realize it had been well over a year if not more since I had spoken with her.

The day of graduation, I raced to school to meet up with Arwen for the ceremony. I walked into the main building where all the seniors were but there was no sign of Arwen. I knew there were other girls like myself that didn't have male walking partners. We were told earlier in the week we would be walking at the end of the line, so I made my way down the line as everyone gathered next to his or her walking partner. I was waiting for a few minutes when a teacher pulled me out of line. She told me to stand with a guy named Kent Jackson who I knew briefly from my days at Muscatel.

"Actually, I already have a walking partner, Arwen Gordon. She's not here yet," I said to the teacher.

"She'll have to walk with someone else. Kent doesn't have a walking partner and we need to keep the boy girl formation," the teacher replied.

"But I don't want to walk with him, I want to walk with Arwen. I don't want her to have to walk by herself."

"She'll be fine, we'll get her another walking partner."

The teacher moved me up in line next to Kent. A few minutes later, we were just about to march onto the football field when I noticed Arwen bolting up the hall in her cap and gown. The same teacher that paired me with Kent stopped her. Arwen pointed at me and pleaded with the teacher to let her go. I looked at the formation of the line behind me and Arwen wasn't going to have a partner. She was going to have to walk the field alone, dead last. She stood there looking at me with her arms crossed. I put my hands in the air and mouthed the words "I'm sorry". She shot me a dirty look and turned away. I felt awful.

As I walked onto the field in my cap and gown, I thought I would be relieved that my school days were finally over. I always hated everything that had to do with school. I couldn't stand doing homework or getting up early in the morning. But when I looked around at the rest of my classmates, many that I had known since my days at Janson, a wave of sadness came over me. Everything I had taken for granted and wanted to leave behind for so long, were suddenly things I desperately wanted to hold on to.

After the ceremony, I went to find Arwen. I tried to explain it wasn't my idea to walk with Kent, but she wasn't having it. She felt I had jumped at the opportunity to ditch her and stormed off.

Arwen wasn't the only grumpy one at my graduation. I stood on the football field for almost an hour, chatting with other classmates and my family as I waited for Sheldon to rear his platinum blond head. I expected him to shower me with graduation gifts and congratulations, but he was a no show.

When I came home to change after the ceremony, I had a message from Sheldon waiting for me on my answering machine. He said he couldn't make it to my graduation because he had to go to a Scorpions concert at the Forum to promote an upcoming Dancer show. I couldn't believe he had the nerve to use that as an excuse. The concert wasn't until later that evening and he knew damn well my graduation was taking place in the afternoon. I desperately needed to blow off some steam, and I knew all the seniors were going to a graduation party at my friend, Dave's house. So I did what any other scorned teenage girl would do. I went to the party and got drunk off my ass.

I didn't have a set plan after graduating high school. But the last thing I wanted to do was go to college right away. Without having a steady schedule of school or work in my life, it left a lot of free time for me to hang out in Hollywood, which Sheldon obviously wasn't happy about. He was still hounding me about not going to the Strip anymore, and I kept right on ignoring his demands.

On the same note, Dancer had a show coming up at Gazzarri's, and Sheldon wanted to know what I was doing after the show. Dancer usually threw after parties at their rehearsal studio following most of their shows, which he knew I always went to. So I found it a little strange that he would ask me what my plans were for the night. I told him I planned on going to the after party if there was one, and he abruptly told me there would be no after party. He said he was going home right after the show and badgered me to do the same.

The night of the show, I picked up Faye and we made our way out to Hollywood. When we walked into Gazzarri's, I spotted Sheldon's ex-girlfriend, Evie, who Faye happened to be good friends with. I was about to duck out and go to the bathroom when Faye insisted I come with her to say hi, which I reluctantly did.

I had seen Evie around the Strip from time to time, but we never officially met until Faye introduced us that night. My initial first reaction should have been to dislike her, but she seemed very nice and was extremely soft spoken.

Despite the lack of tension between Evie and I, it was still a bit awkward trying to partake in casual conversation with her. I tried to give subtle hints to Faye about relocating to another part of the club, but she didn't catch on. We ended up standing with Evie throughout the entire Dancer set.

When Dancer finished their last song, Alan walked onstage and threw out a handful of flyers to the audience. I glanced at one that had fallen beside me and quickly realized it wasn't a flyer. It was a map with directions to a Dancer after party that wasn't at their rehearsal studio.

I saw Sheldon after the show and questioned him about the after party. He said it was a last minute thing that was planned by two random fans (girls of course). The girls were providing all the food and alcohol, so of COURSE he and his band mates had to be nice and accept the invitation. He said he was only staying long enough to make an appearance and would call me when he got home. I was still annoyed, but relented and ended up going home after the show because I wasn't feeling well.

I passed out shortly after I came home that night. When I woke the next morning, I realized Sheldon had never called me as promised. As a matter of fact, I didn't hear from him the entire day. Faye was the only person who reached out to me, from Evie's house of all people. She said they both had things to tell me.

According to Faye, shortly after I left Gazzarri's a girl named Jezebel was hanging all over Sheldon. He allegedly left with her a short time later.

Jezebel was about a year or so older than me and regular on the Strip. I didn't know much about her, other than she was a writer for *Rock City News*. To make matters worse, Evie got on the phone and told me she had slept with Sheldon a few weeks earlier. He told her that he and I were on a "break". She also said it was around the same time that she heard he was hanging out with Jezebel as well. My head was about to explode.

Sheldon called me the next day, so I confronted him about Jezebel and Evie. He said Evie was a lying, disgruntled ex that wanted him back and that Faye was a compulsive liar. He also said nothing was going on with Jezebel and that she was just a friend he caught a ride with to the after party. Against my better judgment, I stupidly believed Sheldon and let it go.

8

EMANCIPATION, CHEATING, AND REBOUNDS

A few months had passed since I graduated high school, and that's when I met Nima's girlfriend, Missy. She was a petite brunette with big brown eyes and straight dark hair that cascaded down to her ass. She had just turned 21 and happened to mention she was looking for a new roommate. I joked around at the idea of moving in with her. I didn't take it seriously because I was only 17. My birthday was still many months away, and Missy suggested I be emancipated. I told her she was nuts.

Although the thought of moving out on my own was beyond exciting, being emancipated made me think of disgruntled child stars that were getting back at their parents for stealing their money. I felt it might be insulting to my mom to suggest such a thing. I also knew there was no way in hell she would ever agree to it anyway.

As for bringing up the idea to my dad, he didn't have much say in the situation. He was already settled into his new life with Pamela and her three sons. It was a major blow because we had always been so close up until the time of my parents divorce. But he had a new life. I figured I should start a new one as well. After a few days of long contemplation, I finally made the decision to ask my mom about being emancipated.

I walked on eggshells as I carefully and respectfully brought up the idea to my mom. To my complete surprise, she quickly agreed to it and wasn't insulted in the least. I didn't have to do any convincing or arguing on my behalf. Hell, she even said there was a notary at her bank just down the street that could draft up the paperwork.

Damn. I didn't think I was that bad of a kid. Her being so open to the idea made me wonder how much of a demon seed I really was.

"Am I that big of a pain in the ass?" I asked.

"Yes," she said without hesitation.

"Thanks a lot."

"Well you are Marisa. You're a stubborn mule. If I don't emancipate you, you'll find a way to move out anyway. I might as well let you go and make your own mistakes."

I didn't appreciate her predicting my failure and intended to prove her wrong.

A few weeks later, Sheldon picked me up along with a few of my meager belongings and took me to my new home in Canoga Park. Missy greeted me at the front door with a piece of chicken in her hand. I noticed all the lights were out in the apartment too. The only thing lighting up the room were a few candles that were sitting on her dining room table.

"Did I interrupt a romantic evening?" I asked.

"Not at all, the electricity was turned off," she said as she let me in.

"How long is it going to be off for?"

"Oh it'll be on tomorrow. I forgot to have the service changed to my name. Here, have a piece of chicken," she said as she pushed a KFC box towards me.

I took a piece of chicken as Sheldon brought in the rest of my things. He left a short time later for band rehearsal, and I enjoyed my first dinner in my new apartment with Missy.

I was stoked to be out of my mom's house. I had no one to check in with and could come and go as I pleased. I could have parties and do whatever I wanted with no more curfews! My only handicap was not having my own car or a job, but Missy had recently handled the latter.

She told me I would be working with her as a hostess at a place called Club Mustang in downtown L.A. She didn't mention what my job duties would be, so I figured it was a standard hostess job. I didn't have any prior experience welcoming or seating people, but how hard could it be?

A few days after moving in, it was time to start my new job. I asked Missy what the dress code was. She said to dress like I was going to a club. I gussied myself up and rode with her to a sketchy area in downtown Los Angeles. We walked through the poorly lit parking lot, and I followed her to the front of an unmarked building. It didn't resemble anything that looked like a club or restaurant. There wasn't even a sign outside to let you know anything was there.

I followed her up a flight of stairs lit only by white Christmas lights that streamed alongside the walls. When we reached the top, we walked into what looked like a nightclub. There was a dance floor, a bar, and a backroom full of couches where people sat around talking. Near the entrance was a counter with a cash register and what looked like a bullpen of girls just sitting around in chairs talking to each other. I continued to follow Missy through the club and into a small office where a grumpy old Asian woman told me to sit down.

"You 18?" she asked.

"Yes," I said lying my ass off.

I handed her my modified drivers license, which Missy and I had illegally altered the night before. She barely glanced at my ID then handed me a W9 tax form and a pen.

"You work any day you want, three day minimum each week. You done filling this out, you go sit," she said and walked out.

"What does she mean by 'you sit'? What am I going to be doing exactly?" I asked Missy.

"You're a hostess. You hang out. You dance, you talk. It's easy money."

"That sounds like a stripper," I said uncomfortably.

"You are NOT a stripper," she said adamantly. "You wear what you have on. You don't take any clothes off, you don't dance on a pole and you don't give lap dances. Sometimes customers will dance with you on the dance floor, other times they'll sit and talk your ear off about how shitty their life is. These losers pay for your time."

"And that's it?"

"That's it. We sit with the other girls in the bullpen. If a guy likes you, you take your time card and clock in. When they're done spending time with you, you clock out."

"That sounds pretty desperate," I said mildly grossed out.

"Fuck them," she said coldly. "You get 80% of the money, and if they're any kind of man they'll tip you too. Oh and one last thing, don't offer any personal information or give them your real name because they will ask."

"I have to pick a fake name?"

"Yes. Pick something that's easy to remember. What's the first name that comes to mind?"

"Nikki Sixx!" I said with a big smile across my face.

Missy rolled her eyes.

"Fine. From now on if anyone asks your name is 'Nikki', and you have no last name. Got it?"

"Got it," I said nodding my head.

I had a bad feeling about that job. Hell, I had a bad feeling the moment we pulled into that creepy parking lot, but I wanted to prove my mom wrong. I was determined to be independent and make it on my own.

I nervously filled out my tax form, turned it in and followed Missy out to the bullpen. I hadn't sat more than ten minutes when a scrawny Asian guy asked for my hand and we ended up dancing to a few awful 70's disco songs. He barely said a word to me and when he did speak, I could tell he didn't speak very good English. After an hour of dancing, twinkle toes had enough. I grabbed my timecard and walked up to the register to clock out. He paid for the time, left me a $50 cash tip and said goodbye. No harm no foul. It was easy money.

About a week or so later, my mom asked how my job hunt was going. I had no intention of telling her what I was doing for a living. Not that I thought I was doing anything that scandalous, but there wasn't a way for me to explain my job without her thinking I was either a prostitute or a stripper. So I lied and told her I had a job at a clothing store.

A few weeks went by, and I reveled in being an independent 17 year old. I had a good paying job and things finally seemed to be going well with Sheldon. The only downside was that I made the most money on the weekends. That meant I couldn't go to the Strip every Friday and Saturday night like I used to. Other than that, things were going great in my world.

On the other side of the apartment though, things seemed to be up and down with Nima and Missy. Right before I met her I knew he was seeing at least one other girl, but I didn't know what he was up to once I moved into the apartment. Ironically, she was always worried about Nima cheating on her. So you can imagine my surprise when she started cheating on him with a guy named Gary.

We met Gary and his friend, Sam, at a Denny's restaurant by our apartment one night after work. They were both 21, clean cut American guys. They had just rented a huge house in Calabasas and made good money running their own business, which was quite the polar opposite of our current boyfriends.

Sam was tall and slender with short brown hair and blue eyes. He was absolutely hysterical. He had a smart, witty sense of humor and had us in tears within minutes of meeting him. Although Gary was the more attractive of the two with his blond hair and hazel eyes, he was dopey to say the least. He would chime in on Sam's jokes thinking he made them funnier when in reality they always fell flat. Not wanting to make him feel bad, the three of us would throw in a few polite chuckles for his efforts.

Missy went from zero to flirting with Gary in a matter of moments. That made it crystal clear to me she had no intention of mentioning anything about Nima. I knew it was a matter of time before she would pair me off with Sam as if we were boarding Noah's Ark, so I quickly mentioned I had a boyfriend. I really liked Sam as a person, but my focus was on trying to make my relationship work with Sheldon.

Over the course of the next few weeks, when Sheldon and Nima weren't at our apartment, Missy and I would go meet up with Sam and Gary. We would go to their company softball games and to parties at their house. It was a blast hanging out with them, although it was a little awkward on nights when it was just the four of us at their place. It was blatantly obvious Missy was hooking up with Gary, whereas Sam and I were most definitely NOT. I'm sure it was annoying for him, but he seemed to be a good sport about it. We would usually watch movies or have drinks out on their humongous patio, laughing our asses off while we waited for Gary and Missy to finish um, whatever they were doing.

While I did enjoy hanging out with Sam and Gary, I was tired of lying to Sheldon and Nima about where we were going, especially to Nima. We had become pretty close since I started dating Sheldon, and he was like a big brother to me. He always looked out for me when I was on the Strip, and he had recently surprised me by fixing up an old electric guitar of mine when I mentioned to him I wanted to start playing again. .

I didn't always accompany Missy when she would go over Gary and Sam's house. But on the nights I stayed home, that put me in the uncomfortable position of having to make excuses to Nima anytime he would call. On a few occasions, he even called in the wee morning hours and I would have to say something dumb like she had a late night Del Taco craving to explain why she wasn't home.

I didn't want to lie to Nima anymore, so I felt the best thing to do was to stop hanging out with Sam and Gary altogether. I also told Missy I wasn't going to cover for her anymore and that she had better figure out what she wanted to do with Gary. Naturally, this caused quite a bit of tension between us.

Shortly after I came to that decision, a rumor began floating around that Nima was cheating on Missy, which made her absolutely postal. Even though I thought she was a total hypocrite, I kept my thoughts to myself because there was enough friction between us already. I just hoped that if I gave the situation enough time it would work itself out.

Meanwhile, I had been making bank at Club Mustang for just over two months when I noticed a rapid decline in my customer base. I couldn't figure out why. At the end of another money challenged day at work, I was grabbing some things from my locker when Tina, a veteran hostess, struck up a conversation with me. Tina had been there for three years. Aside from a casual smile or hello, that was the first time she had ever sparked up a conversation with me.

"Had a slow night?" she asked.

"More like nights. It's been a gradual decline. I don't know why I'm not getting clocked out as much lately," I said.

"You're kiddin right?"

"Not at all. I'm nice to every customer, and I don't have a reputation of being a bitch. I have no idea what's going on."

"Well you're half right."

"About what?" I asked.

"Your reputation honey."

I looked at her cluelessly.

"Do I need to spell it out?" she continued.

"It would help," I said.

"S-E-X. Girl you don't put out, that's the problem."

"WHAT? Wait a minute, who is putting out?"

"You must be walkin around with blinders on honey. Everyone around here knows you gotta do a little something to keep the customers coming back for more."

I felt like retching but kept a straight face. I didn't need Tina dragging me out to the parking lot to beat my ass like she did with another girl that made the mistake of "disrespecting" her a few nights earlier.

"Girl, when you're new you get checked out like mad cuz they wanna see what you're all about. But when they realize there ain't no fire brewin in that oven…well you see what happens," she continued.

What the hell is wrong with me?

I knew something was shady the moment Missy first led me up those steps. I let my good judgment be clouded just because I wanted to be a grown up and move out of my moms house. There was no question on what needed to be done. I had to quit Club Mustang immediately. Instead, I would get the job I originally told my mom about and work in a clothing store. It's what most girls my age were doing for work anyway. It wouldn't be an exciting job, but it was something I wouldn't have to hide from my family and friends anymore.

I was so glad Missy had taken that night off work and wasn't around to hear what Tina told me. I needed time to digest the reality of what Club Mustang was all about. Then it hit me as

135

I drove Missy's car home that night. *How is SHE able to sustain her job at the club for so long?*

When I came home, Missy was in the living room watching TV. I told her I needed to talk to her. When she turned around and looked at me with that sour puss of hers, I realized what a shitty mood she was in and how I couldn't have picked a worse time.

"I'm quitting my job," I bluntly.

"Why?" she asked.

"Well...I haven't been getting a lot of business lately, and Tina told me something tonight that really creeped me out."

"What did she say?"

"She basically said my business was slowing down because I don't fuck around with the customers."

"Oh please, like you didn't know that was going on," she said as if annoyed by naivety.

"How would I know? I've never seen anything happen at the club."

"Of course they don't do anything AT the club, but you had to have known."

"I didn't, I swear!" I squealed.

"Well now you know. God forbid mommy and daddy find out."

"Exactly. I don't want them to know I ever worked in a place like that. That's why I'm quitting."

"So what if they find out? You're an adult now. You can make your own decisions."

"An adult? I'm an emancipated 17-year-old! I'm not going to stay at that fucked up job and start banging the customers like the rest of the girls. Gross," I said as I crossed my arms.

Although I didn't know what or whom Missy was doing at Club Mustang, I was willing to put it aside. I wanted so badly to stay in the apartment and not have to move back to my mom's house.

She bowed her head to me and said, "Oh excuse me, Miss Perfect Statue of Virginity. Is Club Mustang beneath you?"

"You know what? Ever since I stopped lying to Nima for you, you've been a total bitch on wheels. Especially since you found out he was cheating on you. So stop taking your problems out on me!"

"Fuck you, you fucking cunt!" she snapped.

"Go fuck yourself Missy! You're just pissed because at 21 you still don't have the balls that I do at 17 to stand up for yourself!"

Oh shit. Well at least I've given her a justifiable reason for being mad at me now.

"I don't need to take this shit from a jailbait teenybopper," she said as she grabbed her car keys and stomped towards the front door.

She flung open the front door and said, "And stay out of my fucking room while I'm gone!"

"I will because I don't want to get herpes!" I screamed as she slammed the door behind her.

I didn't want to eat crow from my mom. But it had to taste better than the knife crazy Missy would probably plunge into my neck in the middle of the night. I knew I had to move out. Not the next day or month, IMMEDIATELY. I ran to the phone and called Sheldon.

"Hey do you have your car?" I asked.

"Yeah, I just got home from dropping off my mom. Why?"

"I'm moving out, like right now. Missy is straight up *Looney Tunes*. I'm going to have to sleep with one eye open if I stay here."

"Really? Wow baby that sucks."

"Yeah, can you 'wow' your ass over here? She just left and I want to be gone by the time she gets back."

I hung up with Sheldon and ran around the apartment like a panicked Chihuahua, collecting my things as quickly as I could. Luckily, there wasn't much to pack. I didn't have any furniture. The only items I had aside from clothes were my two guitars and a pile of blankets I was using as a makeshift mattress in my bedroom.

I threw everything I had into a suitcase and a few trash bags. I grabbed my guitars and walked out to the living room. I sadly took one last look at my first apartment. Damn, it was such a cute place too.

Am I over reacting by choosing to move out so quickly?

In all honesty, I wasn't comfortable in that apartment anymore and hadn't been for quite a few weeks. I was happiest when Missy wasn't there. Anytime I heard her stomping up the steps to our front door, I would barricade myself in my bedroom like a child hiding from an angry parent.

I peeked into my bathroom to make sure I hadn't left anything behind when I heard knocking on my front door. I opened the door and let Sheldon in. I threw my apartment keys on the dining room table as he began to grab my things. I did one last sweep of the apartment and walked into Missy's bedroom to make sure I didn't forget anything. Sheldon grabbed the last trash bag of my belongings and asked if there was anything else. I told him that was it. I walked back out to the living room and picked up my guitars. I was about to walk out the front door when I thought of how Missy called me a cunt. I walked back in, turned on every light in the apartment and set the A/C to it's coldest setting. *NOW I was a cunt.*

When we arrived to Sheldon's, I thought about calling my mom to tell her what happened, but I decided to wait until the morning. I had enough drama for one night and the last thing I needed was to hear her say, "I told you so."

The summer of 1991 was coming to an end. I found myself jobless and living back with my mom once again. But it wasn't long before I settled into my old routine of borrowing cars from my family and resuming my place once again on the Sunset Strip.

By this time, Dancer had gone through two bass players and just hired their third, a short but cute brunette named Jason. With a new band member, came the need for a new band photo. Nima booked a loft in downtown L.A. to do the photo shoot. I came along to help out with hair and makeup.

Nima and Vince were already at the studio when Sheldon and I arrived. I had just begun to lay out hair product when Jason walked in with two girls that he introduced as his girlfriend, Gina, and her younger sister, Lisa. He politely declined my services, saying that the girls would take care of his hair and makeup. That was fine with me. I had my hands full prepping the rest of the guys anyway.

While I crimped Nima's long black locks, I noticed Lisa looking at Sheldon as he touched up his eyeliner. As a matter of fact, I caught her staring at Sheldon quite a bit over the course of the evening. She even went so far as to be mildly flirty with him, which naturally put me on edge.

And while we're on the subject of photo shoots, let me tell you a little bit about the band wars on the Sunset Strip.

When it came down to promoting a bands show, it was all about being raunchy in those days. The nastier the ad the better, and it wasn't long before Dancer jumped on the debauchery bandwagon. They had a headlining show coming up at the Whisky, so they planned on doing another photo shoot that would eventually be a full-page ad.

The slogan for the ad was, "Miss this one and you're going over my knee!" The premise had a girl lying on the lap of each band member in a bikini bottom with the assumption being that they were about to get spanked. I don't know whose stupid idea that was. I was not happy about it in the least.

Being Sheldon's girlfriend, he obviously asked me to be the girl on his lap. He must have noticed my apprehension because he said I didn't have to do it and would respect my decision either way. He also casually mentioned that Lisa offered to take my place if I wasn't going to do it, SHOCKER. Like I didn't see that one coming. The mere thought of Lisa lying across Sheldon's lap with his hand inches away from her barely covered bottom made me psychotically nauseous.

The photo shoot was fast approaching. I still hadn't given Sheldon an answer on whether I would do the ad. The only reason I was even considering it was to keep Lisa away from him. I sure as hell had no desire to be spread eagle across anybody's lap publicly, even if it was my own boyfriend. Surprisingly, my good sense outweighed my teenage jealousy. A few days before the shoot, I told Sheldon I couldn't go through with it.

I chose to stay home on the day of the photo shoot. I was practically chewing on the edges of my bedpost, wondering at what moment Lisa would be spreading her rat infested private parts across Sheldon's lap. I was nauseous the entire day and breathed a sigh of relief once he called to tell me the shoot was over.

A week or so later, the ad was a full-page spread in *BAM Magazine*. It was worse than I had imagined.

Lisa was spread across Sheldon's lap, bare bottom with her underwear dangling off her ankle. Her hands were near her mouth with an "Oh my!" look across her face, while Sheldon had one hand lifted in the air as if he were about to spank her. I would've loved to burn the pants Sheldon wore on that photo shoot with him in them. But after seeing that raunchy ad, I was more grateful that my rump was still anonymous to the greater Los Angeles area.

I don't know what happened on the set of that photo shoot, but Lisa's flirting with Sheldon became more obnoxious after that ad came out. It became the main subject of many fights between us. He swore nothing was going on, but I sensed otherwise.

Rather than dwell on Lisa, I tried to focus my energies on my 18th birthday, which was just around the corner. Sheldon asked what I wanted to do for my birthday. I said I didn't care, but of course I did! The photo shoot with Lisa had caused quite a bit of friction between us. I wanted retribution damn it!

I didn't want to make plans with my friends just yet because I was hoping Sheldon would put forth the effort to do something special for my birthday, so I waited. I waited for him to tell me he was going to take me out to dinner or throw me a party. Some little something to show he was trying to make things better between us. But the weeks passed, my birthday was just a few days away and he was still asking me what I wanted to do. I sadly relented and went with Hannah's plans, which was to have Sheldon and I over to our friend, Bobby's house for dinner at 8:00pm.

The day of my birthday dinner, Sheldon picked me up and brought me back to his house. He had to leave to band rehearsal but promised he would be home by 7:00pm. So I hung out with Laney that afternoon and made sure I was dressed and ready to go by 7.

By a quarter after seven, Sheldon wasn't home. I figured he was just running a little late. As long as he came home by seven thirty, we could rush to Bobby's and be fashionably late.

Seven thirty passed, eight, nine, and then ten. Shortly before 10:30pm, Sheldon casually walked in the door.

"Sorry, rehearsal ran late. I'm gonna shower real quick, then we can go," he said as he rushed past Laney and I.

Laney followed right on his tail and bitched him out for fucking up my birthday dinner. God bless her, she always stuck up for me more than I stuck up for myself.

A half hour later, Sheldon emerged from the bathroom ready to go. I grabbed my purse and walked out the front door without saying a word to him.

By the time we arrived at Bobby's, it was just past midnight. There were about ten people sitting in the living room, none of which were friends of mine. There were empty liquor bottles and beer cans lying around with a few dilapidating balloons and a half eaten birthday cake on the coffee table in front of me. Hannah peeked out from the kitchen, then ran up and attacked me with a big hug.

"Happy Birthday! Where the fuck have you been? I had a big surprise party planned and everything!" she said as she continued to hug me.

My blood began to boil. I didn't know what to say. I should have called Sheldon out in front of everyone for being an insensitive asshole. Instead, I apologized to Hannah for being so ridiculously late.

"There were like a hundred people here. Watch!" she said as she ran to hook up her camcorder to a TV.

I sat on the floor with Hannah and watched my friends from the Alhambra crowd like Alex, Sasha, Jude, and Dagmar, along with a bunch of kids from Rosemead High that I graduated with. They were all drunk, yelling into the camera "Where are you? You're missing your party!"

I grew livid as I continued watching the footage of my friends partying it up. There they were having a great time while I had been waiting on Sheldon's couch, twiddling my thumbs like an asshole. I wanted to leave the party, but I couldn't. Not after all the trouble Hannah went through. I looked at the faces around the living room. All that were left were the random stoners that didn't give a rat's ass what the occasion was. They were just there to party.

"I can't believe they all left already. I know I'm really late, but it's barely midnight. Where did they go?" I asked.

"We were running out of alcohol, and they figured you had flaked on your own party. So they all went to Dave's to finish off some leftover booze from his last party," she said.

I was ready to put my fist through a wall. Instead, I very calmly asked Hannah to make me a cocktail.

"Ooh sorry, we actually drank all the hard alcohol. We have beer though. You want a beer?" she asked sweetly.

I didn't want a beer.

"Sure, I'll have a beer," I said trying to smile.

I sat on the couch next to Sheldon and didn't say a word. He didn't ask for a drink or even make conversation with me. He just sat there looking bored and annoyed, which made me hate him even more.

I only made it halfway through my beer before telling Hannah I was going to leave. I just couldn't take it anymore. I had done my best to put on a brave face. I didn't want to be around anyone, especially Sheldon, so I asked him to take me home.

When I came home, I walked into my bedroom and flopped down on my bed. I was so grateful that the day was over. What a shitty day and a shitty boyfriend I had. It certainly couldn't get any worse right? That's when I flipped on my TV and it got worse.

There was a news report that my favorite male singer, Freddie Mercury, had passed away that day from pneumonia brought on by AIDS. *Happy fucking birthday to me.*

I didn't talk to Sheldon for a few days. When he did call, it was to tell me that Dancer had been picked up to do a small tour of the Midwest. They would be leaving in a few weeks. He wanted to see me before he left to make amends, so I stupidly gave in and met up with him.

We had a long talk about everything that had transpired over the last few months. He also finally apologized for my birthday debacle. We spent a lot of time together before he left on tour. It was the happiest I had been with Sheldon in a very long time. I was actually starting to believe things were finally going to work out between us. Then a few days before he was set to leave, I was woken up by a call from Laney around 3:00 am on Thanksgiving morning.

"I hate to be the one to tell you this, but I don't want you getting fucked over by my stupid brother anymore," she whispered.

"Why, what's going on?" I asked, still half asleep.

"Lisa's here at the house. He's been cheating on you for weeks," she blurted out.

I suddenly found myself wide-awake and very sick to my stomach.

"Don't tell him I told you or he'll fucking kill me," she said.

I was absolutely speechless. I didn't know what to say.

"Are you okay?" she asked.

"Not really," I said as I got choked up.

"I'm sorry, but I thought you should know. Listen, I gotta hang up. Call the house back and make up an excuse to tell Sheldon you're coming over. I'll help you kick her ass, just get over here now!" she said and quickly hung up.

My heart was racing. I knew I was about to lose my shit on Sheldon. I needed to find a place where I could rip him a new one without waking up the entire San Gabriel Valley. Since Lucy was staying over at Tim's that night, I felt her car was my best option. I grabbed my cordless phone and quietly climbed into her car. I made sure all the windows were rolled up and then I called Sheldon.

To my surprise, he answered his phone. I was already borderline hysterical, so I made up a bullshit story about having a nightmare and blamed my tears on the dream I had. I said I didn't want to sleep alone that night and needed to come over.

"You can't come over," he said.

"Why not?" I demanded.

"Because I'm about to go to sleep in a few minutes."

"You can sleep when I get there. I'll be over in twenty minutes."

"I'm going to sleep after we get off the phone."

"You're falling asleep RIGHT after we hang up? Are you narcoleptic?"

He continued to give lame reasons on why I couldn't come over. I cornered him on every excuse. After a good half hour, I could tell he was exhausted with our Ping-Pong match, and to be honest, I was too.

"Look. I know Lisa's there. That's the reason you don't want me to come over," I said.

"No she's not. I keep telling you, nothings going on with her."

"Don't lie to me, I know she's there!"

"Why would she be here?"

"To fuck you, what else! I know she's there, and you're a fucking asshole for cheating on me!"

"Believe what you want."

"I can't believe you don't even care!"

"I do care, but she's not here!"

"YOU'RE A LYING PIECE OF SHIT AND YOU CAN GO TO HELL!" I screamed and hung up.

I turned on the radio and "Bastard" by Mötley Crüe was playing on KNAC. *How fitting.*

I cried until the sky turned a light shade of purple and the smallest rays of sunshine began to come up over the horizon. My face felt tight from being drenched with salty tears. I was absolutely exhausted, and I knew my mom would be waking up soon. I wiped my face with my oversized sweatshirt and then snuck back into my house and passed out.

I woke up sometime in the late morning to the smell of Thanksgiving turkey overtaking my house. But there would be no traditional sit down dinner with my family that day. It would just be my mom, Ginger, and me. Lucy was spending Thanksgiving at Tim's house, and my dad was spending the holiday with his new family.

I got out of bed to get something to drink. But once I saw my red puffy eyes in the mirror, I climbed back into bed and went right back to sleep.

I woke up a few hours later to the sound of gentle knocks on my bedroom door. It was my mom telling me that Thanksgiving chow was ready. I got up to make a plate of food and spent the rest of the day in bed picking at bits of turkey while watching *The Twilight Zone* marathon.

I remember the *Use Your Illusion* albums by Guns N' Roses were big at the time. "November Rain" was on heavy rotation. Even to this day, every time I hear that song it brings me back to eating Thanksgiving dinner in my old bedroom and watching *The Twilight Zone* episode where William Shatner spots that thing in a fuzzy suit on the airplane wing.

A few days passed with no word from Sheldon. He finally called the night before he left for tour and said we would talk about everything in person when he got back. *Whatever.*

I still loved Sheldon despite the fact he had been cheating on me for god knows how long. At the same time, I was glad to have him leave. I knew if he was around, there was a chance I might forgive him and take him back. I hoped our time apart would help me realize that I really needed to just dump him once and for all.

A few days after Sheldon left for tour, my friend, Mark, invited me to see his band, Electric, play at the Whisky. My first thought was not to go. Not only because Mark's band sucked but I was an absolute wreck over Sheldon. The last thing I wanted to do was be in a club full of people. On the other hand, I was also sick of wallowing in my room, which I had been doing everyday since Sheldon left.

I told Mark I would go to the show. I thought about calling Faye or Sasha to go with me but decided it was best if I went alone. I wasn't sure how long I was going to stay and didn't want to be responsible for ruining anybody's evening.

When I arrived at the Whisky, I talked to my friend, Bear, who was one of the bouncers. He said I looked sad and asked why I was there by myself. I told him I hated boys and needed a drink. I'm sure he knew I was underage, but my ID said I was Lucinda Tellez, age 21. Thank god for older sisters. I had mooched Lucy's ID since I was 15 to get into 18 and over clubs. Now that she was 21? The world was my oyster.

I walked into the Whisky and noticed Heidi Stossel who was married to Teddy, Marks singer. I had always heard crazy stories about Teddy and Heidi's volatile relationship, but in Hollywood you never know what's true and what isn't. I was having that very thought when Teddy walked up to Heidi, and they went from zero to screaming in just under a minute. A few moments later, she threw her drink in his face, punched him in the nose and stormed off. Apparently, some rumors in Hollywood were true.

Teddy and I were friends, but it clearly wasn't the right moment for me to walk up and ask, "Hey, how are you?" as he wiped a drink out of his eyes. I turned on my heels and walked over to the bar to get myself a drink.

Sipping on a fresh cocktail, I walked closer to the stage to check out who was playing. The band sounded a bit like Skid Row, and I suddenly found myself staring at the cute singer with the powerhouse voice. He wore a crushed purple velvet coat with no shirt and black leather pants. He had long black hair cascading down his chest. He must have noticed me staring at him because moments after the end of their set, he walked up to me and introduced himself. He said his name was Larry and the band was Rockhoney, both of which were in town from Chicago.

Within a half hour of meeting Larry, we were walking around the club holding hands and snuggling as if we had known each other for years. We went upstairs and leaned against the rails as he put his arms around me and gave me little kisses throughout the set of Electric. It all felt remarkably comfortable, and there was nothing sleazy about it at all. It was quite sweet actually. It was nice to have that genuine physical affection, which I had not had in a long time. I didn't have one shred of guilt about what I was doing with Larry.

Shortly after Electric finished their set, Larry's band mates were heading out. That meant he would have to leave too, so he walked me to my car. When I pulled my car keys out of my purse, I caught him staring at them. I forgot there was a heart shaped frame on my keychain with a prom picture of Sheldon and I.

Damn it.

Larry asked if that was my boyfriend. I said sort of. He said he had a girlfriend back in Chicago too and that even though he had been hit on while being in L.A., he hadn't cheated on her. Apparently our canoodling wasn't considered cheating in his eyes. Regardless, he said he wanted to see me again and we exchanged numbers. He mentioned he had another Hollywood show the following weekend at the Red Light District and wanted me to go.

I woke up the next morning feeling emotionally refreshed, yet physically hung over. My evening with Larry was exactly what I needed, a simple fling. I threw my bed sheets off of me and a pair of jeans I had worn the night before flew off with change flying out in every direction. I climbed out of bed, picked up the coins, and started going through the back pockets of my jeans. When I pulled out a napkin with Larry's name and number on it, I cracked a smile and gently placed the napkin on my dresser.

Sheldon called that afternoon from Texas and asked what I had been up to the last few days. I told him a few things here and there but left out the part about meeting Larry. He told me Dancer had just played their first show of the tour and were booed offstage. I laughed my ass off, and of course he didn't find that funny. He actually got so angry at my caterwauling that he hung up on me. I rolled my eyes and went on with my day.

A few days later, Sheldon called again. This time, it was to tell me he was on his way home. Apparently, Dancer couldn't make it two weeks on the road together without fighting. He refused to give me specific details about what happened. He only said it was an issue with Nima that couldn't be resolved, and they decided to call it quits for the tour and the band as a whole. Although I didn't say it to him at that moment, I would soon be adding our relationship to that list.

Sure I knew Nima could be controlling when it came to the band, but that had nothing to do with me. I intended on staying friends with him after Dancer came back from tour, which Sheldon wasn't too happy about.

"Well I still want to talk to Nima, but I don't want to be in the middle of whatever fight you guys had," I said.

"You don't even know what happened on tour, and there's no reason for you to stay friends with him."

"Hey, don't take it out on me. Why won't you just tell me what happened?"

"Because it's none of your fucking business what happened."

"You know what? Why don't you talk that way to Lisa? Maybe she'll put up with your bullshit."

"Fuck you," he said.

"Go fuck yourself you cheating asshole!" I yelled and abruptly hung up on him.

Sheldon came home from tour the following day. He wanted to meet up for lunch to talk about things, but I had no desire to see him. I was exhausted from the emotional roller coaster. And to be honest, I really didn't owe him anything. After all, the asshole did cheat on me god knows how many times. I should have just told him to go fuck himself again, but I was curious to hear what he had to say. After some mild contemplation, I agreed to go to lunch with him just so I could state the obvious. We were over.

Sheldon picked me up a few hours later. We had lunch at a Sizzler right by my house. As we sat down, he began to tell me a little bit of what transpired with Nima. At that point, it really didn't matter to me what happened on tour. None of it mattered. I wasn't there to chew the fat with him and see what was new. I just wanted to get it all over with.

I brought up Lisa, and he finally confessed to cheating on me. Apparently it started shortly after he met her. *I knew it!*

One thing I can honestly say about Sheldon is that I never trusted him. As much as I thought I loved him, I was always worried about what or who he was doing when I wasn't around. He justified his cheating by saying that every man cheats. Especially musicians, and I was going to have a hard time finding any guy that would be completely monogamous. After saying that so boldly, he backtracked a little by apologizing if he had hurt me in any way throughout the course of our relationship. He said he really did love me, but I didn't sense an ounce of regret in his voice. It was as if he were reading a pre rehearsed public apology at a press conference. A small part of me felt the best retribution would be to tell him about Larry, but I decided against it. It was pointless to say anything, and I didn't want to drag out that breakup. Our relationship was already emotional road kill anyway.

As we stood up from our table, I sighed a bit of relief. I was walking away from the meal, the restaurant, and from that bullshit relationship. He dropped me off at home, gave me an awkward hug me goodbye and said he would talk to me later. I knew exactly what that meant. I was fine with it.

When I came home, I made a few entries in my journal over what had just transpired and my overall experience with Sheldon and his band. I noticed that little group of friends had slowly been disbanding anyway, even before the band left on tour. Now that the band was broken up, it shut the door on that chapter of my life. No more Dancer shows, after parties and rehearsals. No more psycho, Misha. Aside from the relationship drama, I did have a lot of fun with that group of people. Strangely though, the one person I was really going to miss would be Laney.

Sure she was a little rough around the edges. But she was the only person that had my back when it came to my relationship with Sheldon, even when it meant going against her own brother. I wanted to keep in touch with Laney, but I knew that was highly unlikely. We were just two totally different people. I couldn't see myself being her "backup" the next time the *La Vida Loca* girls decided to do a drive by.

Now that I was without Sheldon, I needed to get back into the social swing of things. Larry proved to be an essential buffer in transitioning my way back to the single life. He was the perfect specimen of a rebound if I had ever seen one. He was cute, affectionate, and most importantly not within driving range of Los Angeles.

The following weekend, Sasha and I went to the Red Light District for Larry's show. When we arrived, we were on his guest list as promised. It was an 18 and over club, which meant I could get in on my own. But I wanted to drink, so I brought Lucy's trusty ID.

When I showed the doorman Lucy's ID, he looked at me, looked at the ID and then looked at me again. I didn't understand what the issue was. Lucy and I looked exactly alike. The doorman asked me what my birthday was. *Ha! Ridiculous! Of course I know her birthday by heart.*

After chirping out her birth date, he asked me for my address. Another inner chuckle I gave to myself. Lucy lived with me, so that wasn't hard information to spout off either.

"Sign your name," he said.

He handed me a pen and a clipboard with a piece of paper on it.

"Excuse me?" I said.

"Sign your name, LUCY," he said snidely.

Now that was a definite problem. I hadn't mastered Lucy's handwriting. It never occurred to me that I would ever have to because we looked like twins. To make matters worse, Lucy's handwriting was neat and consisted of big, googly characters, whereas mine was chicken scratch. He held onto Lucy's ID while he waited for me to sign "my" name. I sloooowly started to sign Lucy's name, trying to remember how she wrote her C's and E's with a particular swirl.

"It shouldn't take you an hour to write your name. Now get outta here," he said as he handed me back the ID.

Larry happened to walk out of the club just as we were walking away. So we followed him around the corner to a side door where he was able to sneak us in.

I spent the week looking forward to continuing our little rendezvous, but while Sasha and I watched Larry's set, something felt off to me. All the excitement I had built up of going to his show was suddenly equivalent to a dilapidating balloon. I figured it was just me being a little uptight over what happened with the door guy, so I grabbed myself a cocktail in the hopes it would loosen me up a bit. But when Larry came to talk to us after his set, I felt the same a distant vibe from him as well. That's when I knew it wasn't just me.

Our chemistry was completely out of whack that night and nothing like it was at the Whisky. As cheesy as it is to say, the magic was gone. Maybe it was never meant to be anything more than a one-night fling. That theory was proven a half hour later when I saw him making out with a hideous Asian girl near the women's restroom when I went to relieve myself.

Larry was completely preoccupied having his tongue down that girl's throat. Needless to say, he didn't notice me when I walked by. After using the bathroom, I grabbed Sasha and told her why we were leaving the club right then and there.

Larry called me a few days later when he got back to Chicago. We spoke for a few minutes, but it was the same drab energy I felt at the Red Light District show. I didn't mention anything about him playing tonsil hockey with the Asian girl. I wasn't upset over it, just mildly grossed out, so I felt there was no need to make a dramatic spectacle about it. I also didn't care to talk to him anymore and was over the whole situation. He must have felt the same way too because that was the last time he ever called me.

I have always believed certain people come into your life to serve a specific purpose and fly right back out as quickly as they came in. I truly feel that Larry was one of those people. He was exactly what I needed at that moment in time to ease the sadness I had over Sheldon. But that was all it was meant to be, and I enjoyed our brief time together.

Meanwhile, my partner in crime Sasha was burning out on Hollywood and going out in general. She wasn't calling me as much as she normally did. I was having a hard time getting a hold of her. After weeks of trying to track her down, she finally called me one evening around midnight. She said she had taken some pills and wanted to kill herself.

Sasha was always a bit outspoken and used to say crazy shit like that from time to time. I wasn't sure if she was telling the truth or just trying to get attention. Not wanting to take any chances, I told her I was coming right over.

When I got to her apartment, she was lying on the living room floor mumbling. I knew it wasn't the doings of alcohol because I had seen her at every stage of a drunken stupor. This was nothing I had ever encountered before. I dragged her to my car and drove her straight to the emergency room.

They ran some blood tests and made her drink a fluid that looked like black liquid coal. After throwing up a little bit of water, I was ushered away by a few nurses who told me they were going to pump her stomach. They kept her overnight for observation and she was sent home the next day.

Later that afternoon, Hannah and I picked up Sasha. We spent the day with her to make sure she was all right and went to a nearby Taco Bell to get some food. When Sasha tried to eat, she said her throat was sore from the tube that was used to pump her stomach. A few moments later, she pulled out a baggy of coke from her purse. She licked her finger, dipped it in the coke and tried to rub it in the back of her throat, I'm assuming to numb it. Yes, she did this right inside Taco Bell.

A few weeks later, Sasha found out she was pregnant by a guy she had been dating for about a month. She did say she was keeping the baby and seemed to be happy about it. As she prepared to nest, she became a recluse. I lost touch with her a short time later. I can only hope that being pregnant saved her life.

By the winter of 1991, I had been licking my wounds over the Sheldon breakup for several weeks. But I was starting to feel like myself again and ready to resume my place as a fixture on the Sunset Strip. Unfortunately, I was finding it hard to leave the warm confines of my cozy home to hang out on the freezing cold boulevard. Okay maybe it was wasn't freezing but as cold as

151

Southern California could get in the winter, which was still pretty damn cold.

Even in 40-degree weather and brisk winds, girls would still dress up in their slinky barely there outfits and shiver their way up and down the Strip in spiked heels. I, on the other hand, opted for the cute and warm look. I would wear my baby doll dresses or plaid skirts with colorful tights and stomp down Sunset in combat boots instead of heels. When it came to gloves, I couldn't find a pair that kept me warm until I stumbled upon a pair of bright, sky blue mittens that worked wonders.

My mittens never matched anything I wore. They certainly were far from sexy. No normal person over the age of 7 should have been wearing them, but I didn't give a shit. They kept my hands warm…well until half the musicians on the Strip started to borrow them. They would borrow one mitten and move it back and forth on each hand every few minutes to keep both warm as they passed out flyers. Apparently, most of them didn't care about aesthetics either when it came to the cold.

With another chilly weekend ahead of me, I made plans to meet Faye on the Strip. I had borrowed my dad's truck and noticed it was low on fuel, so I stopped at a gas station near my house. I had just begun to pump a whopping $5 in gas when Brandon pulled up to the pump directly behind me.

We had already made eye contact, so it would've looked ridiculous for me to rip the nozzle out of the tank and speed away. I didn't know what to say to him, so I said hi. He said hi back and walked inside to pay for his gas. I looked at the display for my pump and mumbled for it to hurry the fuck up. I was hoping to reach the $5 mark before he came back outside. I only reached $4.05.

"What are you up to tonight?" he asked.

"Going to Hollywood. What about you?"

"I'm just about to head home actually."

Then came the uncomfortable silence. We hadn't seen each other since his graduation over a year earlier. Things obviously were not good between us, and I wasn't about to act like they were by having a friendly exchange.

"So are you still with Grace?" I asked bluntly as I put the nozzle back on the handle.

"Yeah, I am," he said.

"Well I finally got rid of Ronan. He turned out to be a big psycho. I just couldn't take someone trying to control my life ya know? Yeah, of course you know."

"Speaking of Ronan, it was him that caused the problems between you and Grace."

"No, I think it's because Grace is a crackpot and was jealous of our friendship."

"No really, it went down at Kaitlin's grad party."

Kaitlin was a senior in Brandon's graduating class. She had thrown a pool party for the class of 1990 shortly before their graduation. Naturally, myself and a few other juniors mooched in on the celebration.

"You're crazy. Ronan wasn't at Kaitlin's party," I said.

"Not while you were there. He came after you left," he said.

I had to leave Kaitlin's party early because my friend, Brian, ended up throwing me in the pool about an hour after I got there. *Bastard.*

"Ronan never told me he went to that party," I said.

"Of course he didn't because he ended up having one hell of a conversation with Grace."

"Why in the hell would he talk to Grace? They don't even know each other."

"Apparently he had a problem with you and I being friends too. He found out Grace was my girlfriend at the party and told her that you and I had hooked up a few weeks earlier. He said he forgave you for cheating on him but felt she should know about it too."

"What a fucking liar he is! He knows damn well that never happened!"

"Of course he knew that, but he said it to piss her off."

"Well you told her the truth right? You told her that never happened and that he's a psycho liar?"

"Of course I did, but she didn't believe me. She thought I was just lying to get out of being caught cheating."

"Why didn't you tell me this before?"

"Because I just found out about it a month ago."

"So he purposely pissed off Grace, knowing that would put a wedge between you and I."

"Yeah, pretty calculated huh?"

"Of course it's calculated. That's exactly why I dumped him. It looks like he got his wish though, about putting a wedge between you and I."

We stared at each other for a few moments and then a click went off on his gas pump.

"I guess I better get going," he said as he put the nozzle back on the handle.

"Yeah, I guess I should too," I said.

I didn't want to go though. I missed Brandon so much. I really wanted to stay and talk to him. Every time I thought I had purged him from my system, it only took one look at him to get my heart fluttering again.

"Well uhhh, I guess I'll see you around then. Have fun in Hollywood," he said smiling.

"Yeah, thanks. Have a good night," I said smiling back.

That was the last time I ever spoke to Brandon. I heard through the grapevine that he eventually married Grace a few years later and settled down in Arcadia with a few kids.

It was a cold evening that night on the Strip. There was a particularly chilly wind blowing about, and I had only taken one lap down Sunset before it set in. I ran across the street to AM/PM for a warm beverage.

As I walked back toward the Whisky, I was juggling a pile of flyers in one hand and a cup of hot chocolate in the other when a guy by the name of Ash Lee approached me. I nearly choked on my mocha soaked marsh mellows because to me, he was a dead ringer for Nikki Sixx.

He had the same black spiky hair, same body type and the same beautiful green eyes. When he introduced himself, I took a mitten off to shake his hand. I was swooning.

"Do you have room for one more?" he said smiling as he handed me a flyer.

My heart fluttered as he placed a flyer in my mitten.

"If you play bass, I'm going to drop dead," I said bluntly.

"I play guitar actually," he said mildly confused.

Okay, so he's ALMOST like Nikki Sixx.

He said he was in a band called Wikked Gypsy. By far, he was one of the sweetest guys I had ever met on the Strip. He didn't pitch his band or try to sell me tickets to his show like everyone else. We spoke about our favorite bands, how he was from Iowa and well, my random mittens. He rolled up his bundle of flyers, put them under his armpit and blew inside his hands, rubbing them together to warm them up.

"Do you want to borrow a mitten?" I asked innocently.

I wanted to slap myself in the forehead when I heard those words come out of my mouth. *What the hell am I thinking? Of course he doesn't want to wear these butt ugly things.* My mittens were more uncool than the leopard pants and matching headband I wore six years earlier at the Ratt concert.

"Yeah, sure," he said.

Surprised at his reaction, I gave him the mitten I had pulled off earlier to shake his hand. He smiled as he took it, and I turned into a big pool of melted butter.

"Are you gonna be here for a while?" he asked.

"Yeah, totally. I'll be around."

"Okay, I'll come find you in a little bit and bring it back. Thanks!" he said raising his mitten covered hand and walked off.

I figured I would never see that mitten again, but it didn't matter. I had sacrificed it to the hottest guy on the Strip. I took a big sip of my hot chocolate and walked off in the opposite direction to find Faye.

I chatted with a few people as I made my way up Sunset and planted myself on an Astroturf staircase near the pizza place where the bikers always hung out. I was organizing my flyers and polishing off the last of my hot cocoa when a blond rocker walked up and glared at me.

He was extremely thin with blue eyes and long stringy hair. I had seen him on the Strip a few times before. He always wore the same black leather jacket, which had broken pieces of a mirror glued to the back. I was fairly certain he wasn't in a band because he never passed out flyers like every other guy on the Strip. He just always seemed to be lingering around the boulevard, especially near the Rainbow. He continued staring at me for a few moments and asked if I wanted to go with him to his car to do blow.

"No thanks," I said politely as I continued arranging my things.

"You sure honey?"

"I'm sure. I've never done it before anyway."

"Well in that case, I'd be honored to pop your coke cherry."

I started to get irritated and said, "Nah, I'll pass."

"Sweetheart, you don't know what you're missing. How about I give you a quick bump right now to give you a little taste?"

"Am I starring in a bad *Afterschool Special* right now? Fuck off already!"

"Suit yourself Prudence," he said.

He shot me a dirty look and walked off. *Moron.*

I wasn't about to do blow on Sunset Blvd just for some loser to think I was cool. I couldn't give two shits what he or anyone else in Hollywood thought of me. If people couldn't accept me for being a tomboy with horrible blue mittens and a dislike for cocaine, then that was perfectly fine with me.

After getting my things organized, I picked myself up off the stairs and made my way towards the Roxy. I finally ran into Faye who was carrying her very inebriated friend, Pixie. Pixie had her arms wrapped around Faye and could barely walk.

Pixie was a regular on the Strip. Several people had told me that we looked like sisters even though I had never met her before. I only knew of her through Faye.

"Can you do me a huge favor?" Faye asked with hopeful eyes.

"Of course what's up?" I said.

"My ride is picking us up at the Whisky, but there's no way she's going to make it down there. Can you look after her so I can run down and have them drive up here?"

"Um…yeah. I guess so," I said.

"Thanks!" she said as she unloaded Pixie on me like a sack of potatoes.

"Oh and if you see Strange from the Glamour Punks, he's coming with us too. Feel free to leave her with him if you need to take off!" she said as she skipped off.

I noticed an empty bus bench nearby. I dragged Pixie over and propped her up next to me like a puppet. Her head flopped onto my lap, which caused the short miniskirt she was wearing to fly up. I pulled her skirt down over her ass with one hand and used the other to pull her hair away from her face so she could breathe. A few moments later, she mumbled something and sloppily tapped my knees with her hand.

"What?" I asked.

I leaned my head down to hear her, but she said nothing. She started tapping the inside of my knees again as if to separate them. It finally hit me what her taps meant, and I quickly spread my knees right before she barfed between my legs.

I will give her credit though. Even in her wasted stupor she still had the consideration to not barf on me, which would have been completely understandable. I sat with one hand holding her hair and the other holding her skirt down as she lay heaving between my legs.

A few minutes later, Strange walked up and asked me what happened. I lifted my legs to show him the puddle of barf beneath me. He thanked me for taking care of Pixie. After leaving her with Strange, I felt the cold wind was a bit much for my thin California blood, so I decided to leave.

I made my way up the Strip and noticed Ash Lee in front of the Roxy. He was talking to a few people and still wearing my bright blue mitten, which was beaming from his hand like a lighthouse beacon. I felt silly asking for my goofy mitten back. I didn't want to bother him about it, so I kept walking. To my surprise, he noticed me and yelled out my name. I was smiling before I turned around to acknowledge him.

"Are you leaving?" he asked as he jogged up to me.

"Yeah, I'm freezing my ass off."

He pulled my mitten off his hand, gave me a big hug and said, "Well, thanks for lending this to me."

We said our goodbyes, and I floated off to my car.

Over the next few weeks, I settled back into my routine of going to the Strip every weekend. I had purged all things Sheldon out of my system. I was feeling the slightest remnants of being in rebound mode, and that's when I started hanging out with Charlie, the bass player of Electric.

Charlie was a sweet guy I met when I first started going to the Strip. I know it's mean to say he was a rebound, but he was. He wasn't my type of guy. He was a hesher with wavy brown hair that streamed down his back. We had made out a few times, and that was basically the nature of our relationship. I wasn't even really attracted to him, so I certainly had no intention of sleeping with him or trying to make him my boyfriend. God knows if I was in my right mind, I should've been pursuing Ash Lee.

During that time, I began going out with Faye quite a bit too. That was fun for the most part, except when I happened to spot a guy I might like. With her stunning good looks standing next to my goofy ass, I knew I didn't have a chance in hell.

I picked her up one night and we went to see a show at the Whisky. We strolled in during the set of a band called Mudd Jr. and decided to stand a few rows back from the stage. The singer immediately spotted Faye and sang right to her. She smiled at him and started walking towards the stage. When she reached the front of the stage, he squatted down and continued singing to her. They looked at each other for a few moments, then she put her hand behind his neck, pulled him to her and started making out with him. She stopped after a few seconds so he could continue singing his song, and she walked back over to me.

"I take it you know that guy?" I asked sarcastically.

"Oh I totally don't," she said as she wiped her mouth.

"Why did you just make out with him then?"

"I dunno. It was just something fun to do. Lets go to the bathroom so I can fix my lipstick."

I envied Faye for being so bold. I never could have got away with something like that. My braces were still in full effect and scaring guys away by the droves.

After Mudd Jr. finished their set, Faye and I walked outside to get some air. We were standing in front of the Whisky talking about nothing in particular, when to my beautiful eyes did appear the one and only Brent Muscat, one of the guitarists of Faster Pussycat. Visions of scarves and Les Paul guitars danced in my head as the last five years of my life flashed before my love struck eyes.

You can always sense when someone is looking at you. And since I happened to be staring at Brent like a lunatic, he looked over at me. We locked eyes for a few moments, but once his eyes moved over to Faye, I knew it was over.

Sure enough a few minutes later, Brent walked over and introduced himself to us, or rather Faye. He was with Dave Zink, the guitarist of Blackboard Jungle. They spoke about the third Faster Pussycat album that was coming out in a few months. Brent pulled a cassette out of his pocket that had "Faster Pussycat" written on it. He asked if we wanted to hear some new songs, which would later become the *Whipped* album. Of course I said yes. We walked off to Brent's car, which was parked in the Tower Video parking lot about a block away.

Dave opened the car door and Brent immediately hopped in the back seat with Faye. Disappointed, I sadly took my place in the passengers seat while Dave hopped in the drivers seat.

Dave popped in the cassette, and we listened to a rough mix of a song called "Big Dictionary". I was still a huge Pussycat fan, so I was genuinely interested in hearing the new songs. But my interest was overshadowed by the sounds of Brent getting comfortable in the backseat with Faye.

Dave rambled on about the logistics of the track and guitar techniques. I don't know what gave him the idea that I would care to hear those details. I wasn't a sound engineer, and I didn't know what the hell his terminology meant anyway. I nodded as if I was paying attention, when really I was listening to Brent whisper sweet pre-coital nothings to Faye.

Faye made an attempt to start a conversation between the four of us because she knew I had a huge crush on Brent. I appreciated her efforts, but the situation was blatantly clear. Brent was looking for a steak dinner, not a side of baked squash with a set of braces.

After hearing another track, I had enough of what was going on in the backseat. I decided to cock block Brent by saying Faye and I had to leave. Everyone climbed out of the car, and my heart dropped when Brent asked Faye for her phone number. *How can he possibly ask for her number? I'm the one that has loved him since I was 13!*

Faye gave him her number and we said our goodbyes. As we walked away, Faye felt bad that Brent hit on her instead of me and apologized. She said she only gave him her number to be polite and promised me that if he ever called her, she wouldn't talk to him. *Yeah, right.*

Faye and I never really spoke about Brent again after that night. So if she did hook up with him, I never knew about it.

9

I'M SO GOTH, I SHIT BATS

I rang in the New Year by sleeping my way through midnight. And just a few short weeks into 1992, I noticed things start to change drastically on the Strip.

Cops began to put a stronghold on our socializing. We weren't allowed to hang out on the boulevard anymore. If you stopped to talk to people it wouldn't be long before an officer popped up behind you, asking you to "keep it moving". Bands couldn't pass out flyers because the residents were bitching about the amount of litter and loitering in their neighborhood. Those were a few contributors to the impending death of the Sunset Strip. But I would say the most significant was a tidal wave called Grunge.

I remember the first time I heard that song. I was in my bedroom, writing in my journal and listening to a local alternative station called KROQ. I was caught up in my writing and not paying much attention to the song playing on the radio. I figured it was a new track by a band I already knew of. When the song finished, the DJ said the song was called, "Smells Like Teen Spirit" and the name of the band was Nirvana.

Who the hell is Nirvana?

Literally, what seemed like overnight, all of the glam boys cut off their long locks. They threw their spandex pants into their pink glitter caboodles and chucked everything into the garbage. Nirvana had thrown down the grunge gauntlet, and that put every glam band in Hollywood on the chopping block.

And while we're on the subject of death, let me tell you about a gloomy local Hollywood band called The Kids.

The Kids had played around Hollywood for the last few years and dressed head to toe in black. They never really fit in visually or musically to the glam rock scene on the Strip. They were the gothic misfits that were more like the Cure than Poison. I went to one of their shows a few months earlier at the Roxy. They had the stage lit up with candles while their singer, Sebastian, paced the stage singing about love, hate, and other "dark" thoughts while passing out long black stem roses to the crowd.

Despite his small stature, Sebastian always stood out to me because of his platinum blond hair, pale skin, and beautiful crystal blue eyes. I met him around the same time as I did Sheldon. I always saw him around Hollywood, but we were never really friends. I knew he was a buddy of my former nemesis, Casey, because I would always see her buzzing around him whenever he was in the vicinity.

I'm not sure what sparked Sebastian's interest, but the last few times I had run into him he became much more friendly toward me. Maybe I had unintentionally sent out an "I am single" pheromone that he picked up on. Regardless, he suddenly began to chat me up quite a bit, which he had never done before.

One of the last weekends I hung out on the Strip, Hannah randomly decided she wanted to come with me and we ran into Sebastian. We spoke about some of the last few shows we went to. I let it slip that I had gone to see Electric. Without missing a beat, Sebastian said they were a hesher band that sucked. After hearing that rave review, I chose to keep my fling with Charlie to myself.

Sebastian also mentioned he was going to an after hours club later that night called The Church. I had heard a little bit about it over the last few months because it was the latest afterhours hotspot. He invited Hannah and I to go, but I wasn't crazy about driving all the way to valley. Unfortunately, he wasn't taking no for an answer. I relented and told him we would meet him there later.

GREG WARKEL: Faster Pussycat was recording their *Whipped* album at the time, and I was going down to the sessions because I was friends with Muscat. We kept driving by this old church every time we went to the studio, and one day we noticed there was a "For Rent" sign on it. We contacted the guy renting it out and went to take a look. We told the guy we were going to use it as a rehearsal studio when really we were thinking of putting a nightclub together. Neither one of us wanted to give our real names because if things went wrong we didn't want anyone coming after us. We used an alias and said we didn't have ID's on us, but we had cash to pay a few months up front, so he let us sign the paperwork.

KENNY PRICE (Blackboard Jungle): Opening night at The Church was Halloween in 1991. Greg and Brent decided they wanted to do an after hours club with Blackboard being kind of the anchor, so they found a place on Satsuma Avenue in the valley and we would run afterhours there after our gigs.

We used to rehearse at The Church in the balcony area where a choir would've sang. We rehearsed up there and would play till like 2:30 or 3 in the morning. I remember one time we were doing a cover, I think it was "Sweet Transvestite" or "Paranoid", something like that when Duff and I think it was Matt from Guns N Roses walked in. I think maybe John Beaubien was working the door that night. So they heard us playing and Duff was like, "What the fuck is this shit?" and Beaubien said, "It's Blackboard Jungle" and Duff was like, "uhh whatever" and then he came in and drank.

On opening night, Greg and Brent were pissed because a girl got really wasted and ended up pissing in the confessional. I remember one night when Dazzle from Stars From Mars got in a fight because some guys were screaming, "Faggot!" at him. A bunch of us were drunk and ran up behind Dazzle to back him up. Dazzle whipped off his bullet belt, swung it back, and it hit me right in the face because I was standing behind him. I was like, "Oww! Dude!" and he said, "Oh sorry man" and went back to yelling at the guys. "Yeah, man we're gonna kick your ass!"

JOE HOWARD: The work staff at The Church consisted of Eric who was the music guy, John Beaubien and Jay were bartenders, then I worked the front door with a big, black guy named Curtis, and Greg's brother, Jamie. Jamie was more like the security dude. He was built like a brick shit house. He was a monster but the nicest dude ever IF he liked you. Greg was the guy that ran it all, and Brent was more behind the scenes; he wasn't hands on like Greg was.

I remember people used to come to the door and say, "I know Brent Muscat", thinking that would get them in for free. I'd say, "I don't give a fuck." Brent would say, "Dude you gotta let my friends in if they say they know me", and I said, "Everyone in the fucking world comes up and tells me that they know you. Fuck that. They can come in if they pay money and that's it."

One thing about Greg, he was a businessman, so we weren't letting ANYBODY in for free. There's nobody that got into that place without paying. I would've made my own mom pay it didn't matter (laughs). When it started, it was $15 at the door. I told Greg to make it $20 because it was a pain in the ass to deal with change, so he changed it. We were making so much money at the door it was ridiculous.

Greg's meetings were the best. He'd get everyone together and say the same three things every Saturday. "I love you guys, but don't steal from me, don't let anyone in for free and don't give away any alcohol for free." Those were the three rules. It was hilarious.

Being an after hours club, I knew The Church wouldn't get going for at least a few more hours. This worked out perfectly for me. It gave my mom and Lucy plenty of time to drift into a comfy, deep sleep before sneaking back out of the house with one of their cars. Since Lucy had a small 2 door Ford Escort, as opposed to my mom's huge station wagon, Lucy's was the obvious car to steal. I had coincidentally borrowed her car to go out that night. There were always two rules she made me go by when I took her car.

First, she always wanted her car home before 2:00am. The reason being, she didn't want me driving around Hollywood as people were leaving bars. Fair enough.

Lastly, I had to put her car keys back in her bedroom when I came home. She said it was so she could easily find them the next day. I knew damn well it was a preventative measure to keep me from stealing her car in the middle of the night. But unbeknownst to her a few weeks earlier, I had swung by a key shack on the way home from the mall to have my own set of secret keys made for her car.

When I brought Lucy's car home that night, I was happy to find everyone was already asleep, including Lucy. I put her car keys in her room like the good, responsible sister I was, and then quietly began to get ready in my bedroom.

Our house had old hardwood floors. Only through trial and error did I find three areas in the living room with particularly squeaky boards that were loud enough to wake the dead. I memorized where those landmines were and made a mental note not to hit them as I snuck in or out of the house.

About an hour or so later, I grabbed my cordless phone and put it under my pillow to muffle the sound of buttons being pushed. Without being able to see the numbers, I slowly moved my fingers around the pad like I was reading Braille. I joined my phone under the pillow and quietly told Hannah to be outside of her house in ten minutes.

I still didn't have my own private phone line and was continuing to do the "balancing jack" act with the phone cord on the kitchen phone. But I had recently devised a better plan in dealing with late night phone calls.

I had two different phones in my room each serving it's own important purpose. A cord less, and an old school corded phone with a clear case that lit up bright neon orange when I had a call.

My cord less phone is what I used the most. But it had a ringer that woke the dead, so I always unplugged it at night along with the phone in the kitchen. I would rely on the corded neon phone in the late evenings because even with the ringer off, the damn thing lit up my entire bedroom like a searchlight anytime I had a call.

After double-checking my phones, I grabbed my things and slowly opened my bedroom door. I inched and stretched my way through the living room like I was playing a round of Twister, being careful not to step on any of the squeaky land mines that could get me in trouble.

Although I made it safely out my front door, there was a whole new hurdle to leap over in terms of getting my sisters car out of the driveway. Luckily, I had the good sense to leave our driveway gates open when I came home earlier. It was one less thing to do as I executed my escape.

I slowly unlocked the driver's side door to Lucy's car and placed my purse on the passengers seat. I put the key in the ignition and shifted the car into neutral. With one hand on the wheel and all the strength I could muster in my legs, I slowly began to push Lucy's little Ford Escort down our 20-foot driveway.

It was a slow start, but it wasn't long before I had the car moving at a safe manageable speed. Or so I thought. The car was almost out of the driveway when it started veering to the right. I wasn't able to hop in the car fast enough to hit the brake, so the corner of one of the gates gently smashed into the passenger side mirror. I put the car in park and walked over to see the damage. The entire mirror was gone but thankfully, the broken chunks landed quietly onto a patch of grass.

Damn it.

Lucy was definitely going to kick my ass; it was just a matter of when. I knew if I went in the house right then and there my grounding would start on the spot.

OR

I could enjoy one last night of freedom and deal with it in the morning. I walked over to the driver's side, threw it back into neutral and resumed pushing.

The car rolled out of the driveway and onto the street. I hopped in, started up the engine and tore off toward Hannah's.

We didn't have an exact address to The Church. Sebastian only mentioned a general area on Satsuma Avenue in the Valley near Burbank Blvd. I was worried I wouldn't be able to find it since it was in an industrial area. But as soon as we turned down Satsuma, we parked the car and followed the trail of people. They seemed to be walking toward a small white church surrounded by wrought iron gates. I noticed a few people on the roof and also in a small watchtower just to the right of the church.

We walked in and stood just inside the doorway. Beyond the crowded room was a cross-lit up with white Christmas lights on what used to be the altar. I also noticed all the pews were missing. I continued looking around the crowd and figured I would never be able to find Sebastian when he suddenly yelled out my name. He was sitting on the floor in a corner right by the entrance. With him, were a few random people and the guy responsible for my first black eye, Mandie, the singer of The Glamour Punks. Hannah and I walked over to Sebastian, and he immediately pulled me down to the ground to sit next to him.

"That's MandieBamandRonnie," Sebastian slurred out as if it were all one name.

Mandie held a bottle of Jim Beam in his hand and looked up at me.

"She's only here for *la botella*!" he yelled to Sebastian.

Mandie took a swig of the bottle and passed it to Bam. Bam was the drummer of a band called the The Hatebreeders. He was super skinny and stood about 6' 3" with bright purple hair. I remembered seeing him around Hollywood from time to time. Ronnie, however, was not a familiar face. He didn't seem to be in a band and looked quite out of place hanging out with those colorful characters. Regardless of Mandie's outburst, I said hi to the guys and smiled at them with a mouth full of braces. Ronnie laughed as he pulled his long curly brown locks into a ponytail.

"Why are you here?" Ronnie asked.

"Sebastian invited me," I said.

"Do you do EVERYTHING people tell you to do?"

"Huh? Well...no," I said caught off guard.

"Apparently you do," he snapped.

Who is this asshole?

"No, I don't, and what makes you think you're such hot shit?" I barked back.

Ronnie laughed and patted an area of the floor next to him, gesturing for me to sit down. I cautiously moved over and to my surprise, he immediately warmed up to me. I asked why he came off like such an asshole. He said there were so many idiots in Hollywood and it was his way of testing people.

I was about to say something to Hannah who was sitting next to Bam, but they seemed to be in the middle of a deep conversation. Bam took a swig from a bottle of Jim Beam and then passed it to Sebastian without distracting from his conversation. Sebastian took a hit and then handed the bottle to me. I had never tried Jim Beam before. I was more of a vodka person.

Sebastian held the bottle just inches away from my nose and waited for a response. The smell of bourbon was strong and I felt nauseous just thinking of what that would taste like going down my throat.

"I've never tried bourbon before," I said as I took the bottle.

He shoved a liter of Coke in front of me and said, "Here, chase it with this."

I took the liter, filled up half of my mouth with Coke then grabbed the neck of the Jim Beam bottle. I threw my head back till I could taste the bitterness of bourbon touch my tongue and swallowed everything in one gulp. It was pretty bad, but it did give me a warm fuzzy feeling in my stomach a few minutes later. I figured what damage could one shot do? I continued to say that after the 2nd and 3rd shot. It wasn't until after my 4th that I started to second-guess that theory.

I was enjoying my time with Sebastian until the reality set in that I was the one that had to drive Hannah and I home. I was angry at myself for drinking so much. Knowing I needed to sober up quickly, I figured the best thing to do was to stand up and see how bad the damage was.

Before I stood up, I asked Sebastian where the bathroom was. Actually, I yelled over the loud music to see where the bathroom was. He yelled back a response, but I couldn't hear him. I pretended I understood and glanced over to Hannah. I wanted to take her with me, but she was still busy talking to Bam. I decided to venture off on my own.

I slowly peeled myself off the floor when gravity pulled me quite heavily to the right. I almost fell on Bam. He started laughing and caught me. I stood there for a moment and put my hands out as if I were trying to get my balance on a tightrope.

Still laughing, Bam slowly pulled my arm down. As I would start to tip over he'd yell, "timber!" and then catch me. He did this two or three more times. For some reason we found it hysterical. I finally had to tell him to stop or else I would pee all over him.

When I walked away from Bam, I noticed Brent Muscat shuffle by me, or what I thought looked like Brent. He had his hair pulled back in a ponytail and was wearing a black fedora. I wasn't sure if it was really him or just a drunk hallucination. I never saw a pink elephant look so good. I made my way through the crowd and decided to follow him.

I followed Brent to a side room where an Asian girl with a white boa greeted him. She held a video camera in her hand and began filming him as she asked him random questions. I watched for a few moments and quickly realized I was being a stalker. I decided it was best that I walk off and try to find the bathroom.

As I walked around the crowd in my drunken stupor, I didn't realize that a band was playing. I squinted at each band member and quickly realized it was Blackboard Jungle.

I was a big fan of Blackboard Jungle. They were one of the few bands playing in Hollywood that didn't suck. Back then there were so many cheesy Sunset Strip bands with horrible band names to go with their horrible music. But Blackboard stuck out and actually had talent. Their songs were great, all the guys in the band were hot, and the singer, Kenny Price, had a voice like butter that could make a girl slide right off her seat.

JOE HOWARD: Blackboard was really big at the time and some of promoters on the Strip had heard they were playing The Church on a regular basis. They were pissed that they were losing money over them playing some underground club as opposed to one of the clubs on the Strip because we were packing it in. Our headcount one night came to about 1200 people. And it wasn't just Blackboard playing there, we had a bunch of other big Strip bands too. Greg was turning away bands that wanted to play there, and the promoters were pissed that Greg wasn't a legit club owner.

While I watched the show, I brainstormed on ways to sober up and how to sneak back into my house without crashing into everything on the way in. When Blackboard finished their set, it snapped me out of my trance. I had no sense of time and didn't know how long I stood there for. I stumbled over to the bar area to grab a Coke, and made my way back through the crowd to find Sebastian. Luckily, everyone was still where I left them by the front entrance.

Sebastian was throwing back the last shot of Jim Beam when I walked up to him. He said they were going back to his place for more drinks and asked if I wanted to go. I wanted to hang out with him but I simply couldn't do any more drinking. I politely declined and said I needed to get Hannah and myself home.

As we all slowly stood up and stumbled out of The Church, I looked back in the hopes I would catch another glimpse of Brent, but the crowd was thick with people. I was also way too dizzy to focus on trying to pick him out of the crowd. Okay, maybe it was shitty that I was drooling over Brent when I went there to meet Sebastian, but it technically wasn't a date anyway. Besides, I had a previous longstanding crush on Brent. Not to mention, he was totally unattainable anyway, at least in my world. I learned that the hard way when I met him with Faye a few months earlier. The only person that could trump Brent would be Nikki Sixx, of whom my teenage loins still ached for.

Sebastian walked Hannah and I to Lucy's car. I thought he might try to kiss me, but he didn't. Maybe it was my braces that turned him off? I was getting them off in a few short months, so that wouldn't be an issue much longer. He asked if we could hang out sometime, pulled a Kids flyer from his pocket, and asked me to write down my number. I didn't have anything to write with, so he said to call the band hotline and leave my number on their machine. He gave me a big hug goodbye and stumbled off into the night.

Hannah plopped herself onto the passengers seat of Lucy's car and passed out within seconds. I had hoped she would be my wingman and help me focus as we drove home, but so much for that. I sat in the car sucking down the last sips of Coke as if each drop would sober me up. I let out a big burp and looked over to Hannah who was still happily passed out. I shook her a few times to wake her up, but she didn't even twitch. She just laid there like a beached seal on a rock.

Pounding that Coke reminded me that I hadn't gone to the bathroom earlier. I knew I wouldn't be able to make it home without peeing first. I needed my focus to be on driving and not bladder pain. Since we weren't in the greatest area, I didn't want to leave Hannah in the car by herself while I ran back to find a bathroom. So I grabbed some Kleenex from the glove compartment, squatted on the curb in front of Lucy's car, and let the golden showers rain down on Satsuma Avenue.

After I dropped off Hannah, I was so exhausted that I considered just driving right into my driveway. I was going to get in trouble for breaking the passengers side mirror anyway. Strangely though, I had a moment of clarity in my drunken stupor. I realized that getting caught drunk driving AND stealing Lucy's car, in addition to the broken mirror could have me banned from borrowing both of their cars. Needless to say, I decided against that idea and went with my original plan of sneaking the car and myself back to the house.

When I approached my house, I gave the car just enough gas to give it a running start. Then I shut off the lights, the engine, and let the car slowly coast up the driveway. I gently closed the driver's side door, jogged up to my porch and slowly turned the knob to let myself in the front door.

Being drunk, I had momentarily forgotten about the landmines in my living room. Each time I stepped on one, I would whisper for it to "shush" as if that would help. I finally made it to my room and collapsed face first onto my bed when I remembered I had to call and leave my number on The Kids hotline. I quickly did that and put my face back into my pillow. I was just starting to doze off when the neon phone began to light up my room. I wanted nothing more than to sleep, but I thought it might be Sebastian.

"Yeah," I said mumbling into the phone with my eyes still closed.

"Hey baby, how are you? It's been a while!" Charlie said all bright eyed and bushy tailed.

I was immediately annoyed.

"I'm drunk. That's how I am," I said and hung up on him.

I plucked the phone cord out of my wall and passed out with my clothes and shoes on.

I woke up shortly before noon the next day. My mouth felt like I had chewed on a bag of cotton. I was dehydrated, nauseous, and still a bit drunk. Apparently, I was experiencing my first real hangover.

I desperately needed water and had to pee. I was too lazy to get up and do either. I stayed in bed for about a half hour in the hopes I would fall back asleep, but my bladder wasn't having it. I heard my mom and Lucy talking in our living room, so I stood up and braced myself for the shit storm to hit.

After emptying my bladder, I went to the living room and cautiously sat down while my mom made small talk with Lucy. They included me in their conversation, but there was no mention of me sneaking in or out of the house from the night before. *Maybe they don't know I stole Lucy's car and I got away with it?* Even if I were that lucky, there was no getting around the broken rearview mirror.

"Um...so I came out of the club last night and noticed the rearview mirror on the passengers side was broken. I didn't want to wake you when I came in," I said lying through my teeth.

Lucy was angry but relented when she saw how bad I felt. I really did feel bad about it and offered to pay for the repairs. I waited for her to mention me stealing her car, but she didn't say a word about it. I had a feeling I might have got away with it because it's not something she would've hesitated on confronting me about. But I still walked on eggshells for the rest of the day.

By the time dinner rolled around, Lucy still hadn't said anything about me taking her car and that's when I knew I was home free. I was glad that ordeal was over with but I was certainly far from feeling better, at least on a physical level. I was still very hung over, and the moment I tried to eat a salad it all came up faster than I could run to the bathroom.

After hanging out at The Church together, Sebastian and I began talking on a regular basis. I was excited to see where things would go with him until I remembered I still had Charlie to contend with.

Charlie and I hung out a handful of times, but nothing progressed in terms of our relationship, and I use that term very loosely. I hadn't slept with him and had no plans to. We hadn't even got past first base. I was never into Charlie because when it came down to it, we didn't have very much in common. He was into Rush who I hated, and I loved Mötley Crüe who he hated. I honestly don't know how or why we transitioned from being platonic friends to make out buddies in the first place. I suppose not being in your right mind is what rebound mode is all about.

I know I'm a bitch for saying this, but the main thing that irked me about Charlie was that he was way too nice, an absolute doormat. I certainly didn't want to date another asshole; god knows I had my share of those. But I wanted a guy that would call me out on my shit when I was wrong. Someone who would open my mind to try different things and go to places I never would have considered going before. But Charlie rarely had opposing opinions or suggestions on anything. We would go anywhere I wanted to go, do whatever I wanted to do, eat whatever I wanted to eat. He never challenged me what so ever. He was an absolute, total weenie and it got on my last nerve. I knew I had to get out of that situation, but I didn't know how to without hurting his feelings.

The first thing I did was stop returning his calls. Then I felt bad because he would leave concerned messages on my machine, wondering why I wasn't calling him back and ask if I was okay. So I would return a call here and there, then cut him off after a few minutes saying I had to go. When he would ask to hang out, I always said I was busy. I figured he would get the hint and leave me alone at some point, but he didn't. I tried a different approach.

I told him I was having problems at home, which was a lie, and that I needed space to figure things out. He immediately went into counselor mode and kept pressuring me to open up to him about my problems. *Great.*

Sure these were all cowardly approaches in dealing with the situation. I know I was a dick for not being upfront with him. But I felt it was better than telling him he was a rebound. To make matters worse, Valentines Day was coming up. He left a message on my machine saying how he wanted us to spend it together. UGH. That was the LAST thing I wanted to do.

Shortly before Valentines Day, Sebastian invited me to his show at a club called English Acid. Other bands on the bill were Fizzy Bangers, The Ultra's, and Bam's band, The Hatebreeders. I wasn't able to borrow Lucy's car that night, and my dad was using his truck. Hannah's car was in the shop, so the only other option was my mom's station wagon, or as I called it, the "pickle wagon".

The pickle wagon was a burgundy colored, 1980 Dodge Aspen, aka *Titanic* on wheels. I didn't want to be caught rolling that hovercraft into Hollywood, but I didn't have a choice. So the night of the show, I picked up Hannah and we putt putted our way out to English Acid.

Fizzy Bangers were about to go on when I walked into the club with Hannah. I looked around and noticed black lights spread throughout the club. Even the bathroom only had a single red light bulb to illuminate the small restroom. I figured it was pointless to try and touch up my makeup since I couldn't see a damn thing anyway.

Hannah and I stood near the back of the club and took a glance at who was hanging out. A few guys from The Glamour Punks were there. I also noticed Jezebel, one of many girls that fooled around with Sheldon while we were together. She was dancing in front of the stage, drunk off her ass.

Fizzy Bangers finished their set. The Hatebreeders went on next. Sebastian and his friend, Chuck, who played bass in Fizzy Bangers, came over to talk to us. Chuck was Mexican and had taught Sebastian random Spanish words like "*pelo*" (hair), and "*pendejo*" (stupid). They each had Corona's in their hands and referred to them as "Coron nee nee NEE TAS!" in a squeaky voice. Somehow we got on the subject of Disneyland and made a plan for the four of us to go over the next few weeks.

Once The Hatebreeders finished their set, The Kids were up next. Sebastian ran off to start setting up while I walked to the bar with Hannah to buy us a few drinks. It had been well over a year since I last saw The Kids play, so I wasn't familiar with any of their songs. But I quickly became a fan as I watched Sebastian pace the stage and sing with a raw intensity similar to Trent Reznor of Nine Inch Nails.

When The Kids finished their set, Sebastian walked over and gave me a big sweaty hug. He said a few people were going back to The Glamour Punks apartment for drinks after the show and he wanted me to go. He didn't know the address though. He only mentioned it was on Detroit just north of Sunset and described what the building looked like. I told him I would meet him there and bolted out of the club. I didn't want to give him the option of riding in that awful pickle wagon with me.

Hannah and I got caught up talking to a few people outside. By the time I began to pull out of the parking lot, Sebastian was walking out with Mandie and Chuck. Hannah immediately ducked down and tried to hide. My first reaction was to do the same, but it would have looked ridiculous to see a station wagon driving itself.

Sebastian saw me and made his way toward me while Hannah tried to stuff herself in the glove compartment. At that point, I figured to hell with it. It's not like I expected him to be rolling out of the parking lot in a Bentley either. I laid back in the pickle wagon as if it were a low rider and smiled.

"Don't flake out, you better go!" Sebastian said.

"I promise we're going. I'm heading there now," I said.

Sebastian walked off with the guys. Hannah mentioned she was starving, and I was hungry too. We decided to grab some food before heading over to Sebastian's. We stopped at a nearby Del Taco and the stupid pickle wagon began to overheat as it idled in the drive-thru. I didn't want to be stuck in Hollywood if the car broke down and decided it was best if we go home. I was obviously more annoyed than Hannah since that was the 2nd time I had to bail on plans with Sebastian.

A few days later, it was Valentines Day. I would have preferred to do something with Sebastian, but we had only been talking for a few weeks. I felt that having our first official date on Valentines Day might be too much pressure. Instead, I ended up getting a call from Charlie in the afternoon. He left a message saying he wanted to take me to dinner and a movie. I didn't call him back.

I also received a surprise phone call from Sheldon asking if he could take me out to lunch. The last time we saw each other was at Sizzler on the day we called it quits. We had only spoken a handful of times since then. Although most of our talks were vapid conversations, they were still friendly. Since things seemed to be cool with Sheldon, I figured why not. Who was I to turn down a free lunch?

I have no idea what the hell I was thinking. We ended up having a few drinks with lunch and the next thing I know we're back at Sheldon's place hooking up. After it was over, he told me he still loved me. I told him I forgot I had plans with Hannah and got the hell out of there.

I called Faye the moment I got home. I told her all about the huge mistake I just made and how I needed to add Sheldon to the list of guys whose calls I had to avoid.

A few weeks later, The Kids and Fizzy Bangers had another show together at the Whisky for Monday nights No Bozo Jam. Sebastian invited me to go, so I dragged Hannah with me. Faye also called that night, asking for a lift to Hollywood to see a band called Swingin Thing who were playing the Roxy. She offered gas money to pick her up and said she would find a ride home later. Hannah was driving and wanted the extra cash, so we picked up Faye and made our way out to Hollywood.

When we arrived at the Strip, Faye scampered off to the Roxy while I went with Hannah to the Whisky. The Fizzy Bangers were about to go on when we walked in and the floor was packed. We decided to head upstairs for a drink and watch the show from there.

I followed Hannah upstairs and we had almost reached the top when I spotted Charlie at the bar. We quickly turned on our heels, barreled down the stairs and hid underneath the staircase. Sebastian found me a few minutes later and gave me the address to his place. He said he was having a few people over after the show and if I didn't see him after his set, to just head over there.

I managed to avoid Charlie by continuing to hide under the staircase like a troll. The moment The Kids finished, Hannah and I ran out the door. We made a pit stop to get some food and went over to Sebastian's on Martel, just north of Sunset. Hannah buzzed the apartment. To my surprise, Sebastian answered the intercom. I couldn't believe he beat us there.

"Who is it!" Sebastian yelled.

"Hannah and Marisa," Hannah said.

"I wanna hear Marisa!"

176

"I'm here Sebastian," I said.

He buzzed us in, and we made our way up to his apartment. When the elevator doors opened, a random guy and his friends tried walking in before we could get out.

"Are you guys going to the party at Sebastian's?" one of them asked me.

"Yeah, why?" I asked as we walked out of the elevator.

"Don't bother. Mandie is slamming the door in peoples faces and not letting anyone in."

The elevator doors closed, and I heard a door slam from down the hallway. A few seconds later, another small group of people were passing us and heading toward the elevator.

Hannah and I looked at each other as we cautiously walked down the hallway to Sebastian's. I knocked on the front door, and a voice yelled, "WHO IS IT!" from behind the door.

"IT'S MARISA!" I yelled back.

"Sebastian, it's Marisa!" the voice yelled behind the door.

A few moments later, the door opened. Sebastian let us in. I asked what the heightened security was all about. He said they didn't want random people in the apartment, so he was having Mandie turn people away.

When I walked into the apartment, Mandie, Dizzy, and Skitz, one of the guitarists from The Glamour Punks, were there along with Jezebel, Bam, and Chuck. There were also a few other people I wasn't familiar with. I also noticed a girl named Harley that I met earlier in the night at the Whisky. She was super skinny with stringy red hair and beady blue eyes that she outlined in charcoal grey eyeliner. There was something about the way she stared at Sebastian that made me very uncomfortable. Her eyes would follow his every movement as if she were a doctor observing some type of specimen. Casey was also there. When she saw Sebastian put his arm around me, she shot me the dirtiest look. I thought she had a lot of nerve shooting ME looks considering she was screwing around with Sheldon the entire time we were together. I glared back at her with a smile as I put my arm around Sebastian and continued making my way into the apartment.

Before I get ahead of myself though, let me first explain where Sebastian lived.

Technically, it wasn't his apartment. It belonged to a stripper named Angela. Sebastian's living quarters consisted of a makeshift bedroom he created himself. He used a black tarp to section off a small corner of the living room, which contained the only balcony. The space behind the tarp was just wide enough to fit a small twin bed, a stereo, and a few of his other belongings. He recently put up Christmas lights along the small portion of wall he had, which he proudly showed off as if he just redecorated a room in a mansion.

After the tour of his "bedroom", Sebastian offered Hannah and I a drink. Chuck walked up and told us our options were Jim Beam with Coke, or red wine.

"It's vintage 1992, called Chateau de Borracho," Sebastian said as he pulled the cork and waved it under Chuck's nose.

"Ahh that's a very good wine. It must have set you back a whole two dollars," Chuck said.

A brunette with olive skin and long dark curly hair emerged from the bedroom holding a black cat. Sebastian introduced her as his roommate, Angela. Her black cat was Scooby. She was very sweet and welcomed me to her apartment, then left a short time later.

In a matter of minutes, the apartment went from a handful of people to semi packed. Sebastian's bass player, Jack, came in with his girlfriend, Susie, and Vaughn, the singer of Beautiful Destruction, walked in with Strange. One after another, people began piling in. I was having a great time getting to know everyone until I saw Mark and Charlie from Electric walk in.

I happened to be standing near Sebastian's living quarters, so I leapt behind the tarp and fell onto his bed with Hannah in tow.

I had no idea what the hell they were doing there. They were the last people I expected to see. Neither of them were friends with the guys in The Kids or The Glamour Punks, at least not that I knew of. After all, it wasn't that long ago when Sebastian called their band a bunch of heshers.

Apparently Sebastian's opinion hadn't changed because a few minutes later, I heard the word "hesher" being thrown around by Sebastian and Chuck. I peeked out from behind the tarp and saw Charlie and Mark standing by the kitchen. Charlie had put some type of wallet down on the counter and was digging through his pockets for some reason. Mark and Charlie weren't there more than five minutes before they were heckled out of the apartment. I felt bad because they were nice guys, but the last thing I needed to deal with was being caught in a love triangle involving Charlie and Sebastian.

When Hannah and I emerged from behind the tarp, I noticed Charlie left his wallet behind on the counter. I walked over to grab it and quickly realized it wasn't a wallet. It was a personal phonebook divided into two sections, "Dudes" and "Girls".

I began to flip through the "Girls" section. By each girls name was a star rating and comments like, "cute face", "nice tits", and "boneable if really drunk." I happened to see Faye's name and phone number in there with a 5 star rating. His commentary? "Hot, but only 15?"

I was curious to see what he said about me. When I looked myself up, the only items written by my name were my phone number and the address to my house. No stars, no comments, no nothing. Story of my fucking life, baked squash strikes once again.

I closed the phonebook, strolled over to the bathroom and threw it right in the garbage. After reading Charlie's colorful commentary about everyone but me, it became very easy to stop returning his calls without a shred of guilt.

When I came out of the bathroom, Angela had just walked in the front door with Faye, Pixie, and Spazz, the drummer of The Glamour Punks. Angela and Spazz went straight to her bedroom while Faye greeted me with a big drunk hug. Faye told Pixie I was the girl that took care of her on the Strip a few weeks earlier. Pixie thanked me profusely. She wanted to stay but said she needed to leave, so she made herself a quick drink and walked out with Faye.

Over the course of the night, people freely walked in and out of the apartment. A few mentioned they were popping over to Mandie's and would be right back. I asked Sebastian where he lived and he said right down the hall.

About an hour or so later, Faye burst into the apartment and jumped on top of me. She was wearing a jacket that Mandie wore earlier in the evening.

"Hi Marisa! I just came back to say bye!" she said still holding onto me.

"Ohh...uh bye. Are you going home?" I asked.

"No, just back to Mandie's apartment down the hall," she said smiling.

Faye was fairly tipsy when I saw her earlier with Pixie. Now she was straight up drunk. I didn't want her stumbling around the building by herself, so I told her I would walk with her over to Mandie's.

We took a few steps out of Sebastian's when Faye stumbled and fell down in the hallway. I picked her up and told her to put her arm around me, which she did. She took off Mandie's jacket and let it drag in her other hand as she led me down the hall to Mandie's. Right before we reached the door of his apartment, he opened the door.

"Why are you dragging my fucking jacket?" Mandie asked her as he snatched the jacket out of her hand.

Out of nowhere, Sebastian popped up right behind us. Mandie invited us into his apartment, so we strolled in and made ourselves a drink. His place was just as packed as Sebastian's. Mandie mentioned that Sunny and Chris, the guitarists from Swingin Thing, lived on the same floor too. The third floor of the Martel building seemed to be a never-ending party that was referred to as "The Martel Estates". If you became bored at one apartment, you just walked down the hall to someone else's.

CHRIS PENKETH (Swingin Thing): Sunny and I were dropped off on Martel with our bags and had nowhere to live. The car took off, we looked at each other and said, "Where to now?"

I kid you not, a few minutes later, a car pulled up. It was a Japanese girl. I forget her name, but she said, "Chris! Sunny! What are you guys doing?" I said, "We're looking for a place to live." And she said, "You can live with me!" We stayed with her for about a week or so, then we ran into our friends Carrie and Monica who offered us a place to stay, which was on the 3rd floor of the Martel building where Sebastian and Mandie were living.

I remember we used to loot each others apartments looking for change because we'd go down to Rock and Roll Ralphs near La Brea to get the 25 cent burritos. If you were really rich you could get the 35 cent burritos, which were bigger, but you'd have to find that extra dime. If you found loose carts at Rock and Roll Ralphs,

you could return them and get a quarter too. Michael Michelle and I saved a few hookers from some cops one day by hiding them in the Laundromat by a bagel place on the corner. They gave us a dollar for helping them, but we didn't want to spend that dollar because it was our first dollar that hookers actually gave us, so we thought we were pimpin.

SUNNY PHILLIPS (Swingin Thing): Chris and I were living with the Japanese girl, but she had to go back to Japan, so we had to leave her place. I think we were there for a few weeks. When she left, we literally had nowhere to go. We were walking down the street with our bags and our guitars when we saw our friends Monica and Carrie, who offered us a place to stay. The whole thing happened in like five minutes.

About an hour or so passed at Mandie's when I suddenly remembered I left Hannah back at Sebastian's. I could only hope she was having a great time and didn't notice our extended absence. But when Sebastian and I walked back to his place, she was long gone. I couldn't believe she left me stranded in Hollywood.

Sebastian said it was no big deal and that he would take me home a little later. We went behind the tarp and passed out for a few hours. We woke shortly before sunrise and hopped into his black truck, which didn't have a passenger side window. He gave me a jacket to wear on the ride home, but I still shivered my ass off all the way back to Rosemead. When I came home, there was a long message from Hannah waiting for me on my answering machine about how I ditched her. She also said some random girl was being a bitch to her and that some of the guys were hassling her to walk to the corner liquor store and buy them more booze.

After sleeping for a few hours, I called Hannah to apologize. I told her I lost track of time at Mandie's and in no way meant to ditch her. I even offered to pay for her Disneyland ticket if she was still up for going with me, Sebastian and Chuck. She accepted my apology and the Disneyland ticket but said she didn't want to go back to Sebastian's apartment ever again.

A few days later, The Rodney King beating trials began. The Rodney King beating was a huge police scandal that took place in early 1991. L.A.P.D officers pulled Rodney over following a high-speed chase and proceeded to beat him in the middle of a residential street, not knowing that a nearby resident was filming the entire thing.

A few days into the trial, I was sitting in bed watching the courtroom footage when my friend, Joaquin, called. He was the drummer of a band called Smile. He invited me to his show at the Troubadour, where he was opening for a KISS cover band called Cold Gin. Since I hadn't seen him in months, I told him I would go.

While I was getting ready, Sebastian called and asked what I was doing that night. When I told him I was going to the Troubadour, he mentioned he was going there too to see Cold Gin and would meet me there.

When I arrived at the Troubadour that evening, Smile was about to go on and the club was getting fairly crowded. I found a spot near the stage next to a hefty guy that introduced himself as Billy. He asked me if I was there to see Smile. I said yes. He said he knew all the guys in the band and we chatted about how I knew Joaquin.

After chatting with Billy, I glanced around the club looking for familiar faces. A few minutes later, I noticed Sebastian walk in with Chuck, Bam, Mandie, and Harley. His once platinum blond hair was died black, and he had gotten dreadlocks. I barely recognized him.

Sebastian and crew went straight to the bar. I decided to wait until Smile's set finished before I would walk over and say hello. I continued to look around the club and noticed some of the guys from Bullet Boys and Tuff walking around. Chris and Sunny from Swingin Thing were there too, along with Jack from The Kids and some of the guys from The Glamour Punks. I also saw Gene Simmons and Paul Stanley sitting on the first bench of bleachers upstairs, overlooking the club.

During Smile's set, someone kept throwing ice at them from the back bar. Although I couldn't see exactly who it was, I had a pretty good idea that Sebastian and his crew were responsible. Billy was getting agitated and told me if he found out who it was, he was going to beat the shit out of them after the show.

Smile finished their set, and I was about to turn around and look for Sebastian when he popped up beside me drunk off his ass. He said the band that just played totally sucked and that he and the guys were throwing ice at them to get them off stage. I felt Billy looking in our direction, so I quickly changed the subject and asked Sebastian about his hair. He said he wanted to get dreadlocks for a long time. He also said he originally died his hair burgundy a few days earlier but that it looked like shit and decided to dye it black earlier that day.

When Cold Gin went on, Sebastian put his arms around me as we watched the show. I appreciated the nuzzling, but he was being really loud and obnoxious. I could tell Billy was getting agitated too, so I planned to get Sebastian out of there immediately after the show finished.

The moment Cold Gin left the stage, I tried to drag Sebastian away, but he said they were coming back for an encore and wanted to stay. The entire club was chanting, "We want KISS! We want KISS!" Chris jumped up on the shoulders of someone and started chanting with the rest of us when he suddenly fell off and hit the ground. Sebastian and I started laughing.

Cold Gin came back out and finished the show with "Rock and Roll All Night". As the song was finishing, I managed to pull Sebastian into the lobby. I tried to continue dragging him out of the club, but he told me he had to go back inside to get Mandie and the rest of the guys. Just moments after he left to go back inside, Billy came out to the lobby with a drink in his hand. He walked up to me and asked where my loudmouth friend was. I lied and said he left, hoping that would send him away before Sebastian could make his way back outside.

Just then, Sebastian walked out and headed right in my direction. He was with Bam, Mandie, and some of the other Glamour Punks.

"We're all going back to my place for drinks. Did you wanna…" Sebastian began to ask me.

"Yeah, lets go now!" I said cutting Sebastian off as I tried to push him out the door.

"Hey, what's your rush?" he said laughing.

"Were you the one throwing ice at Smile?" Billy asked Sebastian.

Before Sebastian could answer, Billy poured a drink over his head, put one hand around his throat and pushed him against the wall. The guys from The Glamour Punks immediately jumped Billy, security jumped on them, and anyone that was in the vicinity swarmed in to see the fight. Joaquin popped up from out of nowhere, pulled me out of the mess and asked me what happened. When I told him he didn't seem bothered by the ice throwing. He actually thought it was funny and apologized to me for Billy's behavior towards Sebastian.

Security threw all the guys outside. When I finally made my way through the crowd to find Sebastian, he was already far off down the street walking with Mandie and the guys. Billy, who was still out of breath and a bit disheveled, walked over to me.

"You're hanging out with the wrong kind of people little girl," he said.

I shot him a dirty look, said goodbye to Joaquin and went home.

I had just turned off the light in my bedroom and climbed into bed when my neon phone lit up the room and nearly scared the crap out of me. I answered. It was Sebastian.

"How come you didn't come to my apartment after the show?" he asked.

"I didn't think you would be in the mood after what happened. Are you okay?"

"Of course I'm okay. Why wouldn't I be?" he said completely unfazed. "So when are we going to Disneyland?"

10

CRAZY? DON'T MIND IF I DO!

*T*he day we chose to go to Disneyland started out as a beautiful, sunny day. Hannah picked me up in the early afternoon and we darted off to Hollywood to get Sebastian and Chuck.

When we pulled up outside of Sebastian's, I noticed Sunny and Bam hanging out with Mandie on his balcony, which faced the street. Sunny told me the intercom for Angela's apartment wasn't working and that he would run down the hall to let Sebastian know I was there.

A few minutes later, Chuck walked out followed by Sebastian who was holding a plastic cup. After taking a good sniff, I realized it was Jim Beam and Coke. Chuck flipped the passenger seat forward to let Sebastian and I hop in the back. I jumped in first. The moment Sebastian sat down next to me, Chuck flipped the seat back, which hit Sebastian's cup and caused his drink to spill all over him.

Sebastian climbed out of the car and went upstairs to change. When he came back down a few minutes later, he had on a fresh set of clothes and a new drink in hand. He complained about not having any ice cubes left for his drink. Sunny popped into Mandie's apartment and came back out a few moments later with a trey of ice cubes. He dropped a few cubes down to Sebastian for his drink while Mandie grabbed a few and threw them right at Chuck's head.

"That's for wasting a perfectly good drink asshole!" Mandie yelled.

After having a good laugh at Chuck's expense, we hopped back into Hannah's car and made our way out to Disneyland.

On the drive there, Sebastian talked about what a big Dodger fan he was. He and his bass player, Jack, were leaving in a few weeks to see their spring training in Florida. We got on the subject of money and he mentioned how he was going to pay for lunch since we were all pretty broke at the time.

"You guys are on your own," Sebastian said to Hannah and Chuck. "I've got me and Marisa covered," he continued.

"Aww thank you," I said.

"Yeah, just stop by an AM/PM on the way. Two burgers for a buck, I'll sneak them in," he said.

Well it's the thought that counts.

Once we crossed the Orange Curtain and entered the city of Anaheim, the clouds rolled in and the sun slowly started to disappear. By the time we parked Hannah's car at Disneyland, black clouds had completely shrouded the happiest place on earth. It was as if Mother Nature herself was trying to repel us, the evil heathens that dared to cross it's innocent pixie covered gates.

It began to sprinkle when we walked into Disneyland. People started running past us in droves as they covered their heads. I didn't care about walking around in the light mist. Chuck, Hannah, and Sebastian didn't seem to mind either. We continued on our way through the park and stumbled upon the Star Wars ride. By the time we got off the ride, the sprinkles had turned into a light rain and lines for most of the attractions were nonexistent. We had a blast running around the park, getting on and off of rides like The Matterhorn and Space Mountain multiple times in a row.

186

Since our clothes were fairly wet by then, we decided to get on Splash Mountain. Sebastian and I hopped in the back, while Chuck and Hannah sat in the front. When we reached the top of the mountain, I looked down at the long drop below us. Sebastian put his arms around my waist, pulled me towards him and we shared our first kiss. Then the four of us collectively screamed our way all the way down the mountain. Sebastian and I were hit with a light mist when we hit the bottom, but poor Chuck and Hannah were completely drenched.

"Chuck what's up with your *pelo*?" Sebastian asked as he laughed at his hair.

"My *pelo* isn't *pelo* anymore," Chuck said.

"Your *pelo* is *muy malo*!" Sebastian said.

After Splash Mountain, we went on The Haunted House ride to dry off for a bit. We also hopped in a little boat that took us through the It's a Small World ride. The boat was riding too slow for Sebastian, and the constant loop of the "It's a Small World" song was making him crazy. He yelled for the puppets to shut up and would try to jump out of the boat to walk his way out of the tunnel through the shallow stream. By the time we got off that ride it was pouring outside. The temperature had also dropped about ten degrees, so we called it a day and went back to Sebastian's.

On the way to his place, we picked up a fifth of Jim Beam and a liter of Coke. We watched an MTV show called *120 Minutes* while Chuck made us cocktails. I was just finishing my first drink when Hannah whispered in my ear that she wanted to leave. She complained she was getting sick, but I knew she was still bitter about what happened the last time we were at Sebastian's. Since she drove that day and Sebastian was feeling lazy about giving me a ride home, I didn't have much of a choice. So Sebastian walked us to Hannah's car, gave me another kiss and told me to call him later.

While I felt our first semi date at Disneyland was a success, I was tired of meeting Sebastian at clubs and in a group setting. We had yet to have an official date where it would just be the two of us. I nonchalantly brought this up to him, and he suggested I come over to his place the following weekend to watch movies.

I arrived at Sebastian's around 11:00pm on a Sunday evening. I had just parked my moms pickle wagon and was walking towards his building when I saw Angela strolling toward a car idling in the street. We said hello and she seemed to be coughing.

"Are you okay? Are you getting sick?" I asked.

"Just a tiny bit, but I'm fine," she said sniffling.

"How come you're going out? Shouldn't you be in bed?"

"Yeah, but this afternoon Sebastian said he wanted the apartment to himself tonight and to go find something to do for a few hours," she said sweetly.

Only Sebastian could kick someone out of their own apartment.

I apologized to her because it was obvious he did that for me. She said it was cool, hugged me goodbye and then hopped into the waiting car. I continued walking up to the building and buzzed Angela's apartment. I stood there for a few moments and remembered the intercom in her apartment still wasn't working. I was about to walk away and call Sebastian from a payphone next door when I saw the elevator doors open in the lobby. Out came Bam, Mandie, Sunny, Jack, and Susie. *What perfect timing for them to let me in.*

Sebastian was trailing and stumbling behind them as they walked toward the front door of the apartment building. As they walked out one by one, each said hi and greeted me with hugs. Sebastian was drunk and walked right past me.

"Sebastian? Where are you going?" I asked.

"Hey! Oh yeah, we're watching movies tonight right? Heh heh heh...I almost forgot. Come on let's go," he said grabbing my hand and leading me back into the apartment building.

Slightly annoyed, I bit my tongue and followed him into the building. When we walked into his apartment he apologized for being forgetful. He made each of us a drink and asked if I wanted to watch a movie.

"Yeah, I guess," I said still mildly annoyed.

A few minutes into the movie, the house phone began to ring and wouldn't stop. Any calls that were for him he would spend a few minutes on. Those that came in for Angela were told to call back later and hung up on by Sebastian. He didn't want to be bothered by writing down their information.

We made out a little bit during the movie. When it finished, Sebastian said he wanted to watch *120 Minutes*. A few minutes into watching the show, Mandie burst into the apartment with a guy named Spider who was drunk off his ass. I knew that would be the end of my quiet time with Sebastian.

Spider fell face first on the carpet in the living room. With his eyes closed, he began yelling out random things to Mandie, most of which we couldn't understand. After a few more outbursts, we were able to start deciphering Spider's babble. So Mandie decided to mess with him.

"Mandie, leave my drink alone!" Spider yelled.

Meanwhile, Mandie was sitting on the couch at least a good eight feet away from Spider.

"Sorry man, I made you a fresh drink. Here ya go," Mandie said.

"Thanks man," Spider said.

The three of us started laughing.

"Yo how's that drink?" Mandie asked.

"Issss gooood…" Spider mumbled.

"I'm making burgers too. You want one?"

"Yeah."

"Here, how does it taste?"

"It's raw," Spider said.

We all started laughing again.

"Sorry, I thought you wanted it medium rare man. Take this one it's cooked."

"Oh that izzz goooood…"

Theoretically speaking, Spider ended up eating a full meal with three cocktails, all while laying face first on the floor of the living room.

About an hour or so later, Mandie walked out and left Spider behind on the floor. By that time, he had been quiet for a good half hour. We figured he passed out and that was good enough for me. I knew it was the closest we would get in terms of having the place to ourselves that night.

Sebastian and I were about five minutes into our make out session when he said he needed to pee. When he stood up, he fell over. I asked him if he needed help. He said he was fine as he stumbled into the hallway towards the bathroom.

About ten minutes passed and Sebastian still wasn't back. I checked the bathroom, but the door was wide open and the light was off. I walked toward Angela's bedroom and there he was sprawled out face first on her bed passed out.

I slapped him on the butt, which woke him up and told him I was leaving. He stood up and told me not to leave as we walked back to the living room. We cuddled up on the couch and within minutes he passed out again.

Angela walked in the door a few minutes later, and at that point, I just wanted to go home. I slowly peeled Sebastian's arms off me and told him to go back to sleep. He kissed me goodbye and stumbled behind the tarp. I heard him plop himself onto his bed as I walked myself out.

It was about 5:00 am when I hopped into my moms pickle wagon. I wanted to get home before sunrise, but when I went to start the car, the damn thing was dead as a doornail. *Just great. Stranded, cold, and nowhere to go.*

While I considered my options, I noticed Spazz get out of a car and head to Sebastian's apartment building. I got out of the pickle wagon and ran to catch up with him. I figured he was going to see Angela who he was hooking up with at the time. I knew he was my best bet at getting back into the apartment since I knew Sebastian was passed out cold.

I told Spazz the buzzer wasn't working in Angela's apartment. As he told me about his wild night at a Skid Row after party, he began buzzing every apartment in the building repeatedly, figuring someone would let him in. Sure enough, someone did.

When we reached Angela's apartment, he began kicking on the front door. She let us in a few minutes later, and I went behind Sebastian's tarp to tell to tell him what happened. He didn't care because he was still half asleep. He mumbled for me to spend the night and pulled me down to his chest. So we curled up together and fell asleep.

One thing I have to say about Sebastian, even though the music and image of The Kids was dark and angry; he was quite the snuggle bunny. Throughout the night some part of his body was always touching mine. When we weren't snuggled up in each other's arms, he would be holding my hand or have a leg or arm across some part of my body, which I found endearing.

We woke the next morning shortly before noon. Sebastian put on the Dodger game, and called Mandie to come over, which he did a few minutes later. Sebastian was hungry and asked him if he had any breakfast yet. Mandie said he ate a piece of bread with a few toppings that he described like a five star breakfast.

A half hour later, Chuck walked in the door looking a bit disheveled. Fizzy Bangers had a show the night before in Bakersfield at a club called Mars. He said he spent the night at a random hotel with two fat girls he called "animales" and swore up and down that he didn't sleep with them.

When the game finished, I figured I would try and start my mom's car one last time before calling Lucy to come pick me up. I said my goodbyes to everyone and went down to try the temperamental pickle wagon. To my surprise it started right up, so I made my way home.

Weeks passed with no word from Charlie. I couldn't have been happier. Especially after the lackluster commentary he gave me in his little black book. As for Sheldon, well not so much. He had been calling ever since our Valentines Day hookup, and I was avoiding him like the plague. Sebastian and I were dating on a regular basis at that point, so hearing Sheldon's voice on my machine every few days was a constant reminder on what a big mistake I made. I knew I would have to call and resolve the situation with Sheldon sooner rather than later. So on a random Saturday afternoon, I called him and decided to have it out once and for all.

I didn't get more than a few words out before he went into interrogation mode about Sebastian. Apparently, he heard we were dating and was not happy about it.

"What do you have against Sebastian anyway?" I asked.

"He's a slut. He sleeps around all the time and you deserve better than that," Sheldon said.

"Ha! The guy who laid more pipe in Hollywood than the local plumber is calling someone else a slut? Now THAT's funny," I snorted.

Sheldon admitted to screwing up a good thing between us. He said he still loved me and wanted to get back together. I told him he was out of his damn mind and promptly hung up on him.

I talked to Faye later that afternoon and told her what was going on with Sheldon. She said not to believe him because he was chirping the same monologue to his ex-girlfriend, Evie. According to Faye, Sheldon was calling Evie for the past two months, telling her he still had feelings for her and wanted THEM to get back together. Naturally, that didn't surprise me one bit.

Sheldon clicked in on my other line as I was getting off the phone with Faye. He asked why I hung up on him and that he wanted to talk more about "us".

"There is no US," I told him. "And speaking of girlfriends, I just hung up with Faye. She said you're feeding the same line of bullshit to Evie about getting back together with her," I said.

Sheldon paused for a moment and said nothing. I knew I had him. I kicked my feet up on my bed and smiled like the Cheshire Cat.

"Well? What have you got to say foh yohself goovnah?" I said in a snotty English accent as I wiggled my toes.

"Faye is a fucking liar and so is Evie. They're jealous hussies. Evie is the one that's been calling me and saying she wants to hang out."

"Bollocks!" I yelled.

"Why are you talking in an English accent?" Sheldon asked.

A crowning moment in a girl's life is when a guy who has royally screwed her over comes crawling back, and she has no remorse. The taste of that victory is sweeter than any dessert I've ever had. But not as good as finding an awesome pair of designer shoes at a sample sale in your size at half the cost.

As I listened to Sheldon drag Faye and Evie's credibility through the mud, I wondered what I should do about the current situation. *Maybe go into some big grand standing speech and yell at him for being such a douche bag? Be a manipulative bitch and string him along for a few weeks then screw him over?* Considering I was only 18, it would have been justifiable to do either and blame it on a lack of maturity. But I've never been one to deal with such theatrics. Plotting revenge on someone takes up a lot of time and energy that can be used towards something more productive. I didn't have the patience or simply give a big enough shit to do something calculated to Sheldon, even though he certainly deserved it.

"Listen. We're not getting back together. And if you have a problem with me dating Sebastian, then blow it out your ass," I said bluntly and hung up on him again.

I would like my victory sundae with extra sprinkles please.

With another fun filled weekend upon me, I was off to Sebastian's for the night as usual. When I arrived at the apartment, Spider was there along with Elise, Spencer, Harley, and a stripper named Evelyn.

I first met Elise through Sheldon. She and a friend of hers would always go to Dancer shows. I adored Elise because she was a tomboy, which was something I could relate to. She never wiggled around in skimpy clothes or tried to be the center of attention like most of the other girls in Hollywood. She didn't have to. She was comfortable in her own skin and just a friendly, down to earth girl that liked sports. She had long auburn hair, big green eyes and little freckles around her nose. I thought she was the cutest thing ever. Any time she was around, I wanted to jump on top of her and bite her face.

Spencer had long wavy blonde hair and hazel eyes. I didn't know much about her other than we were the same age. I would see her bouncing around the Strip, but we never officially met until that night at Sebastian's. As it turned out, she lived just ten minutes up the street from me in South Pasadena.

And as for Evelyn, she was skinny with a perfectly cut red bob and big brown eyes. She was also a closet stripper. No one was supposed to know that, but of course we all did. If anyone asked her what she did for a living, she would always say she was a secretary for an insurance agency. We all knew that was bullshit because she had her own huge apartment in Hollywood. No 18-year-old secretary would have been able to afford a place like that unless they had rich parents, which Evelyn didn't. No one understood why she tried to hide being a stripper, but nonetheless we went along with her façade.

After having a few drinks at Sebastian's, the seven of us were trying to think of something to do when he suggested we go to the beach. I was fine with group activities at this point and had long given up on having any alone time with Sebastian except for when we were sleeping behind his tarp. With everyone in agreement, we sucked down our cocktails and drove out to Malibu.

We parked on Pacific Coast Highway just past Sunset Blvd. We got out of our cars and looked over the rocks to the ocean waves crashing below. As some of the girls began to take off their shoes, Sebastian snatched one of Evelyn's and threw it over the rocks. It landed safely on the sand below. She started bitching to Sebastian that her shoes were brand new and for him to go and get it. He laughed and told Harley to fetch the shoe, which to my surprise she immediately did. Just like an obedient dog.

I never liked having Harley around because something about her rubbed me the wrong way. Not that she was ever mean to me. She was always quite sweet actually. But I didn't like the way she always lingered around Sebastian.

Once Harley scaled the rocks and fetched Evelyn's shoe, we noticed a stairwell a few yards away that led down to the beach. Spider and Spencer led the way down the steps. I followed behind them. Spencer and I were chatting about how close we lived to each other when I realized Sebastian and the rest of the girls were gone.

That didn't surprise me though. Sebastian always did things like that. He would take off without saying anything and show up later like nothing was wrong. He felt if he was going somewhere for a short period of time, it wasn't worth mentioning because (according to him) he would be back by the time I would notice he was gone.

When Sebastian went AWOL, it was always a crapshoot on how long he would be gone for. It could be a few minutes, which didn't bother me. Then there were times when he would disappear for well over an hour and those instances drove me insane. But I didn't want to come off like a parole officer. I decided I would just chalk it up to being an aspect of his personality that I had to accept.

Knowing that Sebastian would surface at some point in the night, I told Spencer and Spider to continue down the steps to the beach. Sure enough, Sebastian popped up about fifteen minutes later. He was walking down the steps with a cocktail in one hand and a bag of food from Jack in the Box in the other. He said the girls bought him food (I'm guessing Harley) and that

Evelyn was still being a bitch about her shoe and wanted to leave. Since Spencer and Evelyn were the ones with the cars, Harley and Elise decided to take off with Evelyn.

The four of us continued walking on the beach until we spotted a good stack of rocks we could sit on. We snacked on Sebastian's bag of food and chatted amongst ourselves for a bit. After we finished eating, Sebastian wanted to take a walk with me alone on the beach, so we left Spencer and Spider behind. We sat down in the sand and watched a few ducks frolic around in a small pool of water nearby. He talked about how much he loved the Cure and how cool it would be if he were a vampire. Naturally, this made me raise an eyebrow.

His tastes in music were all over the place. He liked everything from Cypress Hill and House of Pain, to alternative bands like Curve, Pighead, Lush, and The Wonderstuff. He asked me random things like if I used a Ouija board before and whether I believed in ghosts.

While I gave him my thoughts on the paranormal and professed my undying love for The Beatles, Sebastian picked up pieces of random garbage around us like broken shells and rocks, then started throwing them at the ducks. I told him he was an asshole and to leave the poor ducks alone. He laughed and threw one more bottle cap.

We shared his drink and somehow got on the subject of us dating. He said he really liked me but wasn't ready for another girlfriend just yet. I was relieved to hear him say that since I wasn't 100% sure what I wanted either. He still wanted us to hang out but was also worried about what I was getting myself into with him. I asked him what he meant by that. He said we would talk about it later and that we should probably get back to Spencer and Spider.

The four of us left the beach a short time later, and Spencer dropped Sebastian and I off at his place. We made some drinks and lay down behind his tarp. He brought up the subject of us dating again as he fed me Reese's Pieces. He seemed to be very concerned about hurting me, so I took that as an opportunity to bring up my concerns about Harley. I told him that her habit of constantly looming around him was getting on my last nerve. He paused for a moment and then admitted to sleeping with her a while back.

195

I was just about to spout off my obvious disapproval when I thought about my own indiscretion with Sheldon on Valentines Day. According to the time frame Sebastian mentioned, both encounters seemed to have happened around the same time, which was when we first started hanging out.

"So are you guys still hooking up?" I asked.

"NO WAY. It only happened that one time because I was wasted," he said.

"You're always wasted," I said bluntly.

"No, but that night was really bad. I haven't been that drunk since, and it's never going to happen again."

He held my hand and looked at me as if he were asking for forgiveness. I didn't know what to say.

"Are you with me?" he asked.

I wasn't sure what he meant by that. Certainly he couldn't mean as a girlfriend. After all, we just had that relationship conversation a few hours earlier at the beach while he was using the ducks as target practice.

"I don't know what you're asking," I said.

"I'm asking if you're with me," he reiterated.

The only thing I could think to say was no. So that's what I said to him.

"Oh so you're NOT with me?" he asked as he unleashed my hand.

"No, no I am. I am with you," I said, waiting to see if I answered correctly.

"Cool, you're with me then," he said.

He grabbed my hand again and popped a few Reese's into my mouth.

What the hell is he even talking about?

Although I was clueless as to what my official relationship status was with Sebastian, I continued to hang out with him. And the more we hung out, the less I saw of Hannah who I was starting to miss.

A few weeks later, Sebastian mentioned The Kids and Fizzy Bangers had a show in Bakersfield coming up. I took it as an opportunity to invite Hannah. I figured a fun road trip was exactly what she and I needed to get in some good bonding time. Boy, was I mistaken.

When I called Hannah to invite her she snapped at me for even suggesting she go to the show. She said Sebastian and his friends were nothing but mooches and that she didn't like any of my Hollywood friends. She had also just started a full time job with "real responsibilities" and wasn't about to drop everything just to go to some dumb show. She ended our conversation by saying I needed to "grow the fuck up". So in a nutshell, the answer was no. She did not want to go to Bakersfield with me.

Borrowing any car from my family that weekend was out of the question. I couldn't drive up with Sebastian because he was already riding in a full car with his band. I was bummed I couldn't go and enjoy the show, but then again we are talking Bakersfield, not Las Vegas.

With Sebastian being in Bakersfield, I made the strange decision to stay home that weekend and organize my bedroom, which was in complete shambles. It was the first Saturday night I stayed home in months.

I was still cleaning my room around 2:00am when Faye called to tell me about her night. She said she went to a party and was yelled out of the house by a bunch of girls that were calling her a slut. She ran outside crying when Vinnie, from Pretty Boy Floyd of all people, happened to be there and comforted her. Once she calmed down, he disappeared and she bumped into Paul, the singer of Swingin Thing who she had a major crush on at the time. Somehow she ended up getting into an argument with him because she was drunk and emotional, so she hopped in a cab and came home. Just hearing her describe her night had me completely exhausted.

She also mentioned Charlie was at the party and he asked about me. I never told Faye the truth about why I dumped him. I also didn't tell her about the high rating and glowing commentary he gave her in his phonebook. She had enough people showering her with compliments. I figured there wasn't anything he wrote about her that she hadn't already heard before.

A few days later, I had just come home from running errands when my mom told me Hannah called. She said she sounded very upset like she was crying and wanted me to call her the moment I got home. I figured she felt bad for being snippy with me about the Bakersfield trip, but I hardly thought it was worth shedding any tears over.

When I called Hannah back she was crying hysterically. It took me a few minutes to finally calm her down just so I could figure out what the hell she was saying.

She said she had just spoken to Ariah and Arwen's mom. Apparently the twins took a trip with some friends to Tijuana that past weekend. There was a car accident. She said everyone in the car was okay, except for Arwen. She wasn't wearing her seatbelt and her head went through the windshield. She died on impact.

I just couldn't believe it. We were only 18. Our birthdays were just two days apart from each other. We had our whole lives ahead of us. How was this even possible?

My first thought was to call Ariah. But Hannah said their phone had been ringing off the hook all day, so I didn't want to be a bother. She mentioned their mom would call her as soon as funeral arrangements were made and give her that info to pass on to any of Arwen's classmates.

About a week later, I went to Arwen's funeral. I arrived a little early and was standing outside the church when Ariah arrived. As I watched her walk up the steps to the church, she looked like a completely different person. It was as if all the light had been sucked out of her. There was no warmth in her big brown eyes anymore. They were completely vacant now. I saw no trace of the girl that ran around Rosemead High like an energetic little spider monkey laughing her ass off and making funny noises. The girl standing before me was basically a zombie.

People walked up to Ariah one by one and gave their condolences. Like a robot, she would say, "thank you" without looking them in the eye. There were quite a few people going up to her, so I felt it was best to wait until after the services to talk to her.

When I walked inside the church it looked like a high school reunion. Each pew was full of my classmates, many that I graduated with almost a year earlier. I took a seat. An usher handed me a memorial card with Arwen's graduation picture sprawled across the front. She looked so pretty in her cap and gown with a big smile across her face.

People continued to pile in and the services began a few minutes later. I have always tried to be the strong person in situations like that. But the moment I heard Ariah have a complete meltdown halfway through the services, it destroyed me.

I pulled myself together by the time the services concluded. When I finally had the chance to go up to Ariah, all I could do was hug her. We held onto each other for a long time. She eventually broke down in my arms. I kept telling her how sorry I was because I didn't know what else to say to her. I felt I didn't have the right to tell her that everything would be okay because I knew it wouldn't be. My heart broke for her and for the fact that I was never able to make amends with Arwen over what happened at our graduation.

When I came home later that afternoon, I fell back on my bed and stared at the ceiling for what seemed like hours. I didn't watch TV or listen to the radio. I also didn't answer any phone calls. I just thought of Arwen. I thought about all the fun times with her and Ariah in high school. Silly things like when they gave me a new wave makeover by dressing me in their funky clothes. When we spray-painted their bedroom walls with skulls while their mom was on vacation. And when Arwen fell into one of the school toilets while climbing a stall to spy on Brandon and Erica for me. There were many random moments we shared that were so unimportant at the time. I didn't realize how special they were until Arwen was gone.

Losing Arwen made me sit back and think about what was going on in my life. I had been flying by the seat of my pants since graduation with no game plan in sight. That had to change. I needed to figure out what the hell I was going to do with the rest of my life.

As the spring flowers started to bloom, so did my relationship with Sebastian, as well as a new shithole right around the corner from his apartment called Thai Ice Café.

Thai Ice Cafe was a small club on Hollywood Blvd near La Brea. On Tuesday nights they sold $1 beers and had bands perform on their teeny tiny stage. Chuck was going there to meet a girl. Since Sebastian and I didn't have any immediate plans we decided to tag along.

I was halfway through my horrible beer when Chuck and the girl he went to meet started arguing. He walked away from her and told us he wanted to leave. He mentioned a party just around the corner on Yucca Street where some of the guys from a band called Alleycat Scratch supposedly lived. I was hesitant on going because that particular area of Yucca was extremely sketchy. There was rarely any parking, which meant you would have to park far way. I knew several girls that were mugged while walking to and from their cars in that area. Regardless, we ended up going there anyway.

When we walked into the party at Yucca it was hardly a party. Michael, the singer of Alleycat Scratch, was there along with Strange. We only stayed long enough to finish a drink and went back to Sebastian's.

When we walked down the hallway to Sebastian's, we noticed Angela standing outside her front door. She told us that Bam was out of control and to keep a good vibe when we walked into the apartment. Sebastian rolled his eyes and walked right past her into the apartment.

When we walked into the apartment, Ronnie was there along with Bam, Jack, and Susie. Bam saw me, put me in a headlock and we started play fighting. We took slow motion punches and kicks at each other and would fly across the room when the other would land a blow. When we both finally landed on the ground, we happened to look over and notice Scooby sitting in corner staring at us. Bam burst out into song.

"Scooby doobie doo. *Donde estas?* He's sleeping in the corner!"

We both rolled over on our sides and cracked the hell up. Ronnie asked us what was so funny, but we were laughing so hard we couldn't talk. For some reason after that night, Bam and I starting calling each other Scooby and never referred to each other by our real names again.

I slowly got off the ground and took a seat next to Sebastian on the couch. He was playing a video game on a Sega Genesis system when Harley bolted in the front door and tore the controller out of his hands. She took away the entire console, said it belonged to her, and abruptly walked out. Sebastian laughed and suggested we go behind the tarp.

We had just sat down on his bed when we heard people yelling from outside, just below his balcony. We went out on the balcony and looked down to find Spider, Chris, and Sunny trying to climb up onto the balcony. They were on someone's balcony below on the second floor.

Sunny climbed onto Spider's shoulders and latched onto the rails of Sebastian's balcony. He pulled himself up and over onto the balcony, climbed over Sebastian's bed and casually strolled into the apartment. Next in line was Chris who also got a boost from Spider. He was hanging onto the rails and yelping, "Someone help me up!" as his long legs dangled below him. We told him to kick his feet up, but he couldn't. Chris dangled for a minute or two, then eventually went around the building and came in through the front door with Spider. Why all three of them didn't do that in the first place? I have no idea.

I know it all sounds like some kind of crazy Fellini movie, but that's just how things went when I hung out with this crowd of people. There was another night when a group of us were walking to a party when Dizzy and Mandie stole a real estate flagpole off someone's lawn and tried pole-vaulting with it on the concrete streets. Random things like that were always happening. I never asked why any of them did the things they did. I just sat back and enjoyed the ride.

And while we are on the subject of crazy, lets talk about the day the city of Los Angeles quite literally lost its damn mind in the spring of 1992.

I was home watching TV and happened to catch live footage of the verdict that was reached in the Rodney King beating trial. The verdict? All officers were found not guilty.

Riots immediately erupted all over Southern California. Shops were looted, businesses were set on fire and people were beating each other in the streets. Every television station was streaming live riot footage taking place all over Los Angeles. I even watched Silo, an electronics store right by Sebastian's place get looted.

"Wow that's right around the corner from Sebastian's house!" I said to my mom as I grabbed my purse and walked toward the front door.

"Where do you think you're going?"

"I'm going to Sebastian's," I said casually.

"Are you crazy? Look at what's going on out there!"

"But…I already had plans to go out."

"*Sufrah!*" she said sternly.

Which basically means, "suffer" in Spanish. But in terms of my mom talking to her foolish daughter, it translated to "tough shit, you're not going anywhere."

Over the next few days, I continued to watch news footage of the ongoing violence and looting that swarmed over the city. It was beyond what the L.A.P.D. could handle, so the National Guard, and the Marines were called in. They bulldozed through the city to regain control and enforced a temporary "dusk till dawn" citywide curfew, which meant no one was allowed to walk the streets after dark.

CHRIS PENKETH (Swingin Thing): We heard machine guns going off on different rooftops. It was crazy. We got up on the roof of the Martel building and were trying to secure it. We filled up empty beer bottles with little rocks that were on the roof, and we watched people coming down, trying to bust into our building. So we started whipping bottles down at them.

We saved the liquor store next door too. Some guys took a trashcan and smashed the liquor store window, so we were whipping bottles down on them too. The next day, the liquor storeowner came by and gave us a case of beer to thank us.

You could see smoke coming from a bunch of buildings, and we actually got busted a day or so later for being out after the dusk/dawn curfew. I remember walking the streets at night. It was so quiet and desolate. It was so eerie.

JOEL PATTERSON (Blackboard Jungle): I was at the Burbank house right when the L.A. Riots broke out. Blackboard had a show in Arizona the following night, so we all met at the house and left from there. We ended up driving on the 10 freeway and it was a war zone. People were on bridges throwing shit down onto the freeway, palm trees were on fire. We were stuck downtown in traffic, but we finally made it out. I don't think we realized it was going to be that bad when we left the house.

One week and one billion dollars worth of damage later, the citywide curfew was lifted. With things finally going back to normal, I borrowed my dad's truck and made my way out to Sebastian's.

My first outing post-riots was a random party in Hollywood. After arriving at Sebastian's, we gathered up the usual's from the Martel Estates and walked outside to the front of the building. Everyone stood at the curb like a bunch of kids waiting for our school bus to arrive.

After standing in silence for a few moments, the bickering began between the few people that actually owned a car. The debate was who should drive, who drove last time and if someone was pinpointed to drive, they bitched at why they shouldn't have to drive. I just wanted to get to the damn party, so I chimed in.

"Well my dad's truck is over there and..."

Before I could finish my sentence, everyone made a b-line for my dad's long bed truck and started piling in the back.

The party wasn't that great, so we only stayed for about an hour. We eventually migrated out of the apartment building and thought about where to go next. While we lollygagged in the street being our usual loud, drunk selves, a woman walked out onto her 2nd floor balcony just above us and started screaming at us to be quiet.

She looked to be in her late 40's or early 50's. I didn't understand why someone so old would be living in that area of Hollywood. It didn't take more than a few seconds for some of the guys in our little group to start yelling back at her to shut up. She quickly disappeared back into her apartment and we resumed our socializing. Normally, I would've felt bad, but it was a Saturday night. It wasn't even that late either, so I don't know why she was so angry.

A few minutes later, she reappeared and began putting small buckets and pots of water on her balcony. Then out of nowhere, she started throwing the water over her balcony to try and hit us. Water was flying towards us and expletives were flying back up to her. In the midst of this craziness, Michael, the singer of Alleycat Scratch, stumbled into the middle of the street completely inebriated.

He looked up to the grumpy neighbor with his hands up in the air and pleaded, "CAN'T WE ALL...JUSSSSS GET ALONG?"

She threw another bucket of water that narrowly missed him as he came scurrying back toward us. I was laughing my ass off until I noticed her go back into her apartment, sans buckets. I had a feeling she wasn't going in to get more water. She was probably going to call the police. Luckily, there were enough of us that had the good sense to wrangle up those that didn't, and we got the hell out of there.

We left the party shortly after midnight, which was way too early for any of us to go home. Without any other ideas, we went with our usual default plan and made our way to Errol Flynn's. Today it goes by the name Runyon Canyon. But back then; before they cleaned it up and made it a canine friendly hiking trail, it was a dilapidating empty park in Hollywood at the top of Fuller Avenue.

I never understood why they called it Errol Flynn's. The late, great actor never owned the land. He was just one of many celebrities that stayed on the property during the late 1950's. Obviously, Errol was long gone as was the entire structure of the house. So we turned it into our own personal nighttime playground.

CASSIDY: It was almost every single weekend we went to Errol Flynn's. And every single weekend, we were walked out by the cops. The cops knew most of us by name, but they never once gave us a ticket.

Everyone hopped the large steel gates of the estate except for me. There was a strange bend between two of the bars in the gate. It was as if Superman himself had pried them apart to trespass for a midnight stroll. Luckily, the gap was just wide enough for me to wiggle my way in.

We walked up the wide dirt road to "the pool" area, which sat just off to the left of the entrance. There were five wide steps leading up to the pool with cactus plants and bushes on either side. I walked up the steps to take a peek. Under the moonlight, I could see that the pool was marked up with graffiti and partially filled with leaves and other garbage. We sat on the steps for a bit passing around a fifth of Jim Beam and a liter of Coke. A few minutes later, we decided to stumble further up the dirt road. We passed the beat up tennis courts with their tattered nets and reached a flat area of the property where the house once stood and overlooked the city.

SUNNY PHILLIPS (Swingin Thing): I went there for a walk with Faye one night when we saw a guy and girl on acid playing tennis on the tennis court. They didn't have a ball, they didn't have any rackets, and they didn't have any shirts on. They were trippin.

The only thing that remained of the old property was the wine cellar or the pool house. There seemed to be a debate on exactly which it was. My argument was for the pool house. It made the most sense because it was a straight shoot through some brush right to the pool steps where we had just been drinking.

It took someone with the balancing skills of a *Mission Impossible* agent to get into. The only entrance was through a square hole in the side of the mountain, which I felt was a possible window from the remaining pool house. To access it you had to slide down the mountain about six feet on your back and sidestep along a narrow dirt path about a foot wide. I was told many tried and fell down the side of the mountain. But the hillside was full of brush, so no one ever tumbled too far without crashing into a tree or bush to break their fall.

SKITZ (The Glamour Punks): The general mayhem that took place behind those gates after hours is enough to fill a book. The one memory that makes me smile the most was when Bam and I were too drunk to walk the whole way down the path to leave. We decided it would be smarter to just run down the side of the mountain. We rolled the whole way, and by the time we got to the street, we had branches sticking out of our pants, our shirts were ripped off and we were covered with dirt.

CHRIS PENKETH (Swingin Thing): Errol Flynn's was always the go to place if there was nothing to do. If we didn't go out every night and party, we felt like we were getting old. We were up there all the time. I don't remember if I fell down the side of the mountain though. I probably did and was just too drunk to remember.

I was curious to see what was inside the pool house and decided to give it a shot. I slid down the mountain on my back and made it to the opening without falling down the hill. When I took a peek inside there was nothing but black, so the guys threw me down a lighter. I still couldn't see anything. I was about to crawl in the hole when I heard the echo of something moving inside. That had me scurrying my way back across the mountainside, squealing for the guys to pull me back up to the house level. After dusting myself off, I overheard a few people talking about going to "the bench." I asked Sebastian what it was.

He pointed to a dirt-covered path with wide wooden steps and said, "It's just a wooden bench further up the mountain at the top of these steps."

The incline for those steps was fairly steep. I only climbed about a quarter of the way up before I began wheezing like an old man and made my way back down. I ended up staying at the house level the rest of the night, along with a few other people that were too lazy to make their way up the steps.

As spring came to a close, so did a major dark point in my life. After six torturous years of withstanding various oral surgeries and wearing headgear that made me look like *The Terminator* without his skin, I was finally getting my braces off!

I sat in my orthodontist's chair rapidly twiddling my feet as she pulled out a tool that looked like elephant sized pliers. I gasped. She said they were for removing the brackets on my teeth. "It won't hurt a bit," she said.

At that point, I didn't care if she was using them to remove my brackets and my spleen. I just wanted my braces off already.

As she cracked off each bracket, I felt like a caterpillar turning into a butterfly. When she popped the last one off and my lips fell over my teeth, it felt like my gums were swollen. I moved them up and down over my gums like a monkey.

"That's just your lips getting used to not going over the brackets. There's nothing wrong with your gums, trust me. You have a beautiful smile now," she said.

When I looked in the mirror, I smiled for a moment and immediately covered my teeth with my lips. It was just a natural reaction because I was so used to not smiling in pictures for the last few years. I would give a meager grin, if that.

Later that evening, I went to Sebastian's to celebrate. When I walked into his apartment, he was with Sunny and Ronnie in the living room.

"I heard you got the braces off. Lets see your choppers!" Sunny said.

I proudly displayed a big Cheshire Cat grin and the guys applauded.

Despite telling myself I needed to get my life together after Arwen's funeral, I hadn't done anything productive to push myself in that direction. Instead, I was going to Errol Flynn's, hanging out at the Martel Estates and going to Hollywood parties with Sebastian till the wee hours of the morning. I was 18, with no job and no plans to go to college. My dream was to be a writer. I knew I had to do something to get me going on the right path.

Shortly after my faux epiphany, things between Sebastian and I started to take a nosedive. He began arguing with me over the silliest things, and I couldn't understand why.

Case in point, I was at Sebastian's place one night with him and Sunny. They spoke about a party their friend, Cassidy, was having, so the plan was to go to her house. The three of us climbed into my sister's car when Sunny decided he wanted to get beer. I stopped by a liquor store next to the Martel Estates, and he ran in while Sebastian and I sat in the car. Sebastian was already drunk. He had been poking at me the entire night with his index finger. It was mildly annoying, so I just kept pushing his hand away. But as we sat in the car waiting for Sunny, he began to poke at me harder. I finally slapped his hand and told him to stop.

"Are you mad?" he asked, as if it were a dare.

"I'm going to be if you don't stop doing that," I said.

"Fine."

He got out of the car and walked home. I rolled my eyes and sat in the car to wait for Sunny. When he came back and saw Sebastian was missing, I told him what happened. He said not to worry and he would handle it.

When we got back to Sebastian's, Sunny was able to talk him into coming back out with us. The three of us got into

Lucy's car AGAIN and made our way to Cassidy's. Sebastian didn't say a word to me the entire way there. When we arrived at Cassidy's, Sunny climbed out with the beer and left me in the car with Sebastian.

"Well, are we going in or what?" I asked.

"It's up to you," he said.

"What do you feel like doing?"

He looked out the window as he twisted one of his dreadlocks around his finger and said, "You're the one driving. I guess it's up to you."

I was already in a shit mood. I really didn't feel like going into the house and fighting with Sebastian in front of everyone.

"Do you want to just go back to the apartment then?" I asked.

"Sure, it's up to you. Whatever you want."

Pain in my fucking ass.

When we got back to Sebastian's, he went to the kitchen and made himself a cocktail. I asked him what his problem was and why he was being so bitchy.

"You knew what you were getting into when you started going out with me. If you can't handle it, well then I guess you shouldn't hang out with me," he said as he shrugged his shoulders.

I said nothing. I stood up and walked towards the front door.

"If you leave, you're an asshole," he said.

"No, YOU'RE the asshole," I said.

I slammed his front door behind me and stomped off to Lucy's car.

I came home a little past midnight and passed out shortly after. About two hours later, the neon phone lit up my room. It was Sebastian. He apologized and said he was really drunk earlier and just wanted to get in a fight. We spoke for about five minutes and then I fell back asleep. A half hour later, he called and woke me up again. He told me he cared about me a lot, more than anyone he dated in quite a while. He said I was one of the nicest people he knew. He also said he didn't want to hurt me and to really think about whether or not I could "hang" with him and his way of living. I said I would think about it and we got off the phone again. But that time I wasn't able to go back to sleep. I was wide-awake and began to think about whether or not I really could deal with his lifestyle.

Based on the few conversations we had about his previous relationships, they all sounded fairly volatile. I seemed to be the most normal girl Sebastian ever dated. I wondered if that was the reason he was starting fights with me over nothing. Was he in a transition period where he wanted to have a normal relationship and was having trouble adjusting? Or was he just one of those guys that thrived on the chaos and were totally incapable of having a normal relationship?

One of the major issues with Sebastian was that he drank too much, which I think I have made abundantly clear. Even he said he was annoyed with how much he drank. If he was sober or even a little drunk things were fine between us. He was funny and very affectionate, which is one of the things I liked most about him. But when he became wasted, he would turn into a demon seed and start shit with me over nothing. He would say I was too nice and needed to get mad more often. I would tell him certain things weren't worth a fight and walk away from him. Naturally, that made him try even harder to piss me off, and he would continue to push until I snapped and yelled at him. Then one of two things would happen. He would either get angry and take off, or he would laugh, give me a kiss and we would continue with our evening.

It all sounds a bit crazy, but I did care about Sebastian, despite the fact I was always on edge. Whenever I called or went to his place, it was always a crapshoot on whether we would get along that day. The smallest things would set him off. But despite the sporadic fights, we would always make up by the end of the night and fall asleep in each other's arms to the *Wish* album by the Cure, which he always put on right before we fell asleep.

As the summer kicked in, Sebastian turned 25, Mötley Crüe got a new lead singer, and The Glamour Punks broke up. Shortly after the latter disbanded, I was over at Sebastian's when Mandie walked in to show off his new haircut. His red locks had been chopped off with the exception of the long bangs that draped over his face. He also shaved the word "BOY" into the back of his head as a nod to his official name, "Screaming 'Boy' Mandie".

MANDIE (The Glamour Punks): The Glamour Punks broke up because we just really didn't get along anymore. We all kinda wanted different things. There was a lot of fighting, drunkenness and general disrespect of each other. There's no way it was gonna last.

SKITZ (The Glamour Punks): By the time we played our last show at the Troubadour, we were way too volatile and in a state of constant chaos. Looking back and knowing what I know now, maybe we could have fixed it and gone on to reinvent ourselves in a way that really could have worked. But I don't think any of us had anything left at that point. It was just time to defuse the situation before one or all of us got hurt. We were just always cranked up to ten. Settling down and saving our energy for the long haul wasn't something that any of us really knew how to do.

Hanging out at the Martel Estates became 100% of my social life. I had grown apart from Hannah, Dagmar, and the rest of the Alhambra crew. The only other girl I kept in touch with was Faye who I only saw sporadically. Without any close girlfriends to hang out with, I naturally gravitated towards the girls in Sebastian's circle of friends.

First, there was Cassidy who I immediately became closest to. She was a year older than me with long brown hair and big brown eyes. She was originally from New York and shared a house in Hollywood on Gardner with her friends Lark, Dexter, and her amazon friend from college named Joelle.

Joelle stood 6'1" with bright blue eyes and wavy red hair that draped down to her shoulders. Everyone called her "the virgin". She did admit to fooling around with guys but considered herself a virgin because she hadn't partaken in actual intercourse yet.

Then there were Emily and Kennedy, the redheads from San Bernardino County. They lived in a small studio apartment on Detroit near Fountain, a few blocks away from Cassidy's house.

Last, but not least were the blondes, Amie and Dina. They lived in the Inland Empire about forty minutes east of me. Since my house was on the way to Hollywood, Amie would always offer to pick me up, which saved me the hassle of having to borrow cars from my family. She was very generous when it came to other people driving her car, especially me. If we were separated over the course of the night, she knew I would always end up at Sebastian's and let me take her car to his place. At some point the next day, she would call me to pick her and Dina up from wherever they spent the night. It worked out perfect for everyone.

Sebastian wasn't thrilled that I befriended the girls. And when I started carpooling with Amie and Dina, things only got worse. I couldn't understand why it bothered him so much. I figured he would be happy I was getting along with everyone. Cassidy even got me a part time telemarketing job where she worked with Joelle and Kennedy too. The four of us would carpool in the evenings to Canoga Park where we would cold call people into selling them timeshares of property in Sedona, Arizona.

My blooming friendship with the girls was just one more thing Sebastian and I would constantly bicker about. I felt he was being ridiculous, so anytime he would give me shit about it, I would him blow off. But the girls weren't the only problem. There were also a few guys in our little circle that became the subject of our fights as well.

Sebastian took a last minute trip to Vegas one weekend, so I called Faye to see what she was up to. She mentioned she was going to the Whisky that Saturday night with her friend, Amy. They were going to see a band called Slamhound. She invited me to come along, so I did.

When I went to Faye's that evening, her and Amy were fully decked out in cleavage bearing tops. Amy was naturally well endowed. Everyone in our circle called her "Amy Hooters". When I made a crack about my lack of an ample bosom, Faye mentioned her rack was mostly an illusion.

"Get outta here. Your boobs are WAY bigger than mine," I said.

"Not really," Faye said.

She grabbed my index finger and used it to poke around the sides of her boobs. They felt hard as a rock. I gave Faye's boobs a few more pokes and realized the secret to her endowments was a wall like Fort Knox built up of padding.

After leaving Faye's we stopped by their friend, Jeff's apartment to have some pre-show cocktails. I didn't know Jeff that well, but the few times I had been around him he was always pleasant with me. Apparently, Sebastian had issues with Jeff. Of course I didn't find this out until after he came back from Vegas. When I told Sebastian what I did that weekend, he was quite vocal about Jeff having any kind of involvement. He also didn't want me hanging around Jeff anymore unless he (Sebastian) was around.

I found his jealousy amusing because I had zero history in the cheating department. Besides, I was totally gaga over Sebastian. The thought of cheating on him never crossed my mind, IF it could be considered cheating. Everything about the way Sebastian and I were with each other would suggest we were in a relationship, yet our official status was something I could never get a concrete answer on. The last time we addressed the issue was months earlier on the evening we went to the beach.

Going back to the subject of the girls, he also didn't like me hanging out with Faye either. He said she was completely out of control and nothing but trouble. But I had known Faye well before him, and I let him know my friendship with her was not up for discussion. He did have a valid point though. Faye was getting out of control. She was only 16 and going out way more than I was, and believe me, I was going out quite a bit. There were also rumors going around that she had already slept with a few guys in Sebastian's circle of friends.

Turns out I wasn't the only one concerned about Faye. When I went to grab her and Amy during Sebastian's Vegas weekend, her father quietly pulled me aside while they were getting ready. He voiced his concerns on several instances when Faye had gone out and didn't come home till the next day. He asked me to have her home by 2:00am.

Truth be told, Faye was going to do what she wanted to do. Of course I couldn't say this to her poor dad, but I think he was already well aware of that. I suppose that's why he came to me personally, figuring I might have a little more influence over her than he would. Faye overheard her dad talking to me and flipped out. She yelled at him about controlling every little move she made and stormed out of the house. I felt bad for him, so I said the only thing I could say, yes. Yes, I would have her home by 2:00am. I ended up getting her home around 2:30 that night, or morning I should say. Sure it was later than what I initially promised, but at least I got her home and even that took quite a bit of wrangling on my part.

The next time I hung out with Faye was at a party in Hollywood. We were having a great time, but I needed to have Lucy's car back by 2:00am. Faye wasn't ready to leave when I was, so she said I could go and she would get a ride home. Of course I didn't want to leave her, but I had no choice. I told her to call me if she needed me, and I would steal Lucy's car to come back out and get her.

I was well into a deep sleep coma when Faye's mom called and woke me around 5:00am. The moment I answered the phone, she asked me why I was at home sleeping when Faye wasn't. She said I was responsible for bringing her daughter home if I picked her up. She also felt I was a bad influence on Faye and banned me from hanging out with her ever again.

I wasn't mad at the verbal lashing her mom gave me because I knew it was coming from a place of frustration. Faye was like my little sister. I was really starting to worry about her when she wasn't around me, so I can't even imagine what her poor parents were going through.

Later that morning, Faye's mom spoke with my mom and also asked to speak with me. She apologized for the harsh phone call just hours earlier and unbanned me from hanging out with Faye. I told her there was no need to apologize, and I was doing my best to keep an eye on Faye when I went out with her. I thought all was well until I got off the phone with Faye's mom and had to deal with my own. My mom was quite disturbed by the things that Faye's mom told her. Oddly enough, she decided to ban me from hanging out with Faye because she felt SHE was a bad influence. Go figure.

Aside from keeping an eye on Faye and maintaining my "relationship" with Sebastian, things were changing up in the Martel Estates. Sebastian was moving out of Angela's and into another apartment on Fuller near Hawthorn with Susie and her friend, Deven.

CHRIS PENKETH (Swingin Thing): When Sunny and I left the Martel Estates, we moved in with a girl named Gabby. We were so

213

stoked to have our own couch space. We were like, "Fuck yeah, this is awesome!" The very next day, there's a knock on the door and Gabby's slave answered the door because she was a dominatrix. So her slave opens the door, and it's Michael Michelle with a few other guys. I was like, "What the fuck are you guys doing here?" Michael said, "Gabby said we could stay here for two weeks." And Gabby was like, "Yeah, it's okay, I told them they could stay for two weeks." Sunny and me were like, "Nooooooo! We finally got our own space!" Because in Hollywood "two weeks" meant INDEFINITELY.

If someone found a place, then everyone who needed a place to stay would hear about it. The next thing you know, there would be ten people in a one-bedroom apartment, so you had to enjoy your space while you had it.

The dynamic between Sebastian and I changed drastically when he moved into the Fuller apartment. Adding to the tension was a new girl that entered our little circle named Bronwyn.

Bronwyn was about a year younger than me. She had long wavy blonde hair, pasty skin and blue eyes. Like a bunch of bloodhounds, the girls in our group immediately pounced, sniffed, and observed the intentions of this newbie. She entered our circle through Robbie, the drummer from Alley Cat Scratch. Within a few short weeks, she moved from Robbie to his singer, Michael, and my skeezer radar went flying off the charts.

Although she was playing musical chairs with the boys in our circle, she didn't look like the typical groupie. She wore these long cloaky witchlike dresses that covered her entire body. She wasn't outwardly sexual either. She seemed to be fairly quiet and very soft spoken.

Shortly after her fling with Michael ended, I found her number written on the back of a Kids flyer that was lying by Sebastian's bed. I immediately took it and flushed it down the toilet, but of course that wasn't the end of that. It wasn't long before I noticed her show great interest in Sebastian. They would chat it up like old friends at every party we went to. Meanwhile, he was still instigating fights with me over the most ridiculous shit. I confronted him about his new found "friendship" with Bronwyn, and of course he denied anything was going on. Anytime she was around me, she would always smile and say hi to me in a sheepish way. I, on the other hand, would shoot her the look of death and walk right past her.

But Bronwyn wasn't the only new addition to our dysfunctional group. A childhood friend of Bam's named Dresden had recently moved to L.A. from New York.

Dresden stood just over six feet tall. He had short black hair with the exception of the long red bangs that hung just below his chin. His eyes were dark brown and his face was chiseled. He reminded me of Johnny Depp with a New York accent.

As the weeks passed and Dresden continued to hang out in our little circle, I noticed he was nice to everyone with the exception of me. He would downright ignore me, and I couldn't understand why. We never had an actual conversation before, so it's not like I could have said something to piss him off. I would overhear him having conversations with people and have to hold back my snickering over the funny things he would say. I found it so frustrating that I couldn't partake in his sense of humor, which seemed very much like mine.

Another weekend was approaching, and I was looking for something fun to do. Sebastian and I had a minor tiff the night before, so I decided to call Cassidy. She told me to put aside my Sebastian issues and go with her and the girls to Pixie's 18th birthday party in Calabasas. I happily accepted her invitation.

It seemed that everyone was going to Pixie's party. I assumed that included Sebastian too. In an attempt to make things copasetic between us, I called him and asked if he was going to Pixie's. He said he was and that he wanted us to go together. I told him I was waiting on a ride from Dina and Amie who were running a little bit late. Aside from picking me up, we also had to get Cassidy too. I told him it might be a while till I could get to his place. He got angry, told me to have fun with the girls and promptly hung up on me.

Amie and Dina finally picked me up and we sped off to Cassidy's. Emily and Kennedy were hanging out in the living room when we arrived, so we had a round of drinks and piled into Amie's little white sedan. Kennedy, Dina, and Amie rode in back. I sat on Cassidy's lap in the passengers seat, and poor Emily was voted to be the driver.

We passed around drinks in the car and caterwauled all the way to Calabasas to random songs like Sophie B. Hawkins "Damn, I Wish I Was Your Lover". We were halfway through "Head Like a Hole" by Nine Inch Nails when Emily made a sharp turn onto Topanga Canyon, almost slamming us into the white pearly gates of Pixie's driveway. Based on the size of the property, it was clear as day that Pixie's parents were rich. She lived in a huge white mansion with big white pillars. At the front of the house was a circular driveway with a beautiful fountain in the center. To me it looked more like a small hotel.

After peeling ourselves out of Amie's car, we made our way to the back of the house. There was a pool and a guesthouse with it's own built in barbecue just outside it's front doors.

Familiar faces like Mandie, Vaughn, Strange, Sunny, and Chris were there to name a few. Sebastian was also there. I saw him off in a corner talking with Dresden. Dresden's eyes widened as I approached them. He shook his head and walked away as if he knew there was going to be trouble. Sebastian glanced over to me and didn't look happy to see me.

"What's up your ass?" I asked.

"Nothing," he said with his arms crossed.

"Are you mad?"

"No. Why would I be mad?"

"Well, you hung up on me that's why."

"I'm fine, why? What's wrong with you? Are you drunk like the rest of your girlfriends?"

"Maybe I am. Is that a problem?"

"No, but I guess I better catch up then," he said.

I rolled my eyes. Sebastian walked away without saying another word as Pixie strolled up to me. She asked if I wanted a drink and a tour of the house. I said yes to both and followed her away from the party. When we walked inside her house, she locked the door behind us. She said her parents didn't want anyone in the house during the party. We walked to her kitchen where she made me a delicious cocktail and proceeded to show me around her humongous home.

We went upstairs and walked out onto her bedroom balcony, which overlooked the entire party. I scanned the crowd to see who else was there and noticed Bronwyn by the pool talking to Sebastian. I gritted my teeth and told Pixie I wanted to go back to the party, so I finished the last of my strong cocktail and we made our way back outside.

By the time we walked outside, I decided not to make a spectacle. Instead, I made myself another drink. When I finished that cocktail, I was too drunk to care what Sebastian was doing. I ignored him the rest of the night until some of our riff raff friends were caught breaking into Pixie's house. Her folks were reasonably upset and told everyone the party was over.

I walked to the front of the house to find Amie's car. It was nowhere to be found. Neither was Emily who no one had seen in the last hour. Some of the girls scattered into different cars. I didn't know what to do until Sebastian came up behind me and told me to go with him. We piled into his roommate, Deven's car, along with Amie, Dina, and Bam. I was still angry that he was hanging out with Bronwyn earlier. But he was being nice on the way home, so I decided not to start a fight.

A few weeks later, Courtney, one of the other rich girls, threw a party at her parent's mansion in Malibu. Cassidy and the rest of the girls wanted to carpool together. But in an attempt to mend the recent tension with Sebastian, I asked if he wanted to go to the party together. We ended up going with Cassidy in her car, along with Dresden who she had just started dating.

Courtney's house was incredible and even bigger than Pixie's. She had tennis courts and an indoor pool. I couldn't imagine growing up like that. Many of us couldn't. I was still living in the house I grew up in, and it certainly didn't look anything like Courtney or Pixie's that is for damn sure.

After watching several drunken tennis matches between Sebastian and Mandie, I walked inside to use the bathroom. Upon stumbling around and trying to find a restroom, I noticed Michael and Strange sniffing around the kitchen. I ignored them and continued on my way down a long hallway where I finally found a bathroom. As I made my way back out to the tennis courts, I passed the kitchen again and noticed Strange help Michael into a dumbwaiter. Strange packed in a few items of food with Michael and lowered him down to the garage. I rolled my eyes and continued walking outside.

I was sitting outside with the girls having drinks when a few more of the guys went into the house and didn't come back out. I just hoped they weren't doing what I thought they were doing. Sure enough, when we all left about an hour or so later the trunks of everyone's cars looked like they were on their way to a Goodwill drive. I felt awful about the food that was looted from Courtney's until I became sidetracked by a fight with Sebastian on the way home.

He was annoyed that I became good friends with everyone in our circle, not just the girls. Suddenly everyone was calling me with plans to go out. I would even find out things before he did. When we first started dating, it was always him that called the shots on what we did each weekend. But now that we were on an even playing field, he obviously wasn't happy about that.

"Who cares who finds out first? In the end, you and I are going to end up doing the same thing anyway," I said.

"You know how weird it is, when I'm getting ready to go out and you're already there knowing everything that's supposed to happen for the night?"

"You should be happy I get along with everyone."

"It's like you're not even my girlfriend anymore. You're just another one of the girls that hangs out in the crowd now."

Oh so NOW I find out I'm his girlfriend? Great.

What the hell was I supposed to do? There was no ulterior motive in me becoming friends with everyone. It just sort of happened, especially with the girls. We were all around the same age, and they really were a lot of fun to hang out with. I couldn't help that I immediately bonded with them. Nonetheless, over the next few weeks, I continued to try and appease Sebastian by letting him choose what we did on the weekends. But of course even that didn't make him happy.

I soon stopped making any effort with Sebastian, and he didn't seem to care the more Bronwyn hung around. I could see we were heading down the break up path. There was nothing I could do to stop it, so I shifted my focus over to my friendships with Cassidy and the girls. It was only a matter of time before Sebastian and I ended things. And when that happened, I knew I would be in desperate need of some serious girl time.

It was a Saturday night when Cassidy called. She asked why I didn't come out with Dina and Amie who were on their way to her house. I told her I had another squabble with Sebastian the night before and planned on staying home since I was in a bad mood. She told me she hadn't planned on going out that night and that I should come over to her place to have drinks with the girls. That sounded like a plan to me, so I borrowed my dad's truck and made my way out to Cassidy's.

As I pulled up to Cassidy's, I saw Sebastian's truck pull out of her driveway. I know he saw me, but he didn't acknowledge me.

When I walked into the house, Dizzy and Vaughn were sitting at the kitchen table playing a board game called Pass Out while Cassidy stood at the kitchen counter setting up her home style lemon drops.

A normal lemon drop usually has vodka, lemon juice, and sugar mixed in a shot glass. Cassidy's consisted of a large plate of sugar, a bowl of sliced lemons, and a bottle of vodka with a stack of shot glasses. Feeling anxious from seeing Sebastian, I helped myself to a lemon drop and took a seat at the kitchen table. I mentioned Sebastian pulling out of her driveway and asked what he was doing there. Cassidy said he came to pick up Dresden and Mandie for a little get together at his place. I was hurt that he was having people over and didn't think to invite me. Dizzy must have noticed the distraught look on my face too because he immediately grabbed me by the shoulders, shook me and said not to let Sebastian have that effect on me. About a half hour later, Sebastian called Cassidy's house and asked to talk to me.

"So are you coming over with everyone else?" he asked rather annoyed.

I decided to play dumb.

"Coming over where?" I asked.

"To my place. Where else?"

"How would I know you're having people over? You didn't invite me until now, and nobody here mentioned they were going to your house," I said casually.

"Oh. Well if you guys want to come over you can."

"Let me see what everyone here wants to do. I'm sure we'll end up going over."

"Well excuse me if you're too cool to come over here then," he said with a bitchy tone and hung up on me.

The lemon drop wasn't calming my feelings of anxiety, so I did another. I dipped the lemon wedge into the mound of sugar, threw back a shot of vodka and battled with my conflicting thoughts as I chewed on the lemon wedge. I knew deep down it wasn't a good idea for me to go to Sebastian's. On the other hand, I didn't give a shit if it went badly. Our relationship had dragged on for long enough. I was sick of being stuck in an emotional limbo. I wanted some sort of resolve either way, and I didn't care how it happened. So once Dina and Amie arrived, they squeezed themselves into the front cab of my dad's truck along with Cassidy, and I drove us to Sebastian's.

A handful of people were in the living room when we arrived. Mostly the regulars like Ronnie, Bam, Mandie, Sunny, and Dresden. There were also some randoms I didn't know and to my disgust, Bronwyn.

My claws came out the moment I saw her. Not wanting to cause a scene, I turned on my heels and went to the kitchen where Cassidy was setting up lemon drops. I turned my back to the living room and threw back the first shot she set up. I knew damn well Sebastian saw me walk in with the girls, but he didn't come to the kitchen to say hi to me. He just sat on the couch chatting with Dina and Amie who joined him in the living room.

About an hour and three lemon drops later, I turned around to face the living room. Sebastian and Bronwyn were missing. I knew they didn't leave because the kitchen was near the front door. I would have noticed if they walked out. My heart began to race.

There is NO WAY in HELL Sebastian would humiliate me like that in front of our friends.

I walked around the small apartment, checking both bedrooms and the balcony. The only closed door was the main bathroom. I was immediately sick to my stomach. That's when I knew all the paranoid thoughts I had for the past few weeks weren't my anxiety anymore. I wondered how long Sebastian was

cheating on me with Bronwyn.

I went back to the kitchen to vent my frustrations to Cassidy. I was bitching to her for a few minutes when Bronwyn and Sebastian came out of the bathroom. I was beyond livid. I glared at him as he walked out, but he wouldn't make eye contact with me. He just walked over to the couch and started talking to Mandie as if nothing were wrong. Bronwyn walked off to the side and adjusted the cloak she was wearing. I caught a view of her buffalo butt and realized that was why she always wore those big cloaks.

CASSIDY: I don't remember much of Bronwyn because she never talked. I only remember she had a big fat ass, wore big dresses and had good hair. She was built like a pear.

A few minutes later, Sebastian walked up to me and told me we needed to talk. We walked out onto the balcony and closed the sliding glass door behind us.

"You better tell the girls to back off," he said.

"Excuse me?"

"They've been shooting dirty looks to Bronwyn since you guys got here."

"I didn't tell the girls to do anything. And who gives a SHIT about Bronwyn," I said coldly.

"I told Dina if her and the girls didn't stop their bullshit, I would never speak to you again."

I was seething.

Why does he care so much about what happens to Bronwyn? Fuck her. Oh that's right, he probably just did.

"You know what? Fuck you and fuck her! I don't need this shit!" I yelled.

I threw open the balcony door and slammed it behind me as I stomped back into the apartment. Sebastian flung the balcony door back open.

"Fuck you for slamming my patio door!" he yelled.

"FUCK YOU FOR BANGING THAT WHORE IN THE BATHROOM!" I screamed back.

I couldn't believe those words came out of my mouth. It's safe to assume by the shocked look on everyone's faces that they were just as surprised as I was. Cassidy ran up to me, told me to calm down, and suggested we go back to her house. I wholeheartedly agreed and walked towards the front door.

"If anyone wants a ride back to Cassidy's, I'm leaving NOW!" I yelled.

In addition to the girls, a stampede of footsteps followed me out the door consisting of Mandie, Dresden, Ronnie, and Bam.

Although the guys had become my friends too, I knew damn well they weren't leaving in support of me. It was because the alcohol supply ran out at the party, and Cassidy always had an ample stash at her place. Not to mention she had a house to hang out in as opposed to a small stuffy apartment like everyone else.

I continued stomping down the hallway and up to the elevator. I anxiously punched the elevator button repeatedly as if that would make it arrive faster. My face felt like it was on fire, and my heart was racing. I wanted nothing more than to tear the long tresses out of Bronwyn's head and hang her over the side of Sebastian's balcony.

We walked to my dad's truck, and the girls stuffed themselves into the front cab with me while the boys piled into the back of the truck bed. This was long before it was illegal to have people riding in the back of an open truck cab, or maybe it wasn't. But at that moment, I was too angry to care about anything.

The truck and my emotions were racing down Sunset Blvd. I erratically drove over various potholes and heard bodies flying around in the back cab. I thought it was my crazy driving until I saw Mandie and Dresden body slamming each other through my rearview mirror. I rolled my eyes and took a sharp left onto Gardner, which sent Mandie and Dresden tumbling toward the right side of the cab. They regained their balance and continued wrestling.

Kennedy showed up to Cassidy's house shortly after we arrived. I sat at the kitchen table with her and Dizzy while Cassidy set up another round of Pass Out and lined up lemon drops. Dizzy purred out comforting words on how I deserved to be treated better and that everything would be okay. It was funny to hear such sweet words from a guy that completely towered over my tiny frame. I remember staring at the three tongue piercings rattling around in his mouth as he spoke. I adored him for taking the time to console me, but I didn't need any convincing. When Sebastian walked out of the bathroom with Bronwyn, I knew without a doubt it was over. I think I came to that conclusion weeks before, I just didn't want to admit it to myself.

Sebastian called me a few days later and denied doing anything in the bathroom with Bronwyn. He said the reason he didn't go up to me when I arrived was because he felt I walked in there with an attitude. He also said he was sick of everyone telling him what a great couple we were. Apparently, everyone was giving him accolades on how cute we looked together and how much they liked us being a couple. He said he didn't want everything to be perfect and cutesy between us. He found it nauseating. He wanted things to go back to the way they were when we first met, before I became tied in with everyone.

I didn't know what to say to him. Obviously, things could never go back to the way they were. I had become friends with everyone. I certainly couldn't ignore people if they called me or wanted to hang out. Overall, he didn't apologize for anything he said or did the night of our fight and ended our call with an ultimatum.

"I can't be just 'friends' with you because I'll never consider you as just a platonic friend. So if we're not going to be more than friends, then I can't talk to you anymore," he said.

"I guess we won't be talking anymore then," I said without hesitation.

Sebastian paused for a moment and then hung up on me.

11

DON'T LET THE DOOR HIT YA WHERE THE GOOD LORD SPLIT YA!

A few weeks after my blowout with Sebastian, Cassidy decided to throw a party at her house for no other reason than to throw a party.

The first thing that came to mind was Sebastian. I wondered if he and Bronwyn were going to show up. I wasn't sure how this was going to work now that his friends were my friends. I couldn't imagine going out and having to see Sebastian and Bronwyn together on a regular basis, but Cassidy assured me he wouldn't go the party. She said he was avoiding the girls like the plague ever since our fight at his place. I also heard through the grapevine that he and Bronwyn were having quite the tumultuous relationship, which didn't surprise me. There was one rumor that they ended up brawling on the floor backstage at the Whisky after a Kids show. The physical aspect of it surprised me because he never once laid a finger on me while we were together. Then again, he probably knew better than to pull that

225

bullshit with me. I wasn't a passive person like Bronwyn, and there's no doubt I would have knocked his head off. I figured that having a turbulent relationship with Bronwyn was what he wanted after all. I guess the reason things didn't work out with us is because I was way too normal for him.

CASSIDY: Sebastian and Bronwyn fought all the time. I remember she lived in a weird, random home. It was like a home for girls or another families home and had a curfew of like 11:00pm. That's why Sebastian could never go over there. They never hung out at her place. She had a weird story, and I don't really know exactly what it was. She was just a weird chick.

The night of Cassidy's party, all the regulars showed up including Harley who I hadn't seen much of since I stopped dating Sebastian. She wasn't part of the normal group of girls I regularly hung out with and rarely ever went to Cassidy's. I didn't understand why she was there and not off lingering around Sebastian as she always did. Dresden was there too, which surprised me because he and Cassidy had recently stopped dating. But it was nice to know at least someone in our circle was capable of an amicable breakup.

A few hours passed, and I was having drinks in the living room with Dina and Amie. While most of us indulged in hard alcohol, Amie rarely ever did. She was always a beer drinker. Whenever we went to parties, she would buy herself a case of Lucky Lager bottled beer with the little riddles underneath the bottle caps.

Amie, Dina, and I were riddle solving with a handful of bottle caps when we heard yelling coming from Cassidy's bedroom. After freshening up my cocktail in the kitchen, I walked down the hall to see what the fuss was all about.

Kennedy and Lark were sitting on Cassidy's bed while Cassidy pounded on her bathroom door. I asked Kennedy what was going on, and she said Dresden and Harley were locked in Cassidy's bathroom. A few moments later, Lark started yelling and pounding on the door too. Considering I had just starred in my own personal spectacle at Sebastian's a few weeks earlier, I took myself and my freshly made cocktail back to the living room and resumed riddle solving with Dina and Amie.

Moments later, I heard a scuffle in Cassidy's bedroom, followed by the sounds of Cassidy, Harley, and Lark yelling. This continued down the hallway and into the living room. The next thing I know, Harley is being thrown out the front door like a bag of garbage. Everyone in the living room, including yours truly jumped out of our seats to find Harley lying like road kill face down in the driveway. She slowly lifted her head, and I noticed half of her front tooth was missing. Lark immediately slammed the front door, leaving Harley outside.

CASSIDY: The jist was that Harley locked herself in my bathroom with Dresden and wouldn't come out. We were knocking on the door for like twenty minutes and then the frustration just got annoying. I think maybe Vaughn came in and took the door off the hinges? I remember Lark being on top of her in the hallway punching her, like sprawled out over on top of her. Then I remember Harley somehow getting to the front door. I threw her out, Lark kicked her in the ass, and she went flying across the porch. I can't remember if she chipped her tooth on the ground or if she hit a car that was parked in the driveway.

If Harley were bleeding, I would have absolutely gone outside to help her. But aside from a badly chipped tooth, she seemed to be okay. I know it sounds harsh, but I didn't feel bad for Harley. After all, she did sleep with Sebastian when she knew we were dating and continued to pursue him the entire time we were together.

As the winter season began to set in, the girls proved to be excellent rehabilitation in helping me get over Sebastian. They planned girly, anti boyfriend outings, and we also spoke about what to do for my 19th birthday, which was rapidly approaching.

Although I felt better about things, I still wasn't 100% over Sebastian. I also didn't feel like having a blow out party to celebrate my last year of being an official teenager. Cassidy told me not to worry about it and that she would handle the arrangements. But before I knew it, the week of my birthday arrived and the girls still wouldn't tell me what we were doing to celebrate.

In all honesty, I didn't really care at that point. My emotions were sidetracked when Dizzy was admitted to Cedars Sinai Hospital just a few days earlier for having seizures. I asked the girls if they wanted to come with me to visit him. But every one of them had a different excuse as to why they couldn't go, which I found strange. The only person who offered to go with me was Joelle, which I also found odd since she barely knew Dizzy. Hell, she barely knew me.

When Joelle and I walked into Dizzy's hospital room, he was sitting up in bed watching TV in a hospital gown with his hair pulled up in a ponytail on top of his head. I gave him a big hug hello, and he seemed to be in good spirits. He said he was feeling better and asked me what I was doing for my birthday. I told him I wasn't sure. I figured the girls would probably drag me to El Compadre, our favorite Mexican restaurant in Hollywood.

Joelle and I stayed with Dizzy for about an hour or so. As we were about to leave, she told me to stay put. She said she had to make a quick phone call and darted out of the room. Dizzy and I looked at each other and raised an eyebrow. He had a phone in his hospital room, so I didn't understand why she didn't use his. Joelle came back to the room a few minutes later. We said our goodbyes to Dizzy and made our way back to the Gardner house.

When Joelle and I got out of her car, I could hear people talking in the living room. That didn't seem like anything out of the ordinary though. That house was always full of people. But when Joelle opened the front door, among all the regulars in the living room were balloons spread out everywhere. Everyone stopped for a minute, looked at me and yelled, "SURPRISE!" I really was surprised because my birthday was still a few days away.

The party was planned out for the last few weeks right under my nose. Even Dizzy knew about it. Cassidy said the girls already went to visit him earlier in the week. The reason they stayed behind was to decorate the house while I was gone. Joelle admitted the reason she darted out of Dizzy's room was to use a payphone and give Cassidy a heads up that we were coming back.

I made my way through the living room, getting birthday hugs from various people and continued into the kitchen. I noticed a big bouquet of roses on the kitchen counter that was sandwiched between bottles of Early Times and Jim Beam.

There were a dozen red roses with one peculiar white rose sitting right in the center of the bouquet.

I knew right away they couldn't be from Sebastian. He would never do anything that nice for me. If he were ever to send me a bouquet of roses, they would be dead and painted black.

"Wow these are beautiful. Who sent them?" I asked Cassidy.

"I have no clue. I found them sitting on my doorstep earlier this afternoon," she said.

On the outside of the bouquet there was an envelope attached with my name badly misspelled. Inside was a note with my name badly misspelled again that read:

Marrissa, Here are some roses, they come in a few. Here they come in a dozen, but there is only one of you.
- A Secret Admirer

I have a secret admirer? That's a first. My mind went into overdrive trying to figure out who it could be. I assumed anyone who would go to that much trouble would also be someone that would want to be at my party. I scanned the room and took inventory of every guy who was there.

I went through the entire male population at my party. The last group of guys I came across was Mandie, Dresden, and Vaughn who were having drinks at the kitchen table. The only person that made sense to me was Vaughn, and only because Cassidy recently told me he thought I was kind of cute. It wasn't much to go on, but no one else there fit the bill. Mandie was like my brother, and it sure as hell couldn't be Dresden because he was still avoiding me like the plague. I didn't even understand why the hell he was at my party anyway. It's not like we were even friends.

"Happy Birthday Marisa!" Kennedy yelled as she slid down the hallway.

"About an hour ago," I said laughing.

"Sorry, I was still getting ready. What music do you want to hear?"

"What do you think?"

"The Beatles coming up!"

I walked into the kitchen to set up a Cassidy style lemon drop when "Help" by The Beatles came on. I loved the back up vocals on that song and always preferred to sing them instead of the lead. As I caterwauled the words to the song, I noticed Dresden singing them too. He caught me looking at him. We stared at each other for a few moments as we continued to sing and then I looked away. When the song was over, I grabbed my roses off the kitchen counter and carried them into the living room to put them in a vase.

After arranging my roses, I picked up an acoustic guitar that was sitting nearby and sat on the couch. I started to play bits of songs I learned from my guitar class days in high school when Dresden walked over and sat down next to me.

"What do you want?" I asked.

"Go ahead and play. I'm just going to sit here and listen," he said.

"I don't need an audience."

"Why? You don't know how to play?"

"Are you always this annoying?"

We hazed each other back and forth a few times when suddenly the tone of our cracks became a bit lighter, more playful. We ended up having a fun little chat about how we both loved The Beatles. We also talked about him being from New York and how I've always wanted to go. He didn't seem like such an asshole after all.

A few days later on my actual birthday, I went over to Cassidy's and planned on having a chill night in with the girls. I was sitting on the couch talking with Kennedy when Cassidy brought in a birthday cake for me. The girls sang happy birthday to me. I blew out my candles. They took the cake away and said it was time for my gift. Cassidy told me to close my eyes and put my hands by my sides. I told her if she shoved the cake in my face while my eyes were closed I would kill her. She promised she wouldn't, so I closed my eyes.

I felt something plop onto my lap and start to move around. I freaked out and immediately opened my eyes to see a white and grey rabbit with big floppy ears looking up at me. I grabbed it and hugged it.

"Oh my god, I can't believe you guys got me a bunny! I love him!" I squealed.

230

"HER you mean. She's a recycled bunny," Kennedy said.

"A recycled bunny?" I asked.

"Not a recycled bunny, a Recycler bunny as in the newspaper. A married couple put up a listing for her because they are trying to have kids and the wife is allergic to the bunny. Her name is Bambeloni," Cassidy explained.

"Bambeloni? I think I'm going to have to change that," I said.

The bunny hopped off my lap and started sniffing around the couch.

"I christen thee Sniffy Rabbit!" I proclaimed.

"There's one catch," Cassidy said. "The wife was really upset about having to give her away. She wants to speak with you, just to make her feel better and know the bunny is going to a good home."

So I called the wife and assured her that Sniffy Rabbit was about to live a very charmed life. She thanked me as she choked over her tears.

CASSIDY: I swear I don't remember the birthday party at all, (laughs) wow that was so long ago. I remember the bunny though!

I had grown up with rabbits since the age of 4. We started off with two and that changed literally overnight. I told Cassidy for months that I wanted a rabbit. But the last time I brought up the idea to my mom was when I asked if we could take Faye's rabbit, Chloe, and she said no. My mom was a huge sucker for animals, but she also called them heartbreakers and didn't want any more pets. I wasn't sure how this was going to go over.

Instead of staying at Cassidy's that night, I decided it was best that I take Sniffy home. I usually slept with Kennedy in Joelle's room, but Joelle had a small rat dog named Dog Dog. I had a good feeling that he and Sniffy were not going to get along.

I came home shortly after midnight and closed the door to my bedroom. Sniffy was tucked into a blanket in a cardboard box, but she he kept hopping out. It was the same pattern every few minutes. After hopping out of her box, that would be followed by the soft pitter pat of her fuzzy paws on my linoleum floors, and her chomping on whatever books and magazines that were within biting reach. Although I was exhausted, I knew there was only one bunny proof room in the house we could sleep in until I could set up my bedroom the following day. So I grabbed Sniffy, a sleeping bag with some extra blankets, and we spent the night on the bathroom floor.

After less than a handful of sleep, I snuck Sniffy back into my bedroom in the wee hours of the morning. I tried to think of a way to sweet talk my mom into letting me keep her. But by the time I heard the banging of pots and pans in the kitchen from my mom making breakfast, I still hadn't thought of anything clever to tell her. So I picked up Sniffy, charged into the kitchen and lifted the bunny right up to my mom's face.

"I didn't ask for her. She was a surprise birthday present I swear," I blurted out.

Sniffy let out a sneeze that caused her big ears to flap. My mom melted into a big pile of goo as she reached to pet her. I knew nothing else needed to be said.

I adjusted to having Sniffy in our family along with my new social life, which revolved around staying at Cassidy's house on weekends. Sometimes we would go out. Even when we didn't the house was always full with people anyway. There was rarely a quiet night at the Gardner house.

CHRIS PENKETH (Swingin Thing): Me and Mandie got in a fist fight at the Gardner house one night and destroyed the living room. I was lying on the couch with Dina I think when Mandie came in in the house. He popped me in the face, and we just started kicking each others asses. We broke Cassidy's table too. Every time he and I hung out for some reason, we ended up fighting each other (laughs). But after a few minutes we'd stop because we realized we were friends and it'd be cool. Now our kids hang out together, it's a trip.

DINA PALMER-GOMES: One memory from the Gardner house that stands out was that big car accident. Faye and I were in the bathroom, drunk, talking and crying about girl stuff when we heard a big crash. There was an accident right across the street.

We all ran out there when Bam and I think it was maybe Mandie, pulled two guys from one of the cars because the accident

knocked them out. Then there was the other driver who they hit, a guy driving a jeep. His body flew out of the jeep and went underneath a house across the street. It was below the porch, next to the porch steps. So basically his head and upper body were in the house, underneath the porch and his legs were sticking out.

I was talking to the two guys that were pulled from the car, and they were drunk. They ran a red light and hit the guy in the jeep. More people came outside to see the accident and started screaming at the two guys, "You killed him! You killed him!" The two guys started freaking out, and one of them started screaming and crying on his knees saying, "Dina please tell me I didn't kill him!" I just kept telling both of them to wait till the cops got there, but we all knew the guy driving the jeep was dead. I just remember thinking, "Oh my god, I've never seen a dead body before this is crazy!"

CASSIDY: I was in Vegas with Amie the weekend that car accident happened. It was also the same weekend my hamster, Sexy, died. Mandie was hamster sitting for me that weekend. Well, he was SUPPOSED to be.

MANDIE (The Glamour Punks): I remember Cassidy saying before she went to Vegas, "Nothing better happen to Sexy!" because we used to fuck with that hamster constantly. I'd get it drunk and just fuck with it all the time. But I swear I didn't do ANYTHING to the stupid hamster that weekend. I can't believe it died on my watch.

I continued to spend every weekend at the Gardner house until Cassidy had an unexpected houseguest that sent me on a temporary hiatus. His name was Pediculus Humanus Capitis, aka head lice.

Cassidy called me one morning to tell me most of her roommates had contracted lice. A few even had scabies. I was itching like a dog for the past few days, so I asked Lucy to check my head. The moment she moved my hair around, she told me I had eggs in the nape of my neck. I let out an "Ewwww!" in complete horror.

She bought me one of those home lice kits with the shampoo, the spray, and the little comb. My mom washed every bit of clothing I had. She sprayed my bed with a lice spray while

Lucy drenched my head with an awful shampoo that dried the shit out of my poor hair. She tried to comb the eggs out, but my hair was too fine to grab onto them. So she proceeded to scrape each egg out with her nails, which took her almost 3 hours. Cassidy and her entire house went through the same regimen with the shampoo and the spray. About a week later, I went back to Cassidy's house to spend the weekend. When I came back home I started itching. Lucy took a look at my head and confirmed I had eggs once again.

"This is the last time I'm going to do this. If you get it a third time, I swear I'm going to let them eat you," she said completely annoyed.

While Cassidy spent the next few days thoroughly fumigating her house and her roommates, I spent that time looking for a full time job and trying to get my affairs in order. I still had my part time telemarketing job with her, Kennedy, and Joelle, but I was tired of flying by the seat of my pants. I wanted to get a full time permanent job, so I updated my resume and signed up with a few employment agencies.

It wasn't all that bad spending a few weekends at home though. It made me realize that as much as I enjoyed spending every weekend in Hollywood at Cassidy's, I never wanted to live in Hollywood. I liked being able to leave the madness. I needed to come home to a quiet, sane house where I could sleep soundly without people filtering in and out all hours of the night. I just couldn't imagine that being my life 24/7. I don't know how Cassidy did it.

A few days before my lice hiatus ended, I was sitting in bed late one night going through job listings in the L.A. Times when my phone lit up.

"Hello?" I said.

"Hi," a male voice said.

"Who is this?"

"It's Dresden," he said.

"Uhh…hi. How did you get my number?"

"Emily gave it to me."

I wasn't sure what to make of the situation. We had a good conversation at my birthday party, but it was the first time we ever spoke to each other. After a few minutes of trying to feel out the situation on both our ends, we found ourselves engulfed in a long conversation. We spoke about our families, all the crazy people in Hollywood, and how I thought he was a dick when he first moved to L.A.

"I always thought you were a big asshole because you would talk to everyone but me," I said.

"That's because I liked you," he said.

"Whaaaat?"

"You were with Sebastian at the time, and I didn't want to disrespect him. I avoided talking to you because I liked you."

"And now?"

"I still like you."

I didn't know how to respond, so I changed the subject and asked him about living in New York. After talking for two hours, we finally got off the phone. I couldn't stop smiling. I had little butterflies in my stomach and then it hit me. I liked Dresden as more than a friend.

Cassidy and Dresden had long been broken up, but I still didn't want to make any waves. I tried to make sense of the situation and came to the conclusion that it was a simple case of me being in rebound mode. Dresden was the first nice guy I met since my breakup with Sebastian. I assumed the feelings I was having for him would fade and there was no reason to tell anyone. *Yep, that's it. Dresden is just a rebound, nothing more.*

After swearing that her home was flea free, I began to hang out at Cassidy's again. I was also running into Dresden at parties, only now would actually talk to each other. We also continued talking on the phone too. I didn't say anything to the girls because I was still trying to convince myself (and hoping) that the feelings I was having for Dresden would go away. Unfortunately, my "rebound" feelings continued to grow stronger. I was bursting at the seams to talk to someone about it. Especially when Dresden admitted it was him that sent me the roses on my birthday. I decided to confide in Kennedy since she and Cassidy were my closest friends at the time.

"So what's going on with you guys?" Kennedy asked.

"Nothing actually. All we've done is talk on the phone. Like A LOT," I said.

"You guys haven't hung out yet?"

"Not on our own. The only times I've seen him are at parties."

235

"But you obviously like him right?"

"Of course I do, but I don't want to. I have no idea what the hell I'm going to do about it."

"You better do something either way because it's getting hard not to notice."

"What do you mean?"

"You guys just naturally gravitate to each other at parties now. That never used to happen before. Your feelings for each other are starting to show, and people will start noticing too if they haven't already."

Aside from Kennedy, Cassidy was the person closest to me, and I didn't want to do anything to jeopardize that. I figured since Cassidy and Dresden dated for such a short period of time, maybe she wouldn't be upset if I told her I liked him? After all, she was a direct, straightforward kind of girl. I knew if there was an issue she wouldn't hesitate to come to me directly.

Over the next few days, I thought about my conversation with Kennedy and came to the conclusion that she was right. I needed to come clean with Cassidy and tell her I had feelings for Dresden. She and I made plans to go to a show on Friday night, so I called her that afternoon in the hopes we could hash things out in time to enjoy the weekend.

"Hello?" Cassidy said as she answered the phone.

"Hey it's me. What's time should I come over tonight?" I asked.

Click.

I figured it was a bad connection, so I called her right back. Her answering machine picked up. I left a message.

"Hey Cassidy, it's Marisa. Did we get disconnected? I wanna see what time I should go over to your place tonight. Call me back, bye."

A half hour later, Kennedy called. There was a tremendous amount of background noise like she was standing in the middle of a busy intersection.

"Hey, where are you?" I asked.

"I'm at a phone booth down the street from Cassidy's," she said.

"Why are you calling me from a pay phone? Is Cassidy's phone not working? I tried to call her a little while ago and got disconnected."

"You didn't get disconnected, she hung up on you. I was there."

"Why would she hang up on me?"

"Someone told her you were sleeping with Dresden."

"What! Who would even say that to her? I've never even kissed him!"

"I know you haven't, but someone told her you guys have been having sex in her house for weeks."

"That's the dumbest thing I have ever heard. She doesn't really believe that does she?"

Apparently she did.

My first thought was to call Cassidy back and come clean about everything with Dresden. Kennedy suggested I give her a few days to cool down and that she would try to talk to her, so I did just that.

About a week had passed since Cassidy hung up on me. I called her repeatedly. I left messages. I sent smoke signals and carrier pigeons. I would get her answering machine or one of the roommates telling me she wasn't home when I knew damn well she was. I was blown away that she would believe something so stupid. She was my best friend. I thought at the very least she would have called to confront me, at which point I could explain what was really going on.

I was kicking myself for not telling her sooner. By hiding the fact that Dresden and I were talking on the phone, made things look even worse. I continued to try and get a hold of Cassidy. But as the days turned into weeks, it seemed my blacklisting from the Gardner house was set in stone.

CASSIDY: Kennedy was sleeping over a lot during that time too, and she got Marisa to admit on the phone that she liked Dresden. We were sitting on the bed as Kennedy talked to her, but Marisa didn't know we were listening to the phone call. Kennedy had the phone pulled away from her ear as she was talking to her, so me, Dina, and Amie could hear everything Marisa was saying. That's how we found out.

I never heard the rumor about them having sex in my house. That was probably something Kennedy made up to tell Marisa as a reason to explain why I was suddenly mad at her. It was better than admitting she was playing both sides of the fence and set her up.

The jist is, we were all mad at Marisa because we had a feeling she was lying about things. Not the Dresden thing because nobody cared at that point. Our biggest issue in the group was that she was lying.

I guess it was a blessing that I was forced to stay home during that time. My health wasn't all that great and my eating habits were atrocious. For months I would sleep all day, wake up in the late afternoon and stay out all night until the sun came up. I never ate anything healthy. I lived off of fast food and soda. I did like vegetables and salads, but I was too lazy to prepare them. I was tired all the time and when my mom took me to the doctor for a checkup, she told me my skin tone was grey. After running a few tests, my doctor told me my iron level was a quarter of what it should be. I was bordering on becoming anemic and had high cholesterol, which was completely unheard of considering I was only 19 and underweight.

My doctor put me on a strict diet, which consisted of eating and drinking nothing I was consuming before. She made me a list of all the healthy things I liked to eat and taught me ways to prepare those as my main meals on a daily basis.

For the next two weeks, I ate steamed vegetables with chicken and white rice, freshly made salads, and substituted soda with lemon water. Within days I felt an immediate difference. I had much more energy. When I went back to the doctor for a follow up visit, she told me she knew I was doing better without having to run any tests. I asked her how she could tell. She said it was because I finally had a bit of color in my face.

12

FIRST LOVE...OR NOT

With my physical health back on track, it was time to focus on my mental health.

Many weeks had passed since I last spoke with Cassidy. I gave up on trying to make amends with her, and most of the girls had turned on me except for Kennedy. By that time, she left the studio apartment she once shared with Emily and moved back to her mom's house in Norco about an hour east of me.

I was sitting in my bedroom with Sniffy on another eventless weekend when Sebastian called from out of nowhere. He heard about my exile and said that was the reason he didn't want me becoming friends with the girls. He knew it was a matter of time before some type of blowout would happen, and that was a big part of him wanting to keep me more isolated to him while we were dating. *Great, NOW he tells me.*

With no social life and essentially no friends, I felt I had nothing left to lose. So I let my feelings for Dresden grow, and I quickly fell in love with him. But what I felt for Dresden was nothing I ever felt with Ronan, Sheldon, or even Sebastian. There were no head games and no bullshit when it came to Dresden, which I found refreshing. He would call when he said he'd call. He would open doors and pull out chairs. He was sweet, attentive, and a total gentleman that made me laugh uncontrollably. For the first time ever, I had a man in my life that didn't cause me stress or come with an agenda. We would talk a few times a day and spend a majority of our free time together. So when he formally asked me to be his girlfriend, I squealed with delight.

On the flip side, as great as I thought Dresden was, I sensed something dark about him. It wasn't anything he was doing that gave me that impression. There was just something about his energy that I couldn't quite put my finger on. With previous boyfriends, their behavior was outright, so I knew up front what I was dealing with. But with Dresden, I sensed something hidden. I didn't know exactly what it was. Since I had no evidence to support that theory, I put that concern on the back burner for the time being.

Christmas was rapidly approaching. I couldn't wait for us to spend the holidays together. On Christmas Day, after spending the afternoon with my family, I cut out a little early to spend the rest of the evening with Dresden.

Dresden shared a house just off Melrose near La Brea with Bam. Their living room consisted of little more than a TV, a dining table, and an unused fireplace. When I arrived at Dresden's that evening, the three of us were full of holiday cheer and ready to celebrate by getting smashed. We sat on the floor and talked about what we wanted to do that night.

"Well let's see. We're all broke and it's Christmas Day, which means everything is closed. So the possibilities are endless," I said sarcastically.

"The liquor store is open at the corner," Dresden said.

"Yeah, and Cold Goose is on sale for two bucks a bottle," Bam said.

"HELL NO, we ain't buying no Cold Goose," Dresden said.

"What's Cold Goose?" I asked.

"The nastiest wine you can imagine," Dresden said.

We gathered our money together and put it in a pile on the living room floor.

"What the fuck is that?" Bam said, pointing at our measly pile of money. "That shit wouldn't get a cricket drunk."

"So what are we gonna do?" I asked.

"We've got enough to get about eight bottles of Cold Goose," Bam reiterated.

"Man, that shit is nasty," Dresden said.

"So eat chips as a chaser dick!" Bam barked.

Dresden snatched up our money, gave me a kiss goodbye and left with Bam. I leaned back next to the cold chimney, grabbed the remote, and flipped through the channels until they came back.

I thought Bam buying eight bottles was an exaggeration. But sure enough, they walked in the door with eight clacking bottles of Cold Goose and one bag of crumbs, which I'm sure was chips at some point earlier on the journey home. Dresden grabbed three plastic cups from the kitchen and came back into the living room. He popped open the first bottle of Cold Goose and filled each of our cups.

"Cheers muthafuckas!" Bam said as he lifted his cup.

We all tapped plastic and took a sip of our drinks.

"It's not THAT bad," I said.

Dresden made a bitter face and said, "It's not that GOOD either."

As the night progressed, each bottle of Cold Goose went down smoother than the last. When I watched Dresden top off his cup with the last remnants from the eighth bottle, I realized I was completely and utterly drunk.

Despite being wasted out of my mind, I managed to prop myself up against the side of the chimney. I passed out while the boys chatted amongst themselves. When I woke a short time later, I thought they were gone until I heard them talking and playing video games in Dresden's bedroom.

My eyes felt so heavy. If I closed them, the room would spin, and I would have to force them back open. After a half hour of playing peek-a-boo with myself, the room swayed one final time and that's when I knew I was going to barf.

I tried to stand up but ended up flopping over on my side like a seal. I looked around for a bag, a plate, or even a bowl. Anything within my grabbing reach that I could yack into, but the room was practically empty. I considered taking the easy way out and just barfing in the fireplace. But in a last ditch effort; I decided I would try to make my way to the toilet.

I slowly started to crawl towards the bathroom, but each movement caused me to dry heave. I tried to focus on the ground, stretching my arms and fingers over the dirty carpet. The road to the toilet seemed so far away. I'm almost certain that a turtle passed me along the way.

After what seemed like hours, I finally passed the threshold of the bathroom. The feel of cold tile on my palms was refreshing as I kept crawling towards the throne. I sat on the floor with a leg on either side of the toilet, flopped my arms across the seat and put my head down. Then I waited. I knew I wouldn't wait very long.

"Yo Marisa! Where you at mama?" Dresden yelled repeatedly.

I listened to his voice fade in and out as he walked throughout different rooms of the house. When he found me in the bathroom, he turned on the light and started laughing.

"Aww mama, are you okay?" he asked.

"Water," I blurted out.

I wanted him to leave. I didn't want to throw up in front of my new boyfriend, and it was coming fast. *Oh please, just get the fuck out and get me my water.*

"Ok, I'll be right back," he said.

Dresden took a few steps out of the bathroom when I started to barf. Luckily, it only took a few good heaves to get most of the Cold Goose out of me.

I quickly wiped my mouth, flushed the toilet, and fell back on the cold bathroom floor by the time Dresden came back in. He picked me up off the ground and carried me to his bedroom. After tucking me into his bed, he put the glass of water near me, kissed my forehead and picked up where he left off on his video game with Bam.

A few days later, I found that trying to get a hold of Dresden was like pulling teeth. He wasn't calling as much as he usually did and was turning into a big flake, which was totally out of character for him. It wasn't even a gradual turn either. It literally seemed like someone flipped a switch in him and his personality changed overnight. He didn't seem to be the least bit mad or grossed out that I was wasted on Christmas, so that couldn't be the problem. Any time I asked him what was wrong; he would insist everything was fine. The only thing I could think of was maybe he was having family problems. He mentioned a few weeks earlier that his mom was having issues with his younger brother and seemed to be very upset about it. I knew in my gut something was very wrong, but I didn't want to keep pushing Dresden. Whatever it was, he obviously wasn't ready to talk with me about it yet. I decided to back off and figured he would just tell me in his own time.

With New Years being just around the corner, I asked him what he wanted to do to celebrate. He was less than enthused about making plans and said he wanted us to spend a quiet night at his place, which I was fine with. I didn't care what we did as long as we were together. I just hoped that whatever issues he was having could be worked out and left behind so we could enter the New Year on a clean slate.

When I arrived at Dresden's on New Years Eve, he continued to be distant. Still not wanting to pressure him, I pretended like everything was fine. I suggested we go to the market to get a few things and make lemon drops. When we came back from the market, I set up a shot for each of us. I figured a little bit of booze might loosen him up a bit. But as we continued to do shots, he became more withdrawn. My patience with his sudden mood swings was also wearing very thin. The person he became over last seven days wasn't the person I fell in love with. It was a side of him I never saw before and I decided I wasn't going to placate him any longer. I demanded to know what was wrong.

Dresden became agitated as I continued to press him for answers, but I wasn't giving up. If something happened that radically changed how he felt about me, I wanted to know what it was. Even if it meant that (gulp) he didn't have feelings for me anymore.

We got into an argument that lasted for hours. I chased him from room to room on the verge of tears, trying to find out why he was shutting me out of his life. At some point during the fight, I glanced at a clock and noticed it was a quarter after midnight. There would be no confetti, champagne, or New Years kiss for me. The only thing Dresden gave me to ring in 1993 was a broken heart.

I couldn't take any more of his half assed answers, so I told him he was a selfish asshole who never loved me. He insisted he did. I told him if he did, he wouldn't be treating me like that and stormed out of his house. I slowly stomped my way to Lucy's car due to my heels. I hoped my snails pace would give him enough time to come out and stop me, but he never did. I took off in Lucy's car and cried all the way home.

Dresden never called me after our fight. And when I tried to call him, he was conveniently never home. I knew damn well he was getting Bam to screen his calls for him. I just wanted to know what I did wrong.

A few weeks passed with no word from Dresden. Naturally, I pressed Bam for details. He didn't want to break guy code since Dresden was one of his closest friends. But he did tell me that Dresden was moving back to New York in a few weeks. My heart immediately sank.

Against my better judgment, I wrote Dresden a letter. I also made him a mixed tape of Beatle songs that reminded me of him. I planned to take everything to him at Bleeker Bobs on Melrose where he usually worked on weekends.

The following Sunday, I called Bleeker Bobs in the early afternoon. When Dresden answered, I quickly hung up. I threw the tape and letter I made for him into a paper bag and drove out to Hollywood.

By the time I approached Melrose my heart was racing. I sat in the car wondering if I was doing the right thing. I knew I wasn't, but for some strange reason I wanted the chance to say goodbye to him.

I walked down Melrose and panicked when I saw Bleeker Bobs come into view. I jumped inside a nearby phone booth and called Kennedy for reinforcement.

"You don't have to do this honey. It's not like he even deserves this from you," she said.

"You're totally right. I don't even know why I'm here. He's the one that blew me off. What am I even thinking? God I'm pathetic."

"You're not pathetic honey. You just want closure. And if this will help you get it, I say do it."

Just then, Dresden walked outside the store and lit up a cigarette.

"Oh god! He just walked outside! What do I do?" I yelled into the phone.

"It's perfect timing. Go talk to him now before he goes back inside, go!"

"Okay I'm going!" I said and quickly hung up on Kennedy.

I ran across the street, and Dresden took a long drag of his cigarette as I continued walking toward him. He didn't seem surprised to see me. As a matter of fact, he wasn't giving me the cold look like he had on New Years. It was more endearing like when we first started dating. We both looked at each other for a few moments, and I knew there wasn't going to be any more fighting.

"Are you almost done with your break?" I asked.

"I will be in a few minutes," he said.

"I won't be here that long. I'm done asking for any kind of explanation."

"But you deserve one."

"I think I do too, but I beat that dog to death on New Years. I'm not here to start that futile argument again."

He paused for a moment.

"Look, it's nothing you did its me," he said.

"Oh for fuck sake, talk about relationship 101..." I said rolling my eyes.

"No listen," he said interrupting me. "I found out I had to move back to New York, so I was trying to distance myself from you."

"Why didn't you just tell me you had to move back?"

"I didn't know how to because I was pissed when I found out. Either way, there was no point in us still hanging out."

"The point is we love each other and should be making the best of the time you have left here."

"Why? So we can get more attached to each other?"

"And this is better? You cutting me out of your life?"

"I'm not cutting you out of my life. I would never want that."

"I don't want that either but that's how you've been acting. Like you want nothing to do with me," I said getting choked up.

"Of course I want you in my life. But it's hard for me to be around you right now," he said.

He tore off a piece of the paper bag I had in my hand, pulled out a pen from behind his ear and wrote his New York address and phone number down.

He handed me the piece of paper and said, "I was going to call you when I got back to New York just so you know."

"How would I have known that?" I asked.

I could feel myself getting heated again but refrained from saying anything else. I didn't have the strength to fight with him anymore. There wasn't anything else to say anyway. So I gave him the bag, told him I loved him as we hugged goodbye and then walked away.

A few days later, Sebastian called. He didn't mention anything about the girls or Dresden. He told me he moved out of Susie and Deven's apartment and was now living on Franklin and La Brea with two girls named Tina and Marla. Bam, Strange, and Michael were supposed to be moving in with them too. They didn't have a phone turned on in the apartment yet, but when they did it would be a restricted line. All incoming calls would be allowed, but there would be a lock on the outgoing, local calls only. I don't blame the girls for doing that with all those crackpots living there. He said he would give me his new number once he had it. But for the time being, if I needed to get a hold of him I could leave a message on the Kids band hotline.

CASSIDY: Bronwyn was around a lot more when Sebastian moved in with Tina and Marla. And that's when he started cheating on her with me (laughs).

I found the conversation with Sebastian odd. He was talking to me like we spoke on a regular basis. When or why would I need to get a hold of him at any point in my life, much less in the next few days?

I asked him where he was calling me from and he said Cassidy's house. I told him he was out of his mind for doing that. He said it was fine because she wasn't home and proceeded to invite me to a Kids show coming up at the Coconut Teaszer in the next few weeks.

I hadn't been around any of that crowd for the last few months. I found it strange that Sebastian would invite me to his show. Especially after his grandstanding speech just months earlier about us being more than friends or nothing at all. That coupled with him calling me from Cassidy's house AND his insistence on me going to his show set my paranoia into overdrive. *Is he setting me up for an ambush at his show with the girls?*

I wasn't 100% sure I wanted to go, but I said I would just to get him off my back. After I hung up with Sebastian, I thought about what I was getting myself into. There was no doubt the girls would be there. The smart thing to do was to stay away from Hollywood and lay low, as I had been doing.

Over the next few weeks, I reconnected with my high school friend, Hannah. I was staying local around the neighborhood, going to house parties and doing whatever I could to keep my mind off of Dresden. On the evening before Sebastian's show, she asked me to come with her to see a Doors cover band called Wild Child. My first thought was to say no since I was hesitant on going anywhere near Hollywood. I was also still undecided about going to Sebastian's show. But when Hannah told me the Wild Child show was in Anaheim at a club called Jezebel's, I relented and told her I would come along.

On the drive to Anaheim, I filled Hannah in on my recent leper status with the girls and how Sebastian invited me to his show. She said I had just as much right to go as anyone else and would come along for support if I wanted her to. I was so happy and relieved when she volunteered to go with me. Not only because she was always such a good friend to me, but Hannah was a tough bitch. I witnessed her brawl on several occasions, and she could take out a herd of bitches with one swing. Having her by my side was better than having a bodyguard.

When we arrived at Jezebel's, it was a shit show right from the start. Wild Child as a band was cool, but the people there to see them were assholes. Most of them were drunk and trying to start a pit in the center of the floor, which I thought was ridiculous. There was nothing about The Doors music that struck me as aggressive, so I couldn't understand what they were so angry about. Maybe they didn't like living in Orange County?

One guy repeatedly bumped me and even tried to pull me into the faux pit a few times, but I kept pushing him back in. He eventually stopped just long enough to barf on the floor in the front of the stage. A few bouncers stood by, and once he gave his last heave they threw him right out.

Hannah, on that same note, decided to get fairly plastered as well. She had recently started dating a convict named Edgar and was upset about him returning to jail over a probation violation. I had just finished my first drink when Hannah was already on her third. I decided to stick to soda for the remainder of the evening, and it's a good thing I did. She barfed up her sixth drink in the girl's bathroom before we left. She could barely walk, so I drove us back to her house. I'm just glad we lived on the same street since I had to walk myself home.

When I spoke with Hannah the next day, she was a complete disaster. She was so hung over and still barfing, certainly in no condition to go with me to Sebastian's show that evening. *Just great, there goes my bodyguard.*

To make matters worse, Kennedy called me that afternoon with news that Dresden was supposedly still in Los Angeles.

I was just starting to feel better about things between us, but that was under the assumption that Dresden had already moved back east. I figured he was busy getting acclimated in New York and that was the reason I hadn't heard from him yet. We hadn't spoken in weeks, not since the day I went to visit him at Bleeker Bobs. I was crushed at the possibility that he was in L.A. that whole time and never once thought to call me. Now, having to potentially face the girls alone at the Teaszer without Dresden by my side (when he was just minutes away) sent me reeling.

I'm not sure what came over me, but I wanted to make a statement by going to the Teaszer by myself. I wasn't going to let anyone dictate where I could or couldn't go. Cassidy certainly wasn't the mayor of Hollywood. If Sebastian or anyone else wanted me to go to their show or anywhere else in Hollywood, I had every right to go.

When I arrived at the Coconut Teaszer that night, I walked right up to the bar and chatted with Junior, the Mexican bartender, that made stiff drinks. He made me a screwdriver that was virtually clear. I took a sip and gagged for a second. I noticed The Kids were setting up, so I grabbed a stool and took a seat near the right side of the stage. A few minutes later, I noticed Cassidy, Dina and Amie walk in.

Oh boy, here we go.

I took a big hit of my drink and stood my ground. I had no idea what was going to happen with the girls. The last time we saw each other we were all close friends. But in all honesty after losing Dresden, I didn't give a shit about anything anymore. Whatever was going to happen would happen. Whether that be the girls ignoring me or dragging me out onto the patio and beating me next to the Mexican guy that made the delicious tacos.

Shortly after The Kids went on, Elise came up to me and gave me a big hug. We screamed over the loud music for a few minutes and caught up on what each other had been up to. She didn't say a word about my falling out with Cassidy. She ended our conversation by saying it was good to see me and skipped off. I really respected Elise that night. She was the only girl in our circle aside from Kennedy that didn't jump on the "We Hate Marisa" bandwagon. As the show continued, so did the pattern of people walking up and giving me hugs. Of course it was all the guys, but I was still glad they weren't letting the girl's opinions of me get involved in our friendship.

Out of the corner of my eye, I noticed Bronwyn walk up and stand near the left side of the stage by herself. A few minutes later, Cassidy, Amie, and Dina joined her. Cassidy looked right at me while giving her a big hug hello, and that made my blood boil. She knew damn well I hated Bronwyn. Hell, she was right by my side badmouthing her for weeks after the bathroom incident at Sebastian's. Now all of a sudden she was nuzzling Bronwyn like she was a new fluffy puppy.

I spoke with Sunny and Ronnie for a bit after the show. I could feel the girls staring at us, or me I should say. I ignored them and acted happy as a clam. Sunny asked if I was going to stay for the next band. Although everyone had been so nice earlier in the night, I felt it was best that I go home. I went there to prove a point and succeeded in doing what I set out to do. I didn't even say goodbye to Sebastian. I gave Ronnie and Sunny a hug goodbye, then made my way out the door (luckily) in one piece.

While I gave myself a pat on the back for standing my ground, I felt really lonely as I walked out of the Teaszer that night. It was great seeing all my old friends, and I was blown away that everyone was being so nice to me. I missed going to Hollywood and hanging out with everyone, especially the girls.

Sure I could've ignored the girl's dirty looks and resumed going to Hollywood, but it wasn't the same. The whole tide of the scene out there was changing. It wasn't just my issues with the girls that kept me away. It could never be like it once was. And quite honestly, it just wasn't fun for me anymore.

I didn't even have my default social pool of the Sunset Strip to dive back into as I had done so many times before. The grunge scene certainly took care of that. Sure people still went to the clubs on the Strip, but the once crowded sidewalks were now a ghost town. People didn't hang out on the boulevard to socialize or pass out flyers like they used to. It wasn't allowed anymore. For the first time in years, you could actually see the sidewalk.

I left the Coconut Teaszer and decided to drive to Dresden's house. I had no idea what I was going to say to him, if he was even there. I didn't even know why I was driving there, but I just kept on going.

When I pulled up in front of Dresden's house, the porch light was out, and there was a "For Rent" sign on the front lawn. The way the trashcans were spilling over with cardboard boxes and other garbage, it looked like whoever lived there was in a hurry to get out. My heart sank because I knew he was gone. Looking at that dark, quiet house that once bustled with energy was a serious reality check that my time with Dresden was officially over.

So lets sum up my life at that point in time. My first love dumped me, I was jobless, and my social circle consisted of a whopping two people, Faye and Kennedy. I was in a serious social coma that I didn't know how to get out of.

Speaking of Faye, I went shopping with her on Melrose the next day and filled her in on my uneventful night at Sebastian's show. She in turn told me about a guy named Ren she was dating. I wasn't happy that Faye was hanging out with

Ren because he was a well-known junkie around Hollywood. It's common knowledge that you can hang around people that drink and not be a drinker yourself, but heroin is on a whole other level. It's not a casual crowd that you frequent unless you're doing heroin yourself. I lectured Faye like a concerned mom over my dislike of Ren. I told her I didn't want her being around him. She assured me with her beautiful smile that she knew what she was doing and to stop worrying about her. Of course that made me worry even more.

A few weeks had passed since Sebastian's show at the Teaszer. Needless to say, I was bored out of my damn mind. He did invite me to another show at Club Lingerie and even to Michael's birthday party at the Hollywood Palms Hotel, but I politely declined both invitations. I didn't understand why he was suddenly calling and inviting me to hang out when he was still dating Bronwyn. How could he think we were capable of having a "normal" friendship? Even though my social life was on a starvation diet, hanging around him again would be taking steps back into a dark hole. It was stupid of me to go to the Teaszer show in the first place. I already lived through the Sebastian portion of my life, and rehashing that dead dog was not what I wanted to drag into my future.

Although I was technically cut off from the girls, I still had indirect contact through Kennedy who still spoke to Amie and Dina. As far as Cassidy went, Kennedy said they were civil to each other, but she wasn't happy that Kennedy chose to stay friends with me.

Kennedy called me one afternoon after a lengthy call with Dina. According to Kennedy, not only did Cassidy hook up with Sebastian right when we first started dating, but she also hooked up with Dresden shortly before he went back to New York.

CASSIDY: Hooking up with Sebastian was just one of those things that happened all the time. I don't remember the timing of when it first started. I do know that when Marisa and I became friends he and I didn't hook up at all. But I don't know if we were hooking up when they first got together because that was before I knew her. If we were hooking up, it was because I didn't know her yet and didn't know she was in the picture. I never slept with Dresden.

Dina also allegedly badmouthed me to Kennedy. She said Dresden was just like every other man, and I was stupid for choosing a guy over my friendship with Cassidy. Kennedy said she tried to tell her that I never slept with Dresden, but Dina wasn't having it. She said it was like trying to convince her that the sky was green instead of blue.

Going back to Dresden and Cassidy, the thought of them hooking up made me sick to my stomach. My first instinct was not to believe it. After all, this was the same rumor mill that said I was having sex with Dresden in Cassidy's house.

I didn't want to believe Dresden would do such a thing. But I thought about him doing a complete 180 during Christmas, when he went from being the attentive boyfriend to completely cutting me off. What would've happened if I hadn't gone to visit him at Bleeker Bobs that day? Would I never have heard from him again? I didn't know who the real Dresden was anymore. Even though I hated to admit it, there was a good chance what Dina told Kennedy could be true.

And what about my best friend, Cassidy, who hooked up with Sebastian? I wasn't even hurt when I found that out, I was angry. Not because they hooked up, but because she had the nerve to jump the gun over a stupid rumor about Dresden and I that wasn't even true.

The first thing I did was call Cassidy. I wanted to tell her what a hypocrite she was, but I hung up on the 3rd ring. I realized there was no salvaging that friendship. Having it out with her wasn't going to change anything, IF she would even get on the phone with me. A few minutes later, my phone rang.

"Hello?" I said.

"Hello? Marisa?" the voice asked.

It took me a second to realize the voice on the other end was Joelle.

"Hey Joelle! How are you?" I said.

"Did you just call the house?" she said demanding rather than asking.

"No," I immediately said.

I don't know why I said no when I had. It was just a natural reaction.

"Actually, I did but…"

"Why are you crank calling the house?" she said cutting me off.

"I wasn't crank calling. I was calling to..."

"Bullshit, you were totally crank calling. Are you fucking ten years old Marisa?"

"Wait a minute, I wasn't crank calling," I said trying to explain myself.

"Calling and hanging up IS crank calling. Why don't you grow up? And more importantly, why don't you go fuck yourself!" she yelled and hung up on me.

I sat there for a few moments with the phone still in my hand, completely stunned. Not because she told me to fuck off, but how did she know it was me that called? And more importantly, how did she find out so quickly? Remember folks, this was 1993 we're talking about. This was before the days of everyone having Caller ID. Well, me at least.

Five minutes later, my phone rang again. I thought about letting it go to my answering machine. I certainly wasn't in the mood to get bitched at again, but my curiosity got the best of me. I answered, and it was Faye. She laughed as I told her what happened with Joelle.

"You really don't know how she found out it was you?" she asked.

"No, but it sounds like you do," I said.

"Haven't you heard of star sixty nine?"

"I have no idea what that is."

"It's a new call return thingy on your phone. You punch the star button, then six and nine and it automatically calls back the last person that called you."

"Wow, I had no idea."

"Really? Gawd where have you been?"

"Living under a rock apparently."

I chatted with Faye for about a half hour. Luckily, I didn't get any more disgruntled calls from Joelle or the rest of the girls. As for handling Dresden in regards to his supposed hookup with Cassidy, I decided to go a more traditional route and write him a scathing letter. I told him I knew what he did with Cassidy before moving back home, included a few other colorful expletives, and sent it off first class to New York.

Maybe I overreacted by sending that letter to Dresden, but it's not like I had anything else to do with my spare time. I didn't have a social life or a job. All I did was eat and sleep. Playing with Sniffy was the only thing that put a smile on my face, but even she was a reminder of friends that were no longer in my life.

I spent the next few weekends at home, licking my wounds over my breakup with Dresden and fighting a bad case of cabin fever. Occasionally, I would make the long trek out to Norco to visit Kennedy, but the drive was exhausting. The area she lived in was rural. There were no sidewalks along the residential streets. There were horse ranches everywhere. When I turned down the street to her mom's house, I would idle by slowly in my car because people would be riding their horses alongside me. Along with the horses were also the cow ranches. You always knew you were entering the city of Norco by the intense smell of cow shit that overtook the air.

I had just come home from running errands when Kennedy called to tell me I was coming out with her that night. She spoke with Chris from Swingin Thing earlier in the day, and he told her about a party going on in the valley. But before heading over to the party, she wanted to stop by a club called F.M. Station to see her friends play.

I was reluctant about going anywhere the girls might be. I had a good feeling they would be at that party, but Kennedy wasn't taking no for an answer. More importantly, I was sick of staying home every weekend, so I agreed to go.

When Kennedy and I pulled up to F.M. Station that night, I noticed one of the bands on the marquee was Rockhoney. I burst out laughing. Kennedy asked what was so funny. I never told her or anyone about Larry, simply because he was in and out of my life in the blink of an eye. Kennedy pressed me for details, so I filled her in on our brief rendezvous, which at that point had taken place well over a year earlier.

When we walked into F.M. Station, her friend's band was already onstage. So we went to the bar for a cocktail and to watch the rest of their set. As we walked to the bar, I noticed Larry standing nearby, sipping on drink. Considering we didn't end things badly, I figured it would be fine to walk up and say hi.

I was actually happy to see him and figured he would be happy to see me too.

I gave him a little wave hello as I approached him. He smiled at me and waved back, then grabbed my hand and pulled me towards him. Kennedy laughed and ordered us some drinks.

"Hi there stranger! How..." I started to say.

"Hi sweetheart." He said interrupting me. "I would love to talk to you, but I'm about to play. Can I get your number in case I don't see you after our set?" he continued.

"Huh? I haven't changed my number."

"What's your name darlin?" he said with a big smile on his face.

"What are you talking about Larry? You know my name," I said with a raised eyebrow.

"Oh umm...yeah. Wait, we know each other?"

"Um yeah. We met at the Whisky about a year ago the first time you came to L.A.," I said as I took my drink from Kennedy.

"Oh yeah, I remember now," he said with a confused look on his face.

It was clear he didn't remember me. I figured I would jog his memory a bit and give myself a good chuckle at the same time.

"Yeah, don't you remember? We were swapping spit the first night we met. Then you invited me to your show at the Red Light District and you ended up slobbering all over an Asian girl that night by the girls bathroom," I said without missing a beat.

"Oh geez. Wow, I did that?" he asked.

"Yes, you sure did," I said.

This time I was the one smiling like the Cheshire Cat.

"Damn. Sorry about that. So uhh, why don't I buy you a drink?" he said smiling.

"No thanks. Already got one," I said lifting my cocktail.

He quickly changed the subject and went into a long story about how his band relocated to L.A. a few months ago. Even though he didn't remember me, I tried to give him the benefit of the doubt. After all, we hadn't seen each other in so long. It was such a brief time that we hung out, so maybe it was wrong of me to be bitchy to him.

"So um…we're playing a show in two weeks if you want to go?" he said.

"Oh yeah? Where at?" I asked, trying to sound more engaging.

"At the Whisky. Tickets are $15 at the door, but I can sell you some for $10."

Okay, maybe I had the right idea to be bitchy towards him earlier. All his rattling on wasn't to catch up with an old acquaintance. It was only to score ticket sales. What in the world gave him the idea that I was a fan of his band? After forgetting he knew me, the least he could have done was comp me a ticket.

"No thanks, I've already seen your band play twice," I said coldly.

By this time, Kennedy's friends had just finished their last song and walked offstage.

"Well, um, it was great seeing you. But we're on next so we have to go set up," he said looking uncomfortable.

"Have a great show. We can't stick around because we have a party to go to."

I grabbed Kennedy's hand and we left F.M. Station. We made our way out to the party, which ended up being at some bands rehearsal studio in North Hollywood. We saw many familiar faces like Ronnie, Mandie, Bam, and of course Sunny and Chris.

I was having a great time catching up with Ronnie when I noticed Cassidy, Amie, and Dina walk in. I bumped Kennedy's arm with my elbow and motioned with my head towards the door.

"Oh fuck them," Kennedy said. "We have friends here too and have just as much right to be here as anyone else."

"I know. It's just annoying though," I said.

"The whole thing is fucking stupid," Ronnie said.

"Of course it is. I wish someone would tell them that," I said.

"I'm not getting involved. This is between you guys," he said.

I chatted with Ronnie for a few more minutes until he walked off to say hi to the girls. I noticed Dina was drunk because she fell on him as she tried to hug him hello.

I told Kennedy I needed some air, so I walked outside with Chris. Ronnie joined us shortly after. A few minutes later, Cassidy, Amie, and Dina came outside too. The girls walked by me and disappeared down the street. I assumed they were leaving and breathed a sigh of relief as I continued talking to Ronnie and Chris. About fifteen minutes later, the girls reappeared and made their way back up the street towards us. They stopped about ten feet away from us, and Dina suddenly started yelling insults in my direction as if I had engaged her in conversation.

I rolled my eyes and laughed because not one word had come out of my mouth in the last few minutes. I had been standing by listening to Chris and Ronnie's conversation.

Dina continued to bark at me. Any time she yelled something I would start laughing. I wasn't doing it to egg her on. I just honestly thought the whole thing was so stupid that I couldn't help but chuckle.

"Don't laugh at me you bitch!" Dina yelled.

This made me laugh harder, which pissed her off even more. So she walked up to me and began yelling in my face, telling me I was a backstabber, a slut, blah blah.

"Whatever you say Dina. You know everything don't you?"

I made a puppet gesture with my hand in front of her face as she continued yelling at me.

"Fuck you bitch!" she yelled.

Dina gave me a hard shove. I was caught off guard, so I immediately shoved her right back, and Ronnie quickly jumped between us. He pulled me off to the side as Cassidy and Amie did the same with Dina. My heart was racing and my hands were shaking.

"You okay?" Ronnie asked.

"I'm fine, but I can't stop shaking," I said as I raised my trembling, stiff hands.

"It's just your adrenaline. It'll stop in a little bit," he said massaging my hands.

DINA PALMER-GOMES: My memory is so bad. I think we were at a party or a bar, maybe in North Hollywood? And we were outside on a curb and I just remember being so drunk and

being like, "Fuck you Marisa!" And maybe I pushed you? I don't even remember. I think it was Chris who was like, "Stop it! Stop it!" that's all I remember. It's very vague.

Although Cassidy and Amie took Dina off to the side, she was still yelling and told them to let her go so she could kick my ass. Ronnie yelled at Cassidy and Amie to get Dina out of there, and to my surprise they did. As they walked away with Dina, Kennedy ran up to me from around the corner.

"Oh my god, I heard there was a fight!" she said completely panicked.

"Boy, good news sure travels fast doesn't it?" I said sarcastically.

"So there was a fight? What happened honey?"

Ronnie shadowboxed next to me and said, "Yeah, *Rocky*, tell her what happened."

"Oh shut up," I told Ronnie.

"Are you okay?" Kennedy asked.

"I'm fine and there was no fight. Dina shoved me, so I shoved her back."

"Don't lie, it was a full out boxing match," Ronnie said as he took mock swings at me.

"Didn't I tell you to shut up?" I said laughing and taking swings back at Ronnie.

"Well I'm just glad you're okay. I can't believe she did that!" Kennedy said.

"I can't believe it either. Can we go home and get away from these crazy people?" I said.

13

SOCIAL RESUSCITATION

*A*fter a few weeks of seclusion from my mild scuffle with Dina, cabin fever was setting in yet again. Many months had passed since all the bullshit with Dresden went down. I had gone out less than a handful of times since then and was eager to start going out on a regular basis. But my only local friend was Faye, and I knew she went to the same places in Hollywood that the girls did. I certainly didn't want to take a chance running into them now that I knew arm-to-arm combat was on the table. I had to find a group of friends that didn't include those bitches. Luckily, my social resuscitation came in the form of a Japanese girl named Ramie.

Ramie was a friend of Kennedy's that moved to L.A. from Japan a few years earlier. She was skinny with big boobs and a perfectly coiffed black bob. She spoke in broken English with a soft pixie voice and lived in a loft near Sunset and La Brea. Her parents still lived in Japan and would send her gobs of money every month under the assumption she was going to college.

Shortly after Kennedy and I started hanging out at Ramie's, her parents felt she wasn't being productive with her time in Los Angeles. Okay, it was more like they found out she dropped out of college. Not wanting to completely pull the financial rug out from under her, they decided to slice her monthly allowance in half. Since she wasn't able to afford her loft any longer, she ended up moving to a house in Burbank with her Boston friends John, Eric, and Greg. Greg and I met briefly when he used to run The Church. I also knew that he and Brent Muscat were tied in with the Blackboard Jungle crowd because they recently produced an album with them.

BRITT (Blackboard Jungle): We were playing a club called God Save the Queen in downtown L.A. with either Junkyard or Black Cherry, and we had recently given Brent Muscat a demo tape. He said he would come by the show, but we didn't believe him. But that night, there he was in the front row while we were playing "Paint You a Picture". That was a pinnacle changing night for the band. It wasn't long after that we recorded the 'I Like it A lot' album with him and Greg Warkel.

The weekend Ramie moved into the Burbank house, I decided to borrow my dads truck to help her out. As a thank you to Kennedy and I for helping her move, she offered to make us a homemade Japanese dinner later that evening. Once all of Ramie's things were unloaded, I went to the market to grab a few goodies for dinner. But when I tried to start my dad's truck, the damn thing was dead as a doornail.

I came back into the house to complain. Eric said he would call Dave, the guitarist of Blackboard Jungle. According to Eric, not only was he a great guitar player but also a skilled grease monkey that would probably fix my car for the reasonable price of a Big Gulp and some Michelob. Sure enough, Dave showed up to the Burbank house a few hours later. His long red hair was pulled back into a ponytail and he slurped on the last bits of a Big Gulp as he strolled in.

Dave and I walked out to my dad's truck and he popped the hood. After some tweaking around the engine and scratching his head, he mumbled in automotive lingo exactly what was wrong with the truck. What I did understand was that my out of pocket expenses totaled about $100. This included parts for the truck and the labor fee consisting of a 12-pack of Michelob.

I hopped in his car and we talked about our mutual love for *Star Wars* as he drove us to Pep Boys. I figured he only suggested Michelob to save me from spending money on a more expensive beer. I even offered to buy him something else, but he wasn't budging. He wanted what he wanted and that was Michelob.

When we came back to the Burbank house, Dave went right to work and wiggled underneath my dad's truck. I'm not sure why, but I felt the need to keep him company as he worked. I sat on the curb and we talked more about *Star Wars* and how cool it would be if we each owned our own light saber.

An hour later, he crawled out from underneath the truck and lit up a cigarette with his oil-covered hands. He ran his arm over his head to get the small pieces of hair out of his face as he leaned into the engine and began to tug at random hoses. For some strange reason, he started mumbling the lyrics to "Achy Breaky Heart". A few verses in, he sidestepped right into the driver's seat of the truck where he was able to start up the engine.

"You are a genius," I said.

He took a big drag off his cigarette and said, "Yeah, I know."

With the truck back in working order, we walked back into the house, and I helped Kennedy set up the dining table for Ramie's Japanese buffet. We set up dishes and lit a few candles while the boys sat on the couch and drank beer. Ramie mentioned some of the other guys in Blackboard Jungle were supposed to come over later, which made Kennedy squeal with excitement. She had a huge crush on the singer, Kenny Price. Every time someone walked in the front door she would perch up like a prairie dog in the hopes it would be him.

While I continued to set the table, Ramie asked if I ever tried Saki before. I told her I hadn't. Eric and John chimed in. They suggested we do Saki bombs, which is basically dropping a shot of Saki into half a glass of Japanese beer and then chugging responsibly.

While I listened to John and Eric talk, I noticed they had a strange accent. I knew they were from the east coast, but it wasn't a familiar New York accent like Dresden or Bam's that I was accustomed to.

"Where exactly are you guys from?" I asked.

"Boston. What about you?" Eric said.

"So that's where it comes from? I'm from L.A."

"Wheh what comes from?" Eric asked.

"Would you like anothah beeh," I said in a bad Boston accent.

"Um, okay like whateverrr dude," Eric said in valley talk.

"Eww! I don't sound like that!" I whined.

"Like omigod you totally do!"

"Whatevaah, no I don't!"

"Grody to the max you do!"

"I don't have an accent. YOU have an accent!" I barked.

"You like have an accent dudette. Like TOTALLY," Eric said with his hand on his hip.

We stood eye to eye for a moment and started laughing.

"Do I really sound that bad?" I asked.

"No, but you do say 'like' way too much," he said.

Over the next hour, the Saki bombs continued to flow as we stuffed ourselves with freshly made Japanese food. One by one, as food coma set in, everyone made their way to the living room. They sprawled across the furniture like a bunch of beached seals. I was wiping down the dining room table when a random guy opened the front door and shuffled in. In my Saki induced haze, he didn't look remotely familiar.

"Marisa, this is Jamie Scrap," Eric said.

"Hey. Nice to meet you," he said as he threw his jacket and bag on the couch.

The house phone rang. Since I was the closest to it, I answered it.

"Hello?" I said.

"Hi, who's this?" the male voice asked.

"It's Marisa. Who's this?"

"Oh hey Marisa, it's Kenny."

I threw a packet of sugar at Kennedy's head to get her attention.

"Oh HI KENNY, what's up?" I said making kissy faces at Kennedy.

Kennedy's eyes immediately lit up.

"Not a whole lot. Is Jamie there?" he asked.

"Yeah, he just walked in," I said as I passed the phone over to Jamie.

They spoke for a few moments, and then Jamie hung up the phone.

"Is he coming over?" Kennedy asked with hope in her voice.

Jamie wiped the long black hair from his eyes and said, "Nah. He's fighting with his girlfriend again, so he's staying home."

Glossy eyed, Kennedy slowly looked over to Ramie and me.

"Why doesn't Kenny like me?" Kennedy asked.

Oh lord. Drunken tears are the worst.

Kennedy's emotions had a tendency to get heightened when mixed with alcohol. I knew it was only a matter of time before the floodgates opened, so I dove into a conversation with Jamie. We had an interesting Beatles vs. Stones chat. I wasn't that familiar with the music of the Stones, other than songs I heard on the radio. I admitted this to Jamie, and he looked at me like I just spoke a language he didn't understand. He told me he would make me a Rolling Stones fan as he rummaged through his bag. Meanwhile, Kennedy's tears were in full effect on the other side of the living room. I heard her say she wasn't feeling well, so Ramie took her to the bathroom.

After going through his bag, Jamie pulled out a CD and handed it to me. It was Rolling Stone's, *Let it Bleed.* He told me if I was ever going to be a Stones fan that would be the album to suck me in. We talked more about our favorite bands, and Faster Pussycat came up in the conversation. He told me that Brent hung around the Burbank house from time to time.

While the very thought of hanging around Brent Muscat had me frothing at the mouth, I hoped it wouldn't happen that night. I must have had about five or six Saki bombs over the course of the evening. I was on the verge of being a lush and certainly in no condition to make a positive impression on Brent. I casually asked Jamie if he knew whether or not Brent was

263

coming over that night. He told me he was in Vegas for the weekend. *Hallelujah!*

A little while later, a funny character named Joe Howard strolled in the door. He had these hysterical one-liners and we somehow got on the subject of the afterhours club, The Church.

JOE HOWARD: I remember the first time the cops came to The Church. They said, "Hey what's going on in here?" And we had to put up signs that said, "Brent Muscat's Birthday Bash". So Greg said every week we're going to have a new birthday party. One week it was Greg's birthday, the next it would be mine, then John's. It was hilarious. We called the $20 entrance fee "a donation". If you wanted booze it was a $5 "donation". But everyone knew what the drill was, if you didn't pay, you weren't getting shit.

We always had someone in the tower with a police scanner too. Usually it was Greg looking out. One time he was like, "Dude you gotta get up here!" So I went up to the tower because he thought the cops were onto him. They were saying some kind of code like, "the location, the location" and Greg is like, "Dude they're talking about us!" because they were saying, "Why are all these cars parked in middle of nowhere? These people have to be going somewhere." He ran downstairs, grabbed about $15,000 in cash, ran back up to the tower and handed it to me. He said for me to stay up there in case we got raided. So I'm sitting up in the tower with fucking $15,000 and here come the cops storming the place. It was fucking scary. I put the money down my pants, climbed down the tower, jumped over the wrought iron fence, and hid in a parked car for an hour. If the cops would've found me, I would've been fucked.

GREG WARKEL: I remember the night The Church got shut down. The guys from Armored Saint were gonna play as a surprise at the end of the set. I think it was Blackboard or Imagine World Peace, one of those bands were closing. We had a bell tower and a couple of guys walking on the roof with headsets. They would tell us what was going on around the street because it was in an industrial area. They called me and said there were ten cop cars sitting at the end of the street, so obviously we knew they were getting ready to raid the place.

I told the bartenders to quit serving, tell everyone the drinks were free and to help themselves. I did it to cause a confusion while me and my guys got out of there, and of course it worked. Once they said, "free drinks!" the bar got mobbed. It was like ants coming out of an anthill. We took all the money from the bar and the door. I was just about to walk out the front door when I saw the cops coming through the gate, so I went out the bathroom window.

Cops were trying to grab people, so I jumped into some girl's car. I had no idea who she was, I just told her, "Go go! Drive!" We took off, and she ended up dropping me off at my place where I met up with the rest of the guys.

The next afternoon, I think it was Beaubien that went back there to clean up. A guy wearing normal looking clothes walked in and asked him if he owned the place. Beaubien knew it was an undercover agent, so he said he wasn't the owner and just got paid to clean the place every Sunday. The agent asked him who paid him. He said he didn't know and that someone just leaves $100 under a rock every Sunday afternoon when he comes to clean. The Church had a good run though, it went for about four or five months.

As spring kicked in, Kennedy and I settled into our new social circle at the Burbank house. She would quietly swoon whenever Kenny popped by. I made sure to always look my best in the event I would run into Brent.

JOE HOWARD: I remember Muscat was at the house one night. I had just started to get to know him, but I thought he was a dick. The beer was running out at the party, and he pissed into one of the bottles and put it in the frig. I don't know why he would do that, but I grabbed it and almost drank it. I was gonna fucking murder him. I told him I was going to kill him, and he ended up leaving the party.

KENNY PRICE (Blackboard Jungle): I remember one night at the Burbank house when I stayed up all night drinking and partying with Britt and Jamie. We were on the couch in the living room being loud, and Eric came out of his bedroom and was like, "Shut the fuck up!" because he had to get up for work early at 5am. And we were like, "Fuck you!" and kept drinking till about 3 in the morning. We finally passed out and then at 5:30 in the morning, Eric got up. He turned on all the lights and started screaming at us in his Boston accent, "EVERYBODY GET THE FUCK UP! IT'S TIME FOR ME TO GO TO WORK! GET UP BITCHES!" What a Masshole.

GREG WARKEL: Eric would do that almost every morning. He and Beaubien did construction back then, so they always had to get up really early for work. I'd come home around 2am or so with a few people, and sometimes they'd get up and drink with us. But then they'd be pissed because they'd have to get up so early for work. I don't know how they got any sleep because this was happening about 5 or 6 nights a week. If Eric had been up drinking with us, he'd come into my room when he was getting ready for work, turn on my light and yell, "Wake up! It's time for me to go to work!" He'd slam doors, turn on music, and bang cabinets.

DAVE ZINK (Blackboard Jungle): I remember hanging out at the Burbank house one night when Greg's Rottweiler, Thaddeus, strolled in. There were a bunch of us hanging out in the living room having drinks, and we noticed the dog was acting weird. He hacked a few times, and I think it was Eric that said, "I think the dog is gonna upchuck."

All of a sudden, this dog cut loose from his rear end with what looked like a fire hose of black coffee that sprayed against the front door and window. It was the most disgusting sight I've ever seen in my life. He shat for an eternity. Greg was in the back room, and we started yelling for him to come out. By that time, Thaddeus must have cut loose with two gallons of shit across the wall. Needless to say, the party was over shortly after that happened. I lived there for a prolonged period of time after that, and every time I walked up to that door I would think, "Was there poo here? Should I not touch there?"

The best thing about hanging out in the Blackboard circle? I didn't have to worry about running into Cassidy, Amie, and Dina. The girls weren't friends with anyone in the Blackboard crowd. They never went to any of their shows or hung out at the places we went to, not even in Hollywood. It was a welcome relief to finally go out and not have to worry about getting into another boxing match.

We used to spend a lot of time at a dive bar down the street from the Burbank house that was run by a crazy, old man named Cecil. He was drunk 100% of the time and charged little to no money for the copious amount of alcohol we would consume. Naturally, it became one of our favorite bars to go to.

GREG WARKEL: We'd always start the night at Cecil's. He was an old drunk. If he passed out while we were there drinking, we'd just go behind the bar and get our own drinks.

DAVE ZINK (Blackboard Jungle): Cecil was a 65-year-old bartender at the Olympia Inn on Victory Blvd. Although the only legible sign outside the bar said, "BEER". He was from Arkansas and drank Coors in a bottle. He had a weird habit of slamming the bottle caps into the ceiling. He would take count of what he drank that night by laying on the floor before passing out and counting the caps that were in the ceiling.

KENNY PRICE (Blackboard Jungle): I think it was Eric that found Cecil's bar. He would do pitchers for like a buck or two. We would get so fucked up there. We'd drink all night long and then at the end of the night Cecil would say, "Uhhh yeah, just give me ten bucks".
Blackboard played there one night, and we had some guy Jeff on the drums because Joel had just left the band. We only had like 60 people there. Joe Howard was going behind the bar to bartend, and some guy said something to Joe's wife. So Joe grabbed the guy, pulled him outside, and slammed his head into a car. He pulled the guy back and had ripped a chunk of the guys hair out. He held the clump of hair in the guys face and said something so simple and funny to him. Damn I wish I could remember what it was.

JOE HOWARD: It was my wife's birthday at the time, and Blackboard was going to do an acoustic set at Cecil's bar. Everyone was there with their girlfriends when some biker guys came walking in. They were sitting at the bar, and it was supposed to be a private night. But we were cool until I noticed them checking out some of the girls we were there with, and they made a few comments. So I said, "Hey man, this is kind of a private thing. So if you're gonna be here just don't be creepin." One guy told me to fuck off, then walked behind the bar to pour himself a drink. I said something to him, he hit me over the head with a mug, so I pulled him over the bar and started whoopin the shit out of him. I took him outside, grabbed him by the head, and ended up ripping a big clump of his hair out as I smashed his face into the side of his '66 Malibu. When I was done I said, "Hey man, here's your hair back."

DAVE ZINK (Blackboard Jungle): I remember we were playing when one of the bikers said something terribly rude to Kristi who was my girlfriend at the time. Beaubien took the guy, flipped him down onto the ground, jammed his boot into his neck, and told the guy, "Don't move." A bar fight broke out, and all of a sudden, I see Joe Howard running out of the front of the bar with some dude that was just helpless. The guy had to be at least a foot taller than Joe but had no idea how to deal with him. I watched Joe take the guy outside, and he starts yelling at him, "Which one is your car!" the guy wouldn't answer, so Joe yells again, "Which one is your car asshole!" and the guy points to a '66 Ford 2 door. It was sapphire blue, beautifully repainted. Joe takes the guys head, smashes it into the right side front fender, and dents the fender with the guys head. I never saw anything like it.

Right when I was feeling at ease with everything, an unexpected blast from the past walked through the doors of the Burbank house on a random evening.

Spencer was always nice to me in the past, but I didn't know her that well. She was never a regular at Cassidy's house either. I hadn't seen or spoke with her since the days of me dating Sebastian.

When she walked into the Burbank house, she gave me a friendly hug. We talked a bit over the course of the evening. Although she didn't bring up my falling out with Cassidy, I was still weary of letting any girls from that group back into my life.

While my overactive paranoia had me keeping tabs on Spencer, Kennedy and I heard through the grapevine that Blackboard and Faster Pussycat had a show coming up at the Palace in Hollywood. My heart began to flutter at the very thought of encountering Brent again. Especially since our last encounter was such a flop due to Faye's excessive beauty getting in the way.

Greg finagled us a few passes the night of the Palace show. We were hanging out in one of the dressing rooms when Brent walked in with a petite blonde.

"That is girlfriend, Selena," Ramie said in her broken English.

DAMN. A girlfriend. Of course he would have a girlfriend.

Selena had long blonde hair and thin-pursed lips to match her skinny frame. She was a standard kind of pretty but nothing stunning as far as I was concerned. Brent and Selena walked up to Greg and Ramie, exchanging hellos and hugs. Greg introduced Kennedy and I to Brent and Selena. They politely said hello, then walked off to chat with other people in the dressing room.

The rest of the evening was fairly uneventful. Blackboard and Faster Pussycat put on a great show, but I didn't have any further interaction with Brent. I knew it was for the best since he had a girlfriend, but it didn't curb the fact that I was crushing on him big time. Although our encounter was brief, I was floating on cloud nine when I went home that night. I couldn't wait for the next outing when I would get a chance to run into him. Luckily for me, I didn't have to wait very long.

The following weekend was Kenny's 25th birthday. The plan was to have a party at Britt's, the bass player of Blackboard Jungle, who had an apartment on Larrabee near the Viper Room.

The night of Kenny's birthday party, I hitched a ride with Kennedy, Ramie, and Greg to Britt's. I scanned the living room when we walked in and recognized a few familiar faces that hung out at the Burbank house. I also noticed one that used to hang out at Cassidy's, Vaughn, from Beautiful Destruction.

I hadn't seen him since my falling out with Cassidy. Although most of the guys stayed neutral, I knew Vaughn and Cassidy were always close. I felt it was best to keep my distance and figured if he wanted to say hi to me he would, which he did just moments later.

While I chatted with Vaughn, I sporadically glanced around the room, hoping for a glimpse of Brent. I finally spotted him standing in a corner of the room and barely recognized him. He wasn't gussied up like he was at the Palace show. He was wearing a long-sleeved black button up shirt and his long dark hair was covered up by a green fedora with a little feather sticking out the side.

Vaughn walked off to chat with a few other people. My gaze at Brent was broken when Greg handed me a beer. He handed one to Kennedy and Ramie as well, then walked off to the kitchen. I noticed an uninhabited couch in the center of the living room, so Ramie, Kennedy, and I walked over and took a seat.

"I'm so excited Brent's here. The only thing that could make this night better is if Nikki Sixx walked through the door," I said.

"Oh my god. Do you see what I see?" Kennedy said to Ramie.

"I swear if you tell me Nikki just walked in, I'm going to walk down to Sunset and throw myself in front of a car," I said holding my stomach.

"No, it's not Nikki. Ramie did you notice?" Kennedy asked.

"Yes, I did," Ramie said with a big smile on her face.

"What? What did you see?" I asked.

"Brent keeps looking over at you," Kennedy said.

I rolled my eyes and said, "You're so full of shit."

"Ramie, am I lying?" Kennedy asked.

"No, he is," Ramie confirmed.

My back was facing Brent. The only way I could look at him was to completely turn around, which was a little too obvious. Kennedy and Ramie were sitting on either side of me at an angle, so it didn't look obnoxious if they took a simple glance in his direction.

"What's he doing now?" I whispered to Kennedy.

"He's just talking to some people, but he keeps looking over here."

"Damn it. I wish I could be facing him right now," I said.

I thought back to the first time I met Brent in front of the Whisky with Faye. I figured he recognized me from back then. Surely, that was the reason he was staring at me.

Not a chance in hell.

He was all about Faye that night. I could have walked out of the Whisky with a purple tail and shot glitter out of my ass, and he still wouldn't have remembered me.

Ramie and Kennedy knew of my longstanding crush on Brent. I figured they were just blowing smoke up my ass by saying he was staring at me. I had to check it out for myself.

I turned around and pretended I was doing a casual glance around the room to see who was there. When my eyes met with Brent's, he gave me a little smile, raising one corner of his mouth ever so slightly. I smiled back and slowly turned around.

"I'm going to die," I whispered to the girls.

As people began to slowly pile into the apartment, I became paranoid of anyone overhearing what the girls and I were talking about, so I developed a plan.

"Listen, anytime Brent looks at me, I want you guys to gently snap your fingers okay?" I whispered to the girls.

Kennedy and Ramie immediately snapped their fingers at the same time.

"Stop it! I said only when he looks at me," I said.

"What? He just did right now," Kennedy whispered.

Jamie Scrap strolled in a few minutes later. He spoke briefly with Brent and they both walked out together.

"Oh no, he can't be leaving already!" I said to the girls.

"No way, it's still early. They are probably just making a run to the store," Kennedy said.

Ramie, Kennedy, and I speculated on where the guys could have gone. About an hour later, Jamie walked in with Brent and his girlfriend, Selena. She walked off and said hello to a few people while Brent hung out near the front door chatting with Kenny and Britt. Despite Selena's presence, the girls resumed snapping their fingers just moments later, which caught me by surprise. Their sporadic snapping continued for another fifteen minutes or so when suddenly it came to a standstill.

"What happened? Why are you not snapping anymore?" I asked sadly.

"Brent walked into the bedroom," Kennedy said.

"Well, I do have to go to the bathroom," I said with a smile.

The three of us walked into the bedroom, which had the only bathroom. Brent and Selena were sitting on a bed and both were talking with a few people that were standing around them. While I waited in line for the bathroom, I could feel Brent staring at me. I didn't make eye contact with him though. I just couldn't. The girls would've had to scoop me up in a bucket after I melted on the floor.

When the bathroom door opened, the three of us piled in. We shut the door behind us and started jumping up and down, squealing like wild piglets. Although music blared throughout the apartment, I was worried about anyone knowing of my crush on Brent. I was still traumatized from being 86'd at the hands of Cassidy and had just settled into having a social life again. I wasn't about to make enemies in my new circle of friends and do something stupid to piss people off. Or would I?

When we walked out of the bathroom, I could feel Brent looking in my direction. I avoided all eye contact and stared straight ahead. Kennedy gently snapped her fingers by my ear as we passed him, and I giggled as we continued our way back into the living room.

"You see Brent look?" Ramie asked, as we sat down on the couch.

"The question is did you see Selena glaring at her?" Kennedy added.

"Oh no! Are you serious?" I asked.

"She totally saw Brent staring at you when we walked out of the bathroom. She was NOT happy," Kennedy said.

"But I didn't do anything. I didn't even look at him," I said.

"Yes you did, you caught her boyfriend's eye. That's quite enough," Kennedy said.

As the night went on and the girls snapped their fingers like hipsters at a poetry reading, my thoughts went back and forth on how to handle Brent. If I was going to continue hanging out in the Blackboard circle, being around him was inevitable. I couldn't very well run out the door every time he came around. So until I could figure out a game plan, I decided it was best to avoid any further interaction with him for the remainder of the night.

I was about to get up and grab myself another beer, when Greg waved us over from across the room and asked if we were ready to head out. We gathered our things and walked over to Greg who was talking to a few people by the front door. Brent suddenly strolled up, said hello and mentioned he remembered me from the Palace show. He smiled as he shook my hand and didn't let it go. He just held onto the tips of my fingers and lightly swung my arm back and forth while he asked me questions like where I was from, how I knew Greg, etc. I was freaking out beyond belief, but I felt I was doing a fairly good job at keeping a cool demeanor. Although Selena was nowhere to be found at the moment, I still felt uncomfortable talking to Brent. Especially after Kennedy mentioned she was giving me the stink eye when we left the bathroom earlier.

I slowly pulled my hand away from Brent's as we continued to chat. A few seconds later, Selena walked into the living room from the bedroom. The close call freaked me out, so I quickly wrapped up my conversation with Brent. He kissed the back of my hand, smiled, and said it was great seeing me again. *Sigh.*

We said our goodbyes to everyone and walked out of the apartment. I held in my excitement until we reached the street, at which point I performed the Snoopy happy dance.

"Oh my god, Selena hates me," I said as I stopped dancing.

"Yeah, but Brent obviously likes you," Greg said.

"Oh my god, what did he say?" I said charging Greg.

"Earlier in the night he told me you were really cute."

"SHUT UP!" I yelled.

"Okay, I'll shut up."

"Don't you dare! What else did he say?" I said clawing at him.

"Nothing really. You happened to walk by when we were talking. He asked who you were and I said you were a friend of Ramie's. That's when he mentioned you were cute, that's all."

It seemed like just yesterday I was a 14-year-old freshman, slobbering over pinups of Brent Muscat on my wall. Now five years later, I find myself at a party with him just a few feet away, staring at me like a lion eyeing a steak. Finally, my baked squash days were behind me! Everything had come full circle...well almost. The day I would come face to face with Nikki Sixx would be the final step in reaching the Holy Grail.

The next morning, I grabbed my typewriter and pounded away on the keys as I described every detail concerning the party at Britt's in my journal. The obnoxious amount of finger snapping between Kennedy and Ramie was too good to be true. It seemed more like a fictitious story I would have written when I was 14, rather than something that actually happened.

I wondered when I would see Brent again. I knew Blackboard and Faster Pussycat would be leaving soon to go on a mini tour of the east coast. Something had to happen before then to bring everyone together. Luckily, it took one call from Ramie to get my answer.

About a week or so later, a bunch of us went to Cecil's bar to hang out. I arrived at the bar before Ramie and Kennedy did. Greg, John, and Eric were there along with a few guys in Blackboard. Brent was there too with Selena. He greeted me with a big hug hello while she gave me the stink eye once again. After saying hi to Brent, I walked off and chatted with Kenny for a little bit about the upcoming tour. Two beers later, my bladder was acting up, so I went to the bathroom. While I was washing my hands, Ramie and Kennedy walked in and greeted me with hugs.

"We noticed Brent outside. Did you get a chance to talk to him?" Kennedy asked.

"Not really. We just said hi and exchanged a hug," I said.

"That's it?" Kennedy asked.

"What was I supposed to do? Give him a lap dance? Selena was right next to him shooting daggers at me," I said.

Selena kept a tight leash on Brent for the remainder of the night. And when I did talk to him, I could feel her eyes burning into me. She must have sensed something was up at Kenny's birthday. Now she was out for blood.

I ran into Brent a few more times before the guys left on tour. Selena would continue to mad dog me every time I saw her. In an attempt to ease the tension, I tried to avoid Brent when we would all be out and about. But he would always come and talk to me, which made her hate me even more. I smiled at her once, but she didn't even crack. She just shot back another one of her many dirty looks. After weeks of trying to extend the olive branch to Selena, it hit me that she was going to hate me no matter what I did. I figured if she already had issues with me for doing nothing, then I might as well be my normal friendly self with Brent.

A few days after the boys left for tour, things were way too quiet in the Burbank house. They were downright boring actually. The only interesting thing that happened was the verdict that had been reached in the Rodney King civil trial. Throughout the duration of the trial, tension was high about the outcome. Everyone was worried another riot would break out across Los Angeles. Commercials were popping up on every TV station with celebrities and police officers repeating the same slogan. "Residents of L.A., Keep the Peace." When the verdict finally came down, two officers were acquitted of the charges, and the other two were sentenced to serve jail time. Luckily, the latter conviction was enough to keep people from starting another riot.

Boring weekend after boring weekend passed as Kennedy and I continued to hang out at the Burbank house while the boys were on tour. We would drink cocktails and make dinners. We complained that Kennedy and I had no one to swoon over with Kenny and Brent being gone. We also kicked around the idea of traveling out to one of their shows. I always wanted to go to New York, and they had a show booked at a popular club called the Limelight. The three of us talked about taking a cross-country adventure on Amtrak to see the show. But when we realized how long it would take and how much money it would cost, that idea lasted all of a few minutes.

I continued to pass the time by writing. Kennedy and Ramie passed their time by reading my writing. I would come up with these random scenarios on how Brent would fall in love with me, and Kenny with Kennedy. I made up funny code names for everyone, so god forbid her or Ramie left one of my stories lying around the house.

The tour only lasted a few weeks, but to us it felt like months. When the guys came home, we welcomed them and our social life back by going to a Blackboard show at the Troubadour.

BRITT (Blackboard Jungle): The Burbank house is where we would go recoup after blowing it out in Hollywood or wherever else. It was like going home to your mom's house. You'd get clean there and just mellow out. I remember there was a big stump in the

middle of the backyard, and that's where I wrote, "Right Down Here with Me" when we came home from the Pussycat tour.

Kennedy, Ramie, and I were at the Troubadour sipping on drinks by the bar when they both decided they had to use the bathroom. I didn't have to go, so I said I would stay put and wait for them. As they walked off, I casually looked around the club to see who was there. When my eyes glanced over to the entrance, I saw Sunny and Chris walk in. I was about to walk over and say hi when I noticed Ronan walk in a few people behind them. Just my fucking luck, Ronan made eye contact with me right away despite the crowd. He smiled as he waved at me and began making his way toward me. I immediately turned away and started shoving my way through the crowd in the opposite direction.

I couldn't believe he was smiling as if everything was fine between us. Did he not remember the last time we saw each other? When he was getting his ass kicked by Alan and Sheldon because he tried to choke me? If he expected me to greet him with open arms after everything he did to me, then he was crazier than I thought.

As I bumped and weaved through people to get away from Ronan, I noticed Jamie Scrap walking down the backstage stairs that lead onto the stage. I ran over to him and begged him to get me backstage and away from my psycho ex. He didn't know the history between Ronan and I, but the panic on my face was enough to convince him, and he quickly led me up the stairs.

Part of the backstage area on the 2nd floor included a wall of glass that overlooked the entire club. I spent the remainder of my night there. Not only to watch the Blackboard show but to keep an eye on Ronan as well.

After Blackboard finished their set, people started to pile out of the club. I noticed Ronan walk over to the exit and wait. Five minutes passed, then ten. I hoped he was waiting for whomever it was he might have come with. Twenty minutes later, the club was almost empty and I knew he was waiting for me. Luckily, I was able to weasel my way down the stairs and sneak out of the band loading entrance without him seeing me.

Aside from the Ronan mishap at the Troubadour and an occasional claw from Selena, things were going great in my world. I had an awesome set of new friends to hang out with, and Brent was there for me to drool over. I enjoyed my routine of hanging out in the Blackboard circle every weekend, and that's when Ramie dropped the bomb that the Burbank house would be no more. Her, Greg, and John were moving to Simi Valley.

Hell, I thought commuting to Burbank was far but Simi Valley? That was in the middle of nowhere, almost a good hour outside of L.A. Regardless, it was a done deal and they ended up moving to Simi a few weeks later.

Shortly after Ramie, Greg, and John settled into the new house they decided to throw a barbecue. Poor Kennedy ended up being stranded in Norco because her car broke down, so I went to the barbecue by myself.

When I arrived at the Simi house, all the Burbank house regulars were hanging out in the backyard. Everyone was drinking beer and picking food off the grill including Brent and Selena. Although I still had a mad crush on Brent, the flirty tension that was once between us was now long gone. I don't know how or when the hell it happened, but somewhere along the line we ended up being platonic friends. I knew it was for the best anyway and hoped it would ease the tension between Selena and I, but of course it didn't. She was still a bitch on wheels every time I saw her.

I said my hello's to everyone and made my way into the house to see Ramie. I found her in her bedroom, watching TV with a friend of hers that came to visit from Japan. I kept telling her to come outside and enjoy some delicious barbecue. It was such a nice day out, but she wasn't feeling particularly social. I, on the other hand, was starving my brains out so I told her I was going to grab some food and come back in.

When I went back outside, Brent was manning the grill and asked me if I was hungry. I told him I was starving and ready to chew my face off. He said the chicken on the grill wasn't done yet, but he had just finished a batch right before I arrived. He led me over to a table where Selena was sitting and chatting with a few people. *Just great.*

The moment she saw me walking up with Brent she tensed up. Sitting on the table in front of her was a large corning ware dish with one piece of chicken all by it's lonesome.

Brent pointed at the chicken breast and asked Selena, "Hey you're not going to eat that are you?"

She paused for a moment and said, "Well, no probably not."

"Ok great, I'm giving it to Marisa then," he said.

He stabbed the chicken breast with a cooking fork, put it on my plate and ran back to the grill to flip some meat. I couldn't believe he just left me there holding the bag, or holding the chicken I should say.

She glared at me like she just caught me having sex with Brent. It was the longest, most uncomfortable five seconds of my life. If she had shown some signs of warmth, I would have tried to engage her in some bullshit "great weather we're having" conversation. But judging by the frostbite she was blowing onto my innocent piece of chicken, I knew she wanted nothing to do with me. I shot her a dirty look right back and walked off.

I don't know why Ramie was in such a funk, but I couldn't get her to leave her bedroom that entire day. I spent my time bouncing back and forth between the barbecue outside and hanging out with her in her bedroom.

Over the next few weeks, I saw less and less of Ramie and Kennedy. Ramie became a recluse in Simi Valley, and Kennedy was still trapped in Norco. I was literally caught in the middle with both living a good hour away from me in opposite directions.

Faced yet again with a deteriorating social life, not to mention being so broke I couldn't afford to pay attention, I spent the next few weekends at home gathering my thoughts and figuring out a game plan on how to get my life back on track.

During that time, I signed up with a few more employment agencies. It wasn't long before I landed my first full time job as a receptionist for a company named Arlen. I was so excited to have a steady gig! That meant I could finally start saving up to get my own car. The only drag about the job was, well, the actual job. I hated answering phones and greeting people. But I was 19 with no other job qualifications, so it would have to do for the time being. It wasn't long before I saved up enough money to buy my first car; a used 1990 blue Ford Tempo.

Arlen was located in the industrial city of Vernon. It was just outside downtown L.A. with a well-known slaughterhouse right around the corner. The murals surrounding the slaughterhouse showed happy pigs grazing in plush, green fields on a spacious farm. My stomach would turn from the stench of dead carcass as I drove down Soto Street every morning to get to work. Not long after I started at Arlen, the company relocated to a nice area of Chino. Driving to Chino would tack on an extra 15 minutes to my commute, but it was worth escaping the stench of dead animals everyday.

While things were great with my job, there wasn't anything happening in my social life to be particularly excited about. The vibe at the Simi house was completely different from Burbank. Nobody really hung out there because it was so far away. I couldn't break Ramie out of her hermit cycle, and while I loved hanging out with Kennedy, the nightlife in Norco wasn't exactly booming. That's when I decided to reach out to Spencer.

I had spoken with her a handful of times since running into her at the Burbank house. Considering she lived just fifteen minutes up the street from me, that made her the perfect partner in crime to start running around with.

I'm not quite sure how it happened, but Spencer and I ended up on several mailing lists to go to "mansion parties". "Mansion parties" were basically a promoter who would throw a huge event at some random mansion in the Hollywood Hills. Girls would get in for free. Guys were charged a stupid amount of money to get in, which they paid because they wanted to be where all the girls were. All the food and drinks were on the house too. Spencer and I would go to these parties and partake in all the complimentary goodies we could put our grubby little hands on.

That was fun for a little while, but it wasn't long before we burned out on the mansion parties too. There were rarely any cute guys there, so we would only go when we didn't have anything better to do. After all, who were we to turn down free drinks?

With my social life once again turning into a snooze fest, I found myself with a whole lot of time on my hands to think. Unfortunately, one of the first people that popped into my mind was Dresden.

We hadn't spoken since that day at Bleeker Bobs. He never responded to the brutal letter I sent him about sleeping with Cassidy either. I was thinking about him way more than I should have and was so angry with myself that I still loved and missed him as much as I did.

14

LET ME CLUB YOUR HEART LIKE A SEAL

I had just come home from work on an early Friday evening. With no plans in sight for the weekend, I decided to take on the painstaking challenge of organizing my journals. It took me well over an hour to find all of them, which were scattered in various boxes and drawers around my bedroom. I pulled pages out at random, both laughing and cringing at all the past memories from the last seven years of my life.

Sometime around midnight, I was in an organizing groove when my neon phone lit up and scared the crap out of me. I answered without hesitation, figuring it was one of the girls calling for a late night cackle.

"Hello?" I said.

No one responded back.

"HELL LOW!" I barked.

"Hi," the male voice said shyly.

"Who is this? I can barely hear you," I said annoyed.

"It's me," he said a little louder.

I immediately knew it was Dresden. I didn't know whether I should tell him I loved him, hated him, or simply say nothing and hang up on him. Not being able to make a decision, I sat frozen.

"Are you still there?" he asked.

"I'm here. Why are you calling me?"

"I don't know. I've been wanting to call you for months."

We walked on eggshells for the first few minutes since neither of us knew how to react to each other. We eventually made small talk about our families and how our jobs were going. But after a few minutes of bullshit formalities, I had enough. I didn't give a rat's ass how the weather was in New York. I wanted to know WHY he hadn't called me since moving back home. WHY he slept with Cassidy before he left, and WHY didn't he answer the letter I wrote to him months ago?

I decided to start with the latter question.

"I did write you back, I just never mailed the letter," he said.

"It only works if you drop it in the big blue box," I said sarcastically.

"I was angry and decided last minute not to mail it because I felt you didn't deserve a response."

"YOU were pissed at ME? You're the one that cut me off and ran away to New York like a big pussy without saying goodbye," I said bluntly.

"What was I supposed to do?"

"You were supposed to stand by the words you told me when you said you loved me."

"And then what? Have a long distance relationship? That shit never works."

Being so young, I was still very optimistic about the power of true love. I saw the world through rose-colored glasses and believed that love conquered all, including three thousand miles of distance between us.

One by one, we asked and answered the questions that plagued us over the past few months regarding our breakup. Then I asked the question that I didn't want to ask but needed to   know   the   answer   to.

"Did you sleep with Cassidy before you left?" I asked bluntly.

"Of course not. I've never slept with her. Not even for the two seconds we were dating," he said.

"I don't believe you."

"If you're not going to believe me, then why ask?"

"Why would the girls lie?"

"How should I know? All you broads are crazy."

"So you really didn't sleep with her?"

"Marisa, when I said I loved you, I fucking meant it. I still love you."

"I still love you too," I said without hesitation.

And just like that the whole tide of our conversation took a radical turn. We had finally cleared the air. In a matter of minutes, we were laughing and joking as if nothing bad ever happened.

After two and a half hours of catching up on our lives from the last nine months, I was on the verge of passing out from complete exhaustion. I had already tucked myself into bed and turned off the lights. As my eyes began to close and I listened to the sound of Dresden's voice, I couldn't help but think of how wonderful the night had been. Not only did I have closure, but I also realized we were still very much in love with each other. *Was all of this REALLY happening?*

I had numerous dreams about having that conversation with Dresden for months. Where we were back in touch with each other and fell in love all over again. Every dream with him was so vivid and real. Everything about the way he looked and what he wore. How he smelled and the way he kissed me. All his little mannerisms were exact, right down to his New York accent. Then I would wake to find it was all just a dream and be destroyed for weeks. I didn't know if I could take another false hope. This time around, I was determined to have some proof when I woke in the morning.

Before we hung up, Dresden mentioned he had a new home number. I slowly rolled over in bed to grab a black marker and Post It note off my nightstand. With my eyes barely open and only the moonlight shining through my bedroom window, I slapped the Post-It Note on the wall next to me and wrote down his new number. I said a little prayer before I fell asleep and hoped that Post-It would still be stuck to my wall in the morning.

When I woke the next morning, I remembered the Post-It that I THOUGHT I had written in the wee morning hours. The wall I supposedly stuck it to was behind me, but I was afraid to turn around. Instead, I just lay there frozen until I found myself distracted by a shirtless poster of Nikki Sixx hanging directly in front of me.

Oh Nikki, so flawless and beautiful...

Wait, what was I just thinking about? Oh yes Dresden, true love, Post-It Note, that's right...

I closed my eyes, rolled over in bed, and let my fingers crawl along the wall as if I were a blind person reading Braille. After not being able to immediately find the Post-It, I panicked and my fingers began to frantically move up and down the wall. I finally took a breath as I felt the paper under my fingers and peeked one eye open to find my hands covering the bright blue Post-It.

Dresden and I began to speak on a regular basis after that initial phone call. He settled back into my life as if nothing ever happened. Talking to him a few times a week had become part of my normal routine, like getting up in the morning to go to work. It was strange to think we hadn't spoken for almost a year, but we put all that behind us. I knew why he did what he did. All was forgiven. We were ready to start over.

Dresden and I were back in touch for about a month or so when he broke the news that he would be coming to L.A. for my 20th birthday. After jumping up and down a few times, I made a list of things for us to do while he was in town. The only thing I scheduled at the time was my birthday party. Cassidy's old roommate, Dexter, had recently moved into a house in Canoga Park. I'm not sure how it came about, but Spencer and Kennedy talked him into letting them have my party there.

SPENCER: I remember how excited Marisa was leading up to his arrival. I was a little bit worried about her hopes and expectations because she had a very clear idea of how she wanted everything to go. I was concerned about that because they hadn't seen each other in so long, and Dresden hadn't seen any of his friends for so long. I felt cautiously optimistic about it all, but I

knew how much it meant to her because it kind of cost her a lot in terms of other relationships.

After weeks of anticipation, the day finally arrived when Dresden was flying into town. I planned to leave work early that day to pick him up at the airport. I made sure to wear all his favorite things, like my little plaid skirt and Red perfume.

When I arrived at LAX airport, Dresden's flight showed as having landed. I ran to an outside gate at the Tom Bradley International terminal where people were already pouring out of the gate. I quickly scanned the faces of people and spotted Dresden in his blue New York Rangers jersey. I ran up to him, he dropped his duffel bag and completely enveloped me in his arms. It felt good to hug him after being apart for so long. Everything about him felt like home. I clung onto him like a spider monkey.

"Oh my god, I can't believe you're here!" I said continuing to hug him.

"Me neither, what a nightmare," he said.

"Oh no! What happened?" I said, letting go of my grip.

He picked up his duffel bag, and we took a seat at a nearby bench.

"Well first of all, we've been sitting at the gate for the last hour," he said as he lit up a cigarette.

"Really? Why?" I asked.

"Who knows," he said. "Oh and the plane was shaking the whole way here. Actually, that was no plane, it was a chicken shack with wings. I'm never flying that airline again."

"I'm just glad you're here," I said as I put my head on his shoulder.

"Me too. You smell nice," he said giving me a kiss on the top of the head.

"You smell like you just ran a marathon," I said making a face.

"Whadya want from me? I almost died on the flight over. It's the sweat of death."

"Come on, let's get out of here," I said.

After leaving the airport, we made our way to the Fame Café in Hollywood where Mandie was bartending that night.

When we walked into the Fame Café, Ronnie was there too. After exchanging hugs and hello's, Dresden and I left with Ronnie back to his and Mandie's place. They had just rented a little house in sketchy area off Hollywood Blvd on Whitley Avenue.

After dropping Dresden's things off at the house, I drove us back to the Fame Café so we could hang out with Mandie. While we sat at the bar having drinks, I looked at Dresden as he talked with the guys. *I couldn't be any happier right now.* I had a decent job, a place to live, a running car, and the man I loved was sitting right by my side. It didn't get any better.

Things were great for about an hour or so. Then just like a cat, I felt the hair stand up on the back of my neck. I looked over to the front door just in time to see Cassidy walk in with Sebastian's roommates, Tina and Marla. They said hello and waved to the guys, then sat down at a table a few feet behind us.

I hadn't seen Cassidy in months. Not since the night of my shoving match with Dina at that party in the valley. I hoped enough time had gone by for things to be copasetic between us. But based on the looks the girls gave me when they walked in, I knew that wasn't a possibility.

For the next half hour, daggers from the girls flew over my head, consisting of sporadic heckling with my name mentioned and endless snickering. I was happy to be with Dresden, but those bitches were ruining my time with him. Not wanting to put up with their commentary any longer, I felt I should head home and give Dresden some male bonding time with the guys. He said he would walk me to my car, so I stood up and gave goodbye hugs to Mandie and Ronnie. When Dresden stood up, he took his jacket off and put it over my shoulders. The girls let out an echoing, "Awwwww..."

I was livid.

Dresden managed to calm me down as he walked me to my car and safely tucked me in. He told me we should get together after I came home from work the next day and that he would call me in the afternoon to make plans.

The next day, I was scraping to get out of work so I could see Dresden. When I arrived at the Whitley house, the strong scent of grilled onions tickled my nose. I walked in to find Ronnie slaving over the stove, while Dresden lounged on the couch watching TV. Dresden told me he had something for me and asked me to come sit next to him.

His arms swam around in a large duffle bag for a few moments, and then he pulled out a small silver box with scotch tape wrapped around it.

"It's nothing special, just an early birthday gift," he said as handed me the box.

After tearing through the scotch tape, I realized it was a necklace. It was a silver gothic style cross with a black onyx jewel set in the center. It was beautiful.

He lit up a cigarette and said, "I had my mom take it with her to the church she goes to. She had it blessed."

"I love it, thank you," I said smothering him with kisses.

We talked about what to do that evening. He suggested we go to Fame Café after dinner to visit Mandie. I figured the girls wouldn't be there two days in a row. But after the bullshit I dealt with from the night before; I wasn't willing to take that chance. Luckily, Dresden was feeling a bit lazy after we ate dinner, so we decided to stay in and snuggle up to some movies. We spoke about the holidays coming up and how I should stay with him for Christmas and New Years. I was so excited to not only be spending the holidays with Dresden but to finally see New York City!

When I went to work the next day, I bought my plane ticket and called Dresden to tell him the good news. We spoke about what to do that night. Of course he wanted to go to Fame Café to hang out with Mandie. I wasn't crazy about going there for obvious reasons, but I wanted to be with Dresden. I relented and said I would pick him up after work.

I raced home after work and called Dresden while I was getting ready. No one picked up the house phone, so I left a message. By the time I finished getting ready, he still hadn't called me back. I was about to call Dresden again when my phone rang. It was Spencer. She said Kennedy was on her way over to her place, and they planned on going to Fame Café that night too. I told her about my minor dilemma with Dresden being M.I.A. She said he probably just lost track of time while being out with the guys. That made perfect sense to me. I didn't want to make a big deal over the situation. She suggested that the three of us just go together, so I grabbed my things and went to pick up Kennedy and Spencer.

When we arrived at Fame Café, Dresden was sitting at the bar with our friends, Stef and Terry, while Mandie served them drinks. Dresden was drunk to put it mildly. He smiled and greeted us with hugs as if nothing were wrong, and then resumed chatting with the guys like we weren't even there.

I vented my frustrations to the girls on how he flaked on our plans, but they continued to talk down the situation. They said it was a slight mishap and that everything would be fine. Not wanting to be a sourpuss the rest of the night, I bit my tongue and didn't yell at him for not calling me back earlier.

We were at the bar for about a half hour until we decided to head back to the Whitley house. Nothing changed when we got back there though. Dresden spent a majority of his time talking with the boys and essentially zero time acknowledging me. Not that I was expecting him to be a lapdog at my side every moment, but he was hardly acting like the guy who said he was head over heels in love with me.

I hoped that having another drink at the house would loosen the stick in my ass, but it didn't. I wasn't having a good time and wanted to go home. I told Dresden I was leaving with the girls. He walked us to my car and apologized for drinking so much. Before I drove off, he promised to spend more time with me before my birthday.

As the days went on and my birthday grew closer, Dresden began to get distant. When I would try to make plans with him he always had something scheduled with the guys. I asked if things were cool with us, and he assured me nothing was wrong and everything was fine. I certainly didn't expect us to spend every moment of his time in L.A. together. But at that point, the ratio of outings was more like 2 to 7 in favor of the guys. Although Dresden's distant behavior was giving me flashbacks from the year before, I wanted to be fair. Not wanting to jump the gun, I felt it was best I give him some breathing room and keep my paranoid thoughts to myself.

Although my birthday party was taking place on a Saturday, my actual birthday was the day before. Since it was on a weekday, I wanted to do something intimate with just Dresden and I. He suggested we go out to dinner and have a mellow night in at the Whitley house. I wholeheartedly agreed. It would be the last opportunity for us to have a quiet night together anyway. He was set to fly back to New York the morning after my birthday party.

On the day of my birthday, I came home from work around 6:00pm. I called Dresden to figure out when I should pick him up from the Whitley house. Ronnie answered, said he was out with Mandie, and that they should be back in a half hour or so. I told Ronnie to have him call me when he came home.

Two hours later, there was still no word from Dresden. I called the house again. Ronnie said they still weren't back yet and he would have him call me the moment he walked in the door. I tried again at 10:00pm. Ronnie gave me the same story. By this time my paranoia was in full gear.

Shortly after midnight there was still no word from Dresden. I decided to call Kennedy and tell her what was going on because I didn't want to keep bothering Ronnie. She said she would find out what was happening and call me right back, which she did about a half hour later.

"Sweetheart, Dresden just came home a few minutes ago and he's completely wasted. He's afraid to talk to you right now because he knows you're mad. He's in no shape to have any type of serious conversation anyway, it would be a waste of time," she said.

"Are you fucking kidding me? What the hell is going on with him?"

"I have no idea. I spent the last ten minutes trying to talk to him, but he's so blitzed he can barely talk. I know you're hurting right now, but there's nothing you can do about it tonight. You might as well just go to bed," she said sweetly.

"How can I possibly sleep right now? I can't believe he's doing this again!"

"Calm down honey. I know you want to call and yell at him, but it's pointless. Just try to get some rest and we'll deal with this tomorrow, okay?"

After hanging up with Kennedy, flashbacks from the previous year began to circle my head once again. Flashbacks of New Years Eve when Dresden freaked out and cut me off because he didn't know how to handle his emotions.

I loved him so much that I tried to find a reason why he blew off our plans. There just HAD to be a reason. There's no way he would put me through that again. He and I spoke about all that. We cleared everything up and were supposed to be in a good place now. Things were going to be okay. I told myself that over and over again until around 3:00 am when I was finally able to wind down and fall asleep.

SPENCER: I remember the days following Dresden's arrival were a little sketchy and her saying over and over, "Why won't he just talk to me? I don't understand. I have no idea what's going on. Why is he freezing me out?"

When I woke the next morning, the first thing in front of my face was the blue Post-It I wrote Dresden's number on a few weeks earlier. I prayed that the day would be better than the previous and tried to pump myself up for my birthday party that evening.

I spent the afternoon running errands and wondering what excuse Dresden could possibly have for blowing off our plans the night before. I had no idea what I was going to say when he called me with his mea culpa.

Apparently, he didn't have anything to say. When I came home later that afternoon, there was no message from Dresden waiting for me when I walked in the door. I immediately called over to Ronnie and Mandie's, but no one answered. I calmly left a message on their answering machine.

"Dresden, it's Marisa. Where are you? I'm coming to pick you up around nine tonight, so call me and let me know where you're going to be. Bye."

He's probably just out with Mandie and Ronnie doing stupid shit. There's no way he would fuck me over. He is NOT going to do this to me AGAIN.

By 8:00pm I was fully dressed and ready to go, but Dresden was still nowhere to be found. I tried the house again. No one answered. I left another message saying I was on my way to the Whitley house to get him, and then made my way out to Hollywood with a knot in my stomach.

On the way there, I thought of every stupid excuse to explain what was happening. The ringer was off, the answering machine wasn't working properly, he was somewhere where he couldn't get to a phone or maybe disgruntled midgets broke into the house and kidnapped him...

I pulled onto Whitley Avenue and parked my car. The guesthouse Ronnie and Mandie lived in was set in the back of an old, rundown apartment building. The only way to access it was to walk down a narrow driveway along the side of the building. As my heels tapped down the driveway and the guesthouse came into view, I noticed all the lights were off and the house was quiet. My heart dropped.

I must have been out of my mind and in complete shock because even though reality was staring me in the face, I continued walking up the driveway. I stepped onto the porch and actually knocked on the front door as if someone was going to answer. I guess I was grasping at any string of hope I could. I was in total denial. I just couldn't believe he did it to me AGAIN.

I stood on the porch by myself for a few moments and looked at my reflection in one of the windows. I looked at the fancy birthday outfit I put together and felt like a complete loser. *What the hell am I going to do? How am I supposed to go to my birthday party and even attempt to enjoy myself after what Dresden did?* The obvious answer was to call Dexter's house and tell Spencer and Kennedy I wasn't coming to the party. I would go home, cry myself to sleep and maybe even pick up some Del Taco along the way, simple enough.

I walked back to my car and climbed in, but I didn't start the engine. I just sat there thinking about every boyfriend I ever dated. I had gone through the typical relationship drama of being lied to and cheated on. Hell, I even survived the psychotic antics of Ronan. But deep down, I never truly trusted any of them except for Dresden.

A million thoughts went through my head as I sat there thinking about what Dresden had done to me. I suddenly became very angry. *Who the hell does he think he is coming to L.A. and turning my life upside down for a second time?*

I decided I wasn't going to let that asshole ruin my birthday party. So just like that, I started up my car and made my way out to Canoga Park without shedding a tear.

After taking a few steps into Dexter's house, I was pounced upon by Kennedy and Spencer. They greeted me with hugs and birthday wishes until they noticed I was by myself.

"Hey honey, where's Dresden? I thought he was coming with you?" Kennedy asked.

That question felt like a bullet.

"Actually, I have no idea where Dresden is," I said calmly.

Spencer and Kennedy looked at each other in confusion for a moment, and then realized what had happened.

"Oh dear," Spencer said in shock. "Let me get you a drink."

Spencer skipped off to the kitchen while Kennedy walked me over to the couch and we sat down.

"What a fucking piece of shit he is. I can't believe he did this to you! Are you okay?" she asked.

I took a deep breath and said, "No, not really."

"It was really strong of you to still come to your party. Good for you honey," she said rubbing my back.

Spencer sprinted back into the living room and handed me a vodka and cranberry cocktail. I took a good hit and gagged for a second. She made it strong, good girl.

Ramie, who I hadn't seen in months, walked up to us with a trey full of Saki shots. She put her trey down on a coffee table in front of me and gave me a big hug.

"Happy birthday! Where's boyfriend Dresden?" Ramie asked innocently in her broken English.

"We don't care because he's a FUCKING asshole," Kennedy said bluntly.

A confused look came over Ramie's face.

"He is?" she asked.

"We'll explain later," Spencer said.

My first drink went down faster than I anticipated, so Spencer made me another. As the cocktails flowed, the girls continued to shower me with accolades on how strong and brave I was to not let Dresden prevent me from missing my own party.

About an hour or so later, as I was finishing up my fourth drink, I looked up to find Dresden, Mandie, and Ronnie walk in the front door. A wave of nausea immediately came over me. I just couldn't believe he had the nerve to show up to my party.

SPENCER: I'm an optimist, so my first reaction when Dresden walked in the door with the guys was, "Oooh okay this is good! He's here after being Houdini for the last few days! This is really good!" Then it some how slapped me in the face that maybe this was definitely NOT good. Maybe Kennedy slapped me in face with it or maybe it was Marisa, I don't remember.

It was such crazy timing too because we were JUST starting to relax and enjoy ourselves when he walked in with the guys. Marisa had a couple of drinks in her, people were starting to show up and she was finally starting to be like, "Okay I can do this!" and then they showed up.

Looking back on it now, it feels kind of juvenile. But back then it was like, "Wow the world is about to end! This is crazy! How DARE he show his face here!" I remember the outrage (laughs).

After shooting daggers at Dresden for the first few minutes, Kennedy and Spencer sprung up off the couch and took him into the kitchen.

SPENCER: When I went into the kitchen with Kennedy and Dresden, I was kinda good cop and Kennedy was definitely more bad cop because she totally confronted him and said, "What the fuck are you doing!"

I remember him feeling really bad, but he knew what he was doing. He was very aware of what he was doing. He just didn't want to face it. He didn't wanna deal with it.

After Kennedy read him the riot act, I talked to him for a few minutes and he said, "You know how much I love Marisa, I love her so much, she's an awesome person, but I just don't think I'm IN love with her." And I said, "You figured that out in 2 days? Was it some sort of fantasy thing you were trying to push?" I didn't understand and kept trying to push him for an answer and he said, "I don't know, I don't know. I just feel a lot of pressure right now." I don't think I told her that, that night. I didn't tell her about that conversation for a long time, not until years later.

He was very sincere and really truly did feel bad. He just didn't know how to handle it. He was stuck in a situation that for

whatever reason was very uncomfortable in and didn't know how to talk to her about it.

He may have come out with one idea of what was going to happen when he got to L.A., and I don't know when it changed or IF it changed. I had no idea what his intentions were. I only knew through my conversations with Marisa and her talking to Dresden that this was supposed to be a love reunion. It was very clear that was what her expectations were and that had to have come from somewhere. I assume it came from the conversations they were having. He wasn't coming out for anyone else's birthday, he was coming out for HER birthday.

I think he was in love with the IDEA of being in love, and it's easy to be in love with the idea of love when it's 3000 miles away. You don't have any obligations or anyone to answer to. So maybe that was it.

While Kennedy and Spencer were in the kitchen with Dresden, my bladder was acting up. But I didn't want to go to the bathroom because I knew if I had a moment alone to myself I would break down. I absolutely hated crying in front of people. So I knew as long as I stayed in the middle of the party, I could keep it together. I had to.

I've always believed the worst thing you can do to a person is ignore them. It's worse than any words you can say or yelling you could ever do, at least in my opinion. I figured I would test that theory with Dresden.

After taking the last hit of my drink, I stood up and walked toward the kitchen. I'm sure Ramie thought I was on a suicide mission to go in there, but I felt I needed to make a point. Regardless of how much I loved Dresden, this was the second time he took a big fat dump on my heart. Therefore, no matter how much it hurt, I needed to show him that he didn't mean shit to me. I would have weeks of crying and eating junk food ahead of me. But at that moment, I needed to be strong to get through those next few hours without shedding a single tear.

When I walked into the kitchen, Kennedy was in the midst of bitching out Dresden. He wasn't yelling back though, he just took what she was dishing out. Maybe it's because he knew he deserved it or due to the fact he was wasted. I'm guessing it was probably a little bit of both.

I grabbed some ice, cranberry juice, and a bottle of vodka. I began making myself a drink, acting happy as a clam despite the ever-growing knot in my stomach. My presence certainly didn't slow Kennedy down. She continued yelling at Dresden, and I could feel him staring at me while I made my drink. A few moments later, I picked up my cocktail and grabbed a straw. I locked eyes with Dresden, shot him the look of death and walked right past him.

I was on my way back to the living room when Ronnie stopped me in the dining room.

"Hey, happy birthday," he said as he gave me a hug. "Are you okay?" he asked.

"I'm fucking fabulous, why do you ask," I said coldly.

"I just didn't expect to see you here."

"Well it is MY birthday party, of course I'm going to be here."

"Look, I know Dresden blew you off, but he's my boy…"

"Yeah yeah, I know all that 'bro' bullshit. Look, I'm happy you're here, but I also wish you would leave and take him with you," I said.

Ronnie gave me a big kiss on the forehead, and I made my way back to the couch next to Ramie. Kennedy and Spencer joined us a few minutes later. Kennedy said it was a waste of time she just spent yelling at Dresden's drunk ass. I told her it was fine and that I had been through the worst of it. He showed up thinking he would probably ruin my night, but I didn't crack. I took a sip of my cocktail and felt proud that I was standing my ground when Cassidy, Dina, and Amie walked in.

UNBELIEVEABLE.

"Oh…my god…" Spencer mumbled under her breath.

"They weren't invited. What the hell are they doing here?" Kennedy blurted out.

"Taking advantage of neutral territory," I said raising my eyebrow.

Switzerland, otherwise known as Dexter, was still friends with the girls and not about to get involved in our little spat. I'm sure they knew this beforehand and decided to take advantage. They knew he wouldn't throw them out if they showed up. It was the perfect opportunity for them to crash my party.

SPENCER: I remember thinking, "Oh my god! What are they thinking?" It was a ballsy move on their part for sure. I think it was for no other reason than to show Marisa that she would feel the effects of their freeze out but Dresden wouldn't. I felt it's the only possible reason they would show up, plus everyone was going to her party. So what were they gonna do if they didn't go? It was a very clear signal that Marisa was going to pay for what happened and experience the fallout but Dresden wouldn't, and that was typical. It was never the guys fault no matter what the situation was, it was ALWAYS the girls fault.

CASSIDY: I don't remember that at all. I wonder why we went? Did we just go to be assholes? Total *Mean Girls!* (laughs)

Taking the girls head on with Dresden by my side was effortless, but not with him and I standing on opposite sides of the room. If the girls didn't already know what was going on, I knew it wouldn't be long until they did, and that made me hate Dresden even more. Not only did he break my heart for a second time and ruin my birthday, but the girls now had the satisfaction of knowing that things were on the rocks between us. *Stupid asshole.*

No one could have predicted that night of Murphy's Law. There were emotional landmines as far as my dilated eyes could see. I decided the best thing to do was plant myself on the couch and drink. I pounded my freshly made cocktail, asked Spencer to make me another and to bring me a shot of vodka. She sprinted back with both in record time.

"Are you okay?" Spencer asked as she sat down next to me and handed me my drinks.

"I'm fine," I said, slamming back my shot and chasing it with my cocktail.

"You might want to slow down on those drinks, you've got to be pretty drunk by now," she said.

"I am not drunk," I said on the verge of being wasted.

"Oh really? You look pretty drunk to me," she said laughing.

"I am not drunk. I'm sedated from my pain," I said matter of factly.

Cassidy, Amie, and Dina stayed at the party for about a half hour or so. Just long enough to make it nice and sparkling clear that they would continue to make my life a living hell. As for Dresden, he looked drunk and miserable the entire time he was there. He ended up leaving shortly after the girls did.

I should have felt better after they all left, but I actually felt worse. I was an emotional masochist for going to my party. I should have just gone home from the Whitley house and bawled my eyes out like any other normal person would.

After I polished off another drink, Spencer and Kennedy disappeared into the kitchen. While they were away, I debated on whether I should sneak out of the party and go home. The moment I stood up off the couch to make a run for it, the girls came back into the living room with a candle-laden cake. They engaged everyone in the room to sing Happy Birthday. I smiled but could feel myself breaking.

When they finished singing, Spencer told me to close my eyes and make a wish. I closed my eyes and took a deep breath. I wished for my 20's to fare better for me than my teenage years and then I blew out the candles.

Keep reading for a preview of:

WALKING CONTRADICTION
The Crackpot Chronicles

The amusing sequel to:

ROCK AND ROLL HIGH SCHOOL
Growing Up in Hollywood During the Decade of Decadence

Now available on AMAZON worldwide!

Visit www.marisatellez.com for details.

1

I HEART NEW YORK!

*I*t was the morning after my 20th birthday party. The sound of my mom dropping something on the living room floor scared me right out of my sleep. I woke up flailing my arms like a wild gorilla and knocked over a glass of water that was sitting on my nightstand. I had no immediate plans to get out of bed and clean it up because I was incredibly hung over.

I was completely out of sorts as I began to wake up. This was much more than the traditional household hangover. I was thinking about the events from the night before and also the last few years of my life that were spent hanging out on the Sunset Strip. Was it all just one crazy, lucid dream or did all of it REALLY happen?

I also thought about how I screwed up my friendship with Cassidy and the girls by letting my feelings for Dresden get in the way. Yes Dresden. My supposed "first love". The man that broke my heart for a second time and ruined my birthday party before cowering back to New York.

I kept telling myself it was all just a bad dream and that none of it ever happened. But when I sat up in bed, I saw the dress I wore to my birthday party from the night before. It was crumbled up in a ball at the corner of my bed. Directly above it was the infamous blue Post-it Note that I wrote Dresden's new number on.

I stood up out of bed and immediately got a head rush. I stabilized myself, pulled the dress off my bed and threw it across the room where it landed in a hamper. I also plucked the Post-it off my wall, crumbled it up and threw it in the garbage. If only everything in life that hurt you was that easy to dispose of. We all know heartbreak doesn't work that way unfortunately.

Had it been any other time of year, the breakup might not have been so painful. Hell, I would have settled for him ruining Valentine's Day. But Christmas and New Years were just around the corner. That, coupled with my recently bought plane ticket was nothing more than a painful reminder now. A reminder of how Dresden asked me to spend the holidays with him in New York shortly before my birthday. An offer which was clearly now, null and void.

After a few days of mulling around, I took Spencer up on her offer to see a show at the Santa Monica Civic. We hopped into her neighbor, Perry's van with Dizzy, Mandie and Ronnie, and made our way to the Cypress Hill and House of Pain show.

A few of us smoked a little bit of erb in the van on the way there. Perry and Mandie wanted to bring a few joints into the venue but we had a feeling all the guys would get searched by security. I don't know how I became the designated hood rat, but they felt Spencer looked more innocent than I did. So they handed her a small Ziploc, which she shoved right down her pants and happily strolled right through security without a second glance.

The air was thick with marijuana smoke as we strolled into the venue. The guys went to the show floor while I went to the bathroom with Spencer so she could dig the green gold out of her pants. We met up with the guys a few moments later by a slowly forming mosh pit. Although we went into the pit together, we lost the guys shortly after. The pit wasn't as violent as most I was in before, maybe because everyone was high as a kite including yours truly. The strangers around us formed a wall to keep us from getting hit and they helped pick up anyone that fell on the floor. There were no fights, no one was shoving or being a dick. Everyone around us was in a great mood and into the vibe of the music.

The show went by in a haze, literally. Half of the venue emptied out by the time we ran into Perry, Mandie, and Ronnie. We all looked at each other wondering what happened to Dizzy. A few minutes later, as more people cleared out, we found him sleeping on the floor near the back of the venue. The guys picked him up and we went back to the van.

Dizzy passed out with his head on my lap as Perry drove us to a nearby Burger King. I would love to say we had a wild night out but everyone was pretty beat by the time food coma set in. So Perry dropped off the guys and we made our way back to Spencer's.

Despite a fun night out with Spencer and the guys, the rest of my holidays sucked. I couldn't stop thinking about how I was supposed to be spending them with Dresden in the snow-lined streets of Manhattan. Instead, I was sitting alone in my bedroom. Despite the plane ticket that was collecting dust on my dresser, the month of December passed by rather quickly.

By early 1994, I still hadn't heard from Dresden. I don't know why I ever expected to. Wanting to break my current state of hibernation, I dragged my stitched-up heart to see some friends play a show at the Roxy in Hollywood.

It had been quite a few months since I went the Strip, or any club in Hollywood for that matter. I saw many familiar faces at the Roxy, yet I still felt a bit out of place. I figured it was a mild case of cabin fever since I hadn't gone out in so long. But the reality hit about a half hour later when I walked outside to get some air. I glanced down the empty sidewalks of Sunset Blvd. and realized it was the end of an era.

Grunge music had successfully invaded Los Angeles. As a result, a majority of the Sunset Strip's glam rock bands packed their things and moved back to their hometowns. Any that remained had done a complete image overhaul in the last few months. The days of every guy wanting to have long hair were gone. Long hair wasn't cool anymore. Many of the guys chopped off their locks and were now sporting stylish short dos or radical Mohawks.

The glitzy, candy-ass band names were changed to something angry and edgy. The music wasn't fun and light hearted anymore, it was serious and grittier. Even bands like Ratt and Poison were being dropped like hotcakes by their record labels in exchange for acts like Soundgarden and Pearl Jam.

And makeup? Oh GOD no. If you were a guy wearing makeup you were made fun of and looked upon like some kind of sad, old relic.

Even Gazzarri's, one of the Sunset Strip's landmark clubs officially closed a few months earlier. The owner, Bill Gazzarri, had passed away in early 1991. Although the club remained open for a few years after he died, it was never quite the same. There were hopes that someone would come along and revive the club. But despite having a generous music history with landmark bands like The Doors and Van Halen gracing it's stage, it was more recently known as a "hair band" club, and no one was willing to invest money in an audience that didn't exist anymore.

In a nutshell, grunge music had come in like a tsunami. It annihilated every glam band off the face of the planet and wiped its ass with whoever was left.

The entire span of my teenage years was spent hanging out on the Sunset Strip during its glam rock era, and now it was officially OVER. I stood there as a twenty-year-old woman, looking around at the skeleton of what was once the biggest ongoing street party in the country.

I grew up in Hollywood during the decade of decadence. It was a time of absolute insanity, gluttony and shamelessness. How the hell was I going to function in a standard social setting? What did normal people do for fun anyway?

When I looked up at the Roxy marquee, I noticed one of the opening bands was called 'Big Apple' something. It reminded me that I still had that unused plane ticket from the New York trip I never took back in December.

My obsession with the city of Manhattan started long before I met Dresden. Despite our falling out or whatever you want to call it, I still wanted to go to New York. I was eager to see The Dakota where John Lennon and Yoko once lived. I wanted to experience a walk through Central Park and stroll through the Lower and Upper East Sides. I wanted to check out the Upper West Side, the backside, front side and every side that the island of Manhattan had to offer.

All I needed was a place to stay and that was quickly taken care of by my old friend, Bam. He had recently moved back to Brooklyn and offered up his place should I ever make my way out there.

I walked back into the Roxy and up to the bar to order myself a cocktail when Ronnie tackled me with a big hug. I hadn't seen him since the night of my disastrous birthday party in November just a few months earlier.

We started chatting and I told him of my tentative plans to go to New York. He told me I was out of my mind to consider going there after the way Dresden treated me. I tried to explain that my reason for going was about seeing New York and not Dresden, but he wasn't buying it. He thought my trip was solely based on going to stalk Dresden.

While Ronnie continued to try and talk me out of going to New York, our friend, Pixie, walked up and overheard our conversation.

"You're going to New York? That's so exciting! When are you going?" she asked.

"I'm not sure when or if I'm going. I have a plane credit that I need to use by December. I've always wanted to go to New York, so I would rather use it on a trip to go there than anywhere else, " I said.

"Well, I'll totally go with you if you decide on New York," she said.

I was caught off guard by her sudden interest.

"Are you serious?" I asked.

"Seriously, I would totally go in one second. I've always wanted to go there too. We just need to find a place to stay."

"Bam said I could stay with him if I ever went out there. Since you know him too, I don't think he would mind both of us staying with him. Do you?"

"He totally wouldn't. Oh my god, I'm so excited! We're going to New York!" she squealed.

Pixie grabbed a pen from the bartender and we exchanged phone numbers on the spot. We spoke about all the places we wanted to go and planned on going in the late spring or early summer. But when I came home from the Roxy that night, I began to second-guess our tentative travel plans.

Pixie and I had several friends in common from Hollywood, but I didn't know her very well. The few times I hung out with her were fun. But taking a trip together was a total crapshoot. Either our personalities would mesh and we would have the time of our lives, or only one of us would live to board the plane back to Los Angeles.

Over the next few months, Pixie and I began talking on a regular basis. We figured out our game plan with Bam and decided we would go to New York for ten days in the middle of August. By that time I just had to be over Dresden! If I weren't, then I would have Pixie choke me until I was.

I filled Pixie in on my soap opera past with Dresden, and I was sick of whining about how he broke my heart. I just wanted to be over him. While she did agree he handled things badly, she very bluntly said it was in the past and to 'get the fuck over it already.' It was a point I certainly couldn't argue with, and the latter statement represented Pixie's personality in a nutshell. She didn't tell you what you wanted to hear, she told you what you needed to hear. If you asked her a question, you would most definitely get a brutally honest answer.

While Pixie and I planned our East Coast invasion, I started dating a guitar player named Karl. Karl played for a J-Rock (Japanese Rock) band from Tokyo, called Gravel.

I met Karl at the Whisky through a mutual friend whose band was opening for Gravel one night. He was a bit lanky with light brown hair and super skinny dreads that draped just past his shoulders. Karl was very sweet, but his personality branded him what Pixie and I would call a "Ralph".

A "Ralph" was a term that Pixie and I made up based on the character of Ralph Wiggum from The Simpsons. Karl, like Ralph, was very nice but super cheesy. He had old man humor, which seemed a bit odd considering he was only 21. Listening to him crack jokes was absolutely painful. I swear you could hear crickets and tumbleweeds following each of his punch lines.

I wasn't sure what to do about Karl. He was a nice guy and I liked him, but there wasn't a wow factor there.

He was like a nicely presented meal that lacked seasoning. So rather than douse Karl in salt, theoretically speaking, I figured I would go with the flow for the time being. I was just glad my New York trip with Pixie was coming up quickly. It was the perfect opportunity to get away from him and hopefully come to a decision about us before I came back to Los Angeles.

My trip was in the planning stages when I began dating Karl, but for some reason he was less than thrilled about me going. Especially since I would be gone for almost two weeks.

I'm not exactly sure what his issue was with me going on the trip. I didn't ask him because quite frankly, I didn't care if he had a problem with it. He wasn't my boyfriend. There was no valid reason in my mind for him to be bitching about my trip anyway. Funny enough, the day after he put his foot down and said he didn't want me to go, is right when I booked my flight with Pixie.

Karl wanted me to call him while I was in New York, which is the last thing I wanted to do. I wanted complete separation so I could get my head straight. Not only in regards to him, but to hopefully get some resolve on my feelings for Dresden once and for all. I knew running into him was inevitable because he and Bam were close friends. But I wasn't about to let that ruin my vacation.

I told Karl I couldn't afford to call him while I was away. He said I could call him collect. I said I didn't want him wasting his money on my collect calls, and after a little more pushing by yours truly he finally relented.

The weeks flew by and before I knew it, I was being dropped off at LAX and rushing to a Delta Airlines gate to meet Pixie. While we sat at the gate waiting to board our red-eye flight, I tapped my foot nervously.

"What's wrong with you?" Pixie asked.

"I've never flown before," I said, still tapping my foot.

"Oh really? Well that's not a problem, lets just have a few cocktails."

"Will that help? I don't want to get sick on the plane."

"Let's get a second opinion and call Bam," she said as she stood up and led me to a phone booth nearby.

She popped in a few quarters, explained the situation to Bam, said "uh-huh" a few times and hung up the phone.

"Exactly what I said before. He said to have a few drinks on the plane and you'll be fine," she said.

"That reminds me, I forgot to bring Lucy's ID with me, dammit!"

"Oh that's so not a problem. I have mine. I'll get us drinks here, but call her right now and have her Fed Ex her ID to Bam's apartment."

I called Lucy, gave her Bam's address and the drinking commenced with Pixie. We had a cocktail at a bar by our terminal and a few more on the plane until we passed out.

We woke up sometime around 8:00 a.m. just as we were landing at JFK airport. We grabbed our bags, walked outside, and almost dropped dead from the scorching temperature and high humidity. It was like walking into a bathroom with the heater on after someone took a scalding hot shower. I never felt anything like it in my life. It was the most horrible weather my thin California blood ever encountered that's for sure.

Already dripping with sweat, Pixie and I flagged down a cab, threw our bags in the trunk and braced ourselves for our ten day adventure in New York City.

"Where ya going?" the cabby asked.

"Take us to Brooklyn!" I said with a smile.

Made in the USA
San Bernardino, CA
14 July 2015